DISCARD

DATE DUE

Moving Images
Effective Teaching with Film and Television in Management

Moving Images
Effective Teaching with Film and Television in Management

Jon Billsberry
Deakin University

Julie Charlesworth
The Open University

Pauline Leonard
University of Southampton

INFORMATION AGE PUBLISHING, INC.
Charlotte, NC • www.infoagepub.com

Library of Congress Cataloging-in-Publication Data

Billsberry, Jon.
  Moving images : effective teaching with film and television in management
/ Jon Billsberry, Julie A. Charlesworth, [and] Pauline Leonard.
      p. cm.
  ISBN 978-1-61735-874-6 (pbk.) – ISBN 978-1-61735-875-3 (hardcover) –
ISBN 978-1-61735-876-0 (ebook) 1. Management–Study and
teaching–Audio-visual aids. 2. Motion pictures in education. I.
Charlesworth, Julie A. II. Leonard, Pauline, 1957- III. Title.
  HD30.412.B55 2012
  658.3'124–dc23

                              2012016447

CONTENTS

SECTION II
CRITICAL ISSUES

SECTION THREE
IMAGINING INCLUSION

DIE ANOTHER DAY

Teaching With Film and Television in the Management Classroom

Jon Billsberry, Pauline Leonard, and Julie Charlesworth

The first decade of the 21st Century witnessed a rapid growth of interest in using feature films and television programs for teaching management and management-related subjects. At the start of the century, there was very little published work advocating the use of moving images in the management classroom. Indeed, this was viewed as something trivial and non-serious; entertainment rather than enlightenment. By 2010, much had changed and work exploring the value of film was commonly being published in journals and could arguably be said to have entered the mainstream. By the end of the decade, the papers published in management education journals had changed in character. It was no longer sufficient to highlight and discuss the benefits of particular feature films and television programs for teaching. Instead, authors had to find new ways of using this media in their teaching.

This book appears at the end of this decade of rapid adjustment and assimilation. We have now identified many useful feature films and television programs for teaching management. We have also worked out how to use

Moving Images: Effective Teaching with Film and Television in Higher Education,
pages ix–xxvii

moving images for different learning outcomes. The purpose of this book is to capture best practice in these areas and provide ideas, guidance, and inspiration on how to introduce moving images into your own teaching. All of the authors have written with you, a management academic interested in using feature films or television programs in your teaching, in mind. As such, it is a practical book and one designed to improve the impact and effectiveness of your instruction.

This book is divided into three sections. The first section records best practice. It looks at how some of the acknowledged experts in the field have used moving images in their teaching. These seven chapters provide inspirational examples of the effective use of film and television and illustrate the wide applicability of this media to teaching. The second section changes tack and the four chapters explore some of the issues surrounding the use of feature films and television programs in management classrooms. These include thinking about the use of visual media from the audience's perspective, technical and copyright issues, and at the nature of the moving images themselves. The chapters in the third section are reminiscent of those in the first section as they look at how feature films and television programs can be used in management education. However, rather than reporting how moving images *are* used in the management classroom, we commissioned chapters that looked at how moving images *might* be used in the management classroom. These authors have taken a step back from 'conventional' teaching approaches and imagined how moving images could be used. Much of the time, of course, these are approaches they have used, but at other times the authors are expanding their horizons and thinking about more inclusive uses of visual media in teaching and learning contexts.

WHY MOVING IMAGES?

One of the weaknesses in the literature on the use of feature films and television programs in management teaching is the lack of theory explaining why this media should be effective in teaching (Tyler, Anderson & Tyler, 2007). Typically, authors tend to advance two or three perfectly sensible reasons why this media works and will demonstrate its effectiveness with reports of student satisfaction or examination results. It is very rare to read replication reports; one notable exception is Billsberry and Gilbert (2008), where a scholar at another university decided to use the same film, *Charlie and the Chocolate Factory* (Burton, 2005) in the same way as the authors and reports it to be effective. This is an important consideration, because the originator of a new teaching technique is likely to have prepared extensively and will bring passion, excitement, and interest to the teaching. Students will always respond to such teaching with excellent feedback. It is only when a colleague 'picks up' and uses the technique in a new context that the relative effectiveness can be examined. As mentioned, there are very few published reports of such disinterested usage. So, although the use of feature films and television programs seems natural, there is still an element of faith surrounding their adoption. Nevertheless, there are many good reasons to think that moving images are both effective and do useful things in ways that that other teaching techniques cannot.

We conducted a review of the literature and were able to identify 11 interconnected reasons why scholars believe feature films and television programs are useful teaching tools for the management classroom. We will briefly describe each of these explanations, which we have clustered in three categories: *Enhancing Teaching, Process of Learning,* and *Medium as Message.*

Enhancing Teaching

This group of explanations views video material as a *supplement* to traditional teaching methods. Here they are used to illustrate theory, provide opportunities for practical application, or contextualize analysis and discussion. In all of these explanations, visual material does not replace other methods; instead it is used alongside them.

Illustration of Theory

The most common explanation found in the literature to explain the use of moving images in the management classroom is its ability to illustrate course theory "given the rather sterile nature of the typical textbook examples" (Hunt, 2001, p. 632). Alvarez, Miller, Levy, and Svejenova, (2004) use feature films to illustrate leadership concepts. Bumpus (2005, p. 792) expands "the current literature by providing motion picture options that feature actors of color in leading roles." Champoux (2001, p. 81) argues that the "strong caricature in animated film can powerfully show concepts." He also uses feature films for illustrative purposes in several of his other articles (e.g., Champoux, 1999, 2005, 2006). Dunphy (2007, p. 179) "proposes using [the...] 'greatest film scenes' for the purpose of illustrating concepts of organizational behavior and management." Kuzma and Haney (2001, p. 34) argue that "film events can provide tangible examples of core course concepts that are sometimes difficult for instructors to convey." Other authors using moving images for illustrative purposes include Comer and Holbrook (2005), Engert and Spencer (2009), Holbrook (2009), Leet and Houser (2003), Sexton (2006) and Tyler, Anderson and Tyler (2007). Huczynski and Buchanan (2004, p. 708) summarize this reason for using feature films and television programs in management teaching; "it has long been recognized that film is a powerful tool for illustrating topics and concepts and for demonstrating the application of theory, providing a source of pedagogical material more stimulating and motivating than conventional methods."

Practical Application

As shown by the previous quote, the illustrative explanation is closely associated with the rationale of practical application. However, we have chosen to separate these in the following way. *Illustration* is when moving images are shown as an example of a theory, an idea or a concept. In effect, moving images are used to help explain the idea to students. *Practical application* differs as it refers to situations when moving images are employed to show the theory, idea or concept 'in action,' that is, being used to bring clarity, insight or understanding to a particular situation. There is little to differentiate the approaches and some authors appear to use the terms 'illustration' and 'practical application' somewhat interchangeably. We decided to separate the two, as our purpose was to provide a complete list of reasons why scholars choose to use feature films and television programs in their teaching. The following authors all advocate the use of moving images for the practical application of theory: Champoux (1999), Comer (2001), Comer and Holbrook (2005), Hunt (2001), Kenworthy-U'Ren and Erickson (2009), and McCambridge (2003).

Providing a Context

Contextualizing course content is another reason why video material is used to supplement traditional techniques. This is more than bringing the outside world into the classroom; it is also about properly framing situations to provide a more complex explanation of events, sensitizing students to the cultural norms, routines, and etiquette of the time in which the events occurred, and facilitating comparison across events, time, and cultures. Bluestone (2000, p. 142), for example, talks about using film to provide a "broader socio-historical context." Champoux (1999) focuses on films that have been remade and has his students compare the original version with the remake. He says, "films spaced many years apart offer observations on cultural mores, roles and relationships in the same culture at two different times. Selected scenes could show the dynamics of value change and highlight, with their differences, what was important at the two periods" (p. 210).

Analysis of Critical Issues

Some authors choose to use film because it allows them to analyze matters that are central to their curricula. Sesonske (1974), for example, is concerned with the aesthetics of film making the use of film almost mandatory. Alvarez, Miller, Levy and Svejenova (2004) focus on leaders and, in particular, conduct detailed studies of leadership in unique situations. Comparing the work of two film directors gives them "an opportunity to compare two distinct sets of backgrounds and styles" (p. 337). Engert and Spencer (2009) are interested in international politics and they use films to provide detailed analysis of particular moments (see Galvin and Hendrickson in this book for a similar application of films to international politics). Kuzma and Haney (2001) are similarly interested in international affairs and use feature films to create "bridges to the past" (p. 35). Billsberry (2009, p. 4) summarizes thus, "in effect, many films are multilayered and multidimensional case studies that focus on a key issue."

Getting Real

Management education is often criticized for being dry and boring (e.g., Mintzberg & Lampel, 2001; Spender, 2007). Management students tend to be confined to the sterile classroom with only occasional forays into businesses (Pfeffer & Fong, 2002). Moreover, business and management tends to be taught through theory, which offers a coldly rational view of the world (Mintzberg, 2004). Feature films and television programs are seen by some as an antidote to the passionless, logical, deductive approach (Bluestone, 2000; Buchanan & Huczynski, 2004; Champoux, 2004; Hassard & Holliday, 1998). Hassard and Holliday (1998, p. 1) believe that using a feature film "offers more dramatic, more intense and more dynamic representation of organizations than management texts."

In addition to bringing the teaching "alive," scholars believe that video material allows a more realistic examination of organizational themes. In particular, this material depicts a more complete and more complex picture of work and working life than management cases and other classroom-bound forms of teaching. Buchanan and Huczynski (2004, p. 312) say that "films depict interpersonal influence as a multi-layered phenomenon, shaped by contextual, temporal, processual, social, political and emotional factors."

> This perspective is valuable for exploring the untidy, complex, and often controversial dynamics of organizational processes, demonstrating how outcomes are shaped, not by the interaction of independent and dependent variables, but by sequences of events in particular contexts. (Huczynski & Buchanan, 2004, p. 707)

Liedtka's (2001, p. 411) "goal was to incorporate a more realistic kind of messy complexity than traditional cases offered, but in a way that educated students without overwhelming them." Mallinger and Rossy (2003, p. 608) used feature films as "a means for appreciating the ambiguity and paradox associated with both national and organizational cultures."

These quotes create an impression that these authors believe that feature films provide a realistic context to study management and management-related matters. Such an impression is misleading because these authors acknowledge that although this media is much more realistic than other media, the 'reality' that is presented is managed, manipulated, and dramatized. Potentially this is quite dangerous, as what purports to be real may be exaggerated, incomplete, and partial, and the mask of reality may 'trick' students and make them unaware that what they are analyzing is itself a fiction. The chapter by Pauline Leonard explores this matter in more depth.

Process of Learning

In this group of explanations, we have clustered those that argue that video material has characteristics that allow it to do something different to other forms of teaching. In effect, these authors argue that this material is advantageous for management educators to use because of the learning process it encourages.

Active Learning

An important theme in management learning over the past four decades has been the idea that learning should involve some element of activity. In particular, there have been many scholars advocating 'active learning' (e.g., Bonwell & Eison, 1991; Honey & Mumford, 2000; Kolb, 1976); i.e., an approach to teaching that encourages students to take responsibility for their own learning usually by creating opportunities for behavioral activity that increases engagement. Recently, some authors (e.g., Kirschner, Sweller, & Clark, 2006; Mayer, 2004) have extended the active learning argument by arguing that cognitive activity, rather than behavioral activity, is more important in creating active learners.

Aware of the potential criticism that their use of feature films is passive (images of sitting in cinemas stuffing popcorn into gaping mouths and couch potatoes glued in front of the box eating TV dinners are very powerful), many scholars (Bluestone, 2000; Holbrook, 2009; Serey, 1992; Serva & Fuller, 2004; Smith, 2009; Tyler, Anderson & Tyler, 2007) advocating the use of visual media have been keen to assert the activeness of the method. Bluestone (2000, p. 141) captures this point well,

> several authors suggest that film analysis may enhance active learning opportunities. … At first glance, that may seem contradictory because most active learning involves a 'hands-on' or discovery process. But active learning also involves a 'minds-on' approach … to stimulate students' active mental engagement with concepts. From that perspective, films, when linked conceptually to the content of a curriculum, can increase students' involvement.

Smith's (2009, p. 462) observations illustrate the active nature of film viewing:

> after numerous and frequent discussions with students through the years, just listening to their conversations gave me the idea for integrating the use of feature films as a key instructional tool. I would hear much active discussion

about current events, music, sports, and movies; and basically no discussion about recent books or articles they read. Many students could recite lines from various popular films, but none could quote passages from their textbooks or assigned readings.

Emotion, Engagement and Retention

Implicit in most of the above explanations for the inclusion of video material in teaching is the idea that such material engages students and thereby aids the retention of learning. Scherer and Baker (1999, p. 143) state that "film provides a familiar attention-capturing visual medium to engage the student and encourage retention." As summarized by Billsberry (2009, p. 4), "films are designed to engage the audience quickly and to swiftly form a bond between the audience and the characters. The narrative arc of a film creates tension, interest, and drama."

Engert and Spencer (2009, p. 85) state that:

> it is widely accepted as scientific knowledge that the human memory stores information in both a visual and an oral form and that a combination of both cognitive capacities helps people access, learn and then remember information.

Kuzma and Haney (2001, p. 34) note that "students retain 10% of what they read, [but] 50% of what they see and hear." They continue, "strong emotions securely imprint information in memory. Given its communicative powers, film amplifies the learning process by engaging viewers' emotions" (Kuzma & Haney, 2001, p. 35). Dunphy (2007, p. 179) says, "Great film moments achieve a life of their own. They seem to hang around in the viewer's subconscious mind begging for clarification or, if nothing else, classification." "Cinema's ability to create a unique experience," says Champoux (1999, p. 207) "gives it unbeatable power as a teaching tool." Billsberry and Gilbert (2008), Bumpus (2005) and Champoux (2001) all make similar points. Interestingly, Ventura and Onsman (2009) found that students were more likely to attend lectures when they knew in advance that they would contain feature films.

Medium as Message

Many of the uses of moving images are concerned with helping students understand the course ideas, or how to apply them, or how to use them critically. In these approaches, feature films and television programs are a supplement to the teaching. The focus is on the course theory; films and programs are just a teaching aid. Others advocate video material because it brings about particular outcomes in terms of engagement and involvement. Another group of scholars see video material being more integral to the teaching process. Rather than being an adjunct to the teaching, these authors argue that the medium and the message are inextricably intertwined.

Critical Thinking

Several authors use feature films to develop their students' critical thinking abilities. Billsberry and Gilbert (2008), for example, do not just use *Charlie and Chocolate Factory* to illustrate different recruitment and selection paradigms; they also want to develop their students' critical thinking skills and have deliberately chosen a fantastic and surreal environment in which to examine management processes. By doing so, they challenge their students to find meaning and to think laterally. Gallos (1993) offers a different approach. She uses feature films to develop her students' ability to see events from different perspectives; a skill she calls 'reframing.' On one level, her students study films, such as *Rashômon* (Kurosawa, 1950), that show an event from different perspectives. But on another level, her students engage in discussion and see how they 'read' the film differently. The point here is that film and teaching are intertwined; the film does not supplement the teaching, it is the teaching.

Student-Driven Curriculum

Several authors (e.g., Billsberry, 2009; Engert & Spencer, 2009; Liedtka, 2001) offer a way to use video material that changes the role of the instructor. Rather than a traditional learning model where the teacher determines the curriculum and the lessons to be learnt, in this alternative model the learners dictate the curriculum based on their readings and analyses of the feature films and television programs. Billsberry (2009) takes a social constructionist approach to leadership and wants his students to discover their own definitions of leadership. He uses film because it

> separates object and subject. Students are the observers and film gives them a common reference point, or objective reality, around which to discuss leadership. Students are the prime creator of their reality and their discussions about the way that leadership is portrayed gives language a prime role (Billsberry, pp. 4–5).

Engert and Spencer (2009, p. 85) similarly use films because they provide "a common reference point to which all participants can refer in order to make their arguments, points and views clear for the other members of the class."

This approach means that instructors lose a lot of control over the learning that takes place (Kuzma & Haney, 2001). Or rather, instructors create learning environments and opportunities, and students dictate the precise foci. Kuzma and Haney (2001, p. 36) explain this well:

The openness of the movies' form affords students great freedom in interpretation, evaluation, and reaction; it also gives viewers room to assign a variety of meanings to any given film. Students are more willing to offer an interpretation and partake in class discussion when they know there is no 'right answer.' … This view privileges learning in the classroom over teaching. This method, as two educators note (Chandler and Adams, 1997, p. 24), requires instructors to 'frame pedagogic content in ways that enable students to discover the relationship of academic concepts to their own life experiences. To use movies and other popular art forms as tools for teaching, and to invite students to explore them as tools for learning, is a risky venture. It requires that we move away from the forms of communication at which we tend to excel to those where we also become students.'"

Moral Development

In the wake of corporate collapses and fraudulent dealings involving individuals with business school educations, there has been considerable debate about the moral compass of management education in the past decade (Birnik & Billsberry, 2008). Appalled by the apparent callousness of senior managers with MBAs, there have been many calls for an ethical dimension being added to management education (e.g., Giacalone, 2007; Leavitt, 2007; Waddock, 2007). This debate has been echoed as a reason to employ feature films in management teaching. Comer and Holbrook (2005, p. 870), for example, argue that this media "cultivates [students'] sense of civic responsibility." In this case, the authors take a stakeholder approach to management, rather than a stockholder one, and have their students analyze *Dr. Seuss* to explore the multifaceted nature of decision-making. This is followed-up with a service learning element in which their students donate books to the local library in return for credit points. Students are encouraged to visit the kindergartens to donate the books and witness the joy of these 'stakeholders.' By carefully selecting appropriate movies and television programs, students can thus be exposed to the impact of decisions.

Media-Savvy Students

Many authors (e.g., Kuzma & Haney, 2001; Liedtka, 2001; Mallinger & Rossy, 2003; Smith, 2009) argue that students' familiarity with visual media in everyday life is a good reason to use feature films and television programs in management teaching. Kuzma and Haney (2001, p. 34) exemplify these arguments,

We teach and live in a culture dominated by film, television, and other visual media. Our students, namely the MTV generation, spend a major portion of their time in front of the television, at the computer, or in a movie theater. Consequently, they are geared to audiovisual rather than written forms of expression and communication.

Mallinger and Rossy (2003, p. 609) concur, "Students today have become accustomed to learning through multimedia and are easily bored or distracted by more traditional pedagogies. As a generation raised on television, film, and computers, they are more receptive to these new forms of information." Smith (2009, p. 464) adds more detail,

> Most of today's college students have a different style of learning than that of their professors. They grew up with computers and television serving as a vital aspect of life, integrated into nearly every facet of living— including education. This 'TV generation' learned about the alphabet and simple relationship skills from watching *Mister Rogers' Neighborhood* and *Sesame Street*. They learned math skills while watching *3-2-1 Contact* and science while watching *Newton's Apple*.

Reviewing the effectiveness of her use of film, Liedtka (2001, p. 411) notes, "our students seemed to like video—they were comfortable with the medium and found it unintimidating and fun."

TEACHING WITH MOVING IMAGES

There are many reasons, therefore, why you might want to consider using feature films and television programs in your own teaching. On one level they 'add color' to your teaching, or they can be used as rich, complex, and multifaceted case studies capable of many different readings. On another level, they offer an active approach to teaching which engages and motivates students. And on yet another level, they have particular qualities that allow instructors to change the learning contract and empower their students.

This book contains examples of management teaching from all of these perspectives. Moreover, the chapters offer a wide variety of different ways of using feature films and television programs in your teaching. These range from ways to illustrate lectures through individual and group work analyzing films. We have stopped short of including teaching approaches where students shoot their own films and instead focused on the use of pre-recorded video material. In the rest of this chapter, we offer brief introductions to each of the chapters. All of these works are new and all have been specially written for this book.

Part One: Inspirational Exemplars

The first section of the book contains chapters that record best practice in the use of moving images in the management classroom. Each chapter records the authors' own experience of using this media in their own teaching. We have deliberately chosen authors who represent a wide range of different approaches to illustrate the options that you have when considering whether or not to use movies or television programs in your own teaching. They include using stills, film clips and whole films, and using this media for illustration, explanation, application, critical awareness, and context. Some of these approaches address individual sessions, other whole semesters. Our goal is to be as broad as possible to fire the imagination about the possibilities.

The person most associated with popularizing the use of movies in management education is Joe Champoux. He has written many books and papers advocating their use and bravely did so at a time when the use of such media was looked upon rather skeptically by 'serious' educationists. But his persistence and persuasiveness won through and now moving images are more mainstream and their use unlikely to destroy your reputation. In this opening chapter, Joe describes the methods he has developed for using feature films in the teaching and learning environment. On this occasion, he focuses on four teaching areas: principles of management, organizational behavior, human resource management, and strategy. He shows how to use this material to explain and illustrate course theories in a lecture theatre setting.

The second chapter does almost the exact opposite to the first one. Rather than focus on mainstream Hollywood films, Thomaz Wood reacts against the conservative and conformist nature of the recommendations in the literature and explores the use of Art House films for management education. He illustrates his points by discussing how *Citizen Kane* (Welles, 1941) and *Terra em Transe* (aka *Land in Anguish/Entranced Earth*; Rocha, 1967) might be used.

Whereas the first two chapters explore the use of moving images with students on 'instructed' courses, the third chapter turns the attention on postgraduate research students. In this chapter, Richard Thorpe and Mark Easterby-Smith describe how they have used clips from television programs and feature films to make research methods more accessible. In particular, they focus on the different approaches used by fictional detectives to conduct their crime investigations, and use these to explain the different ways in which academic management research might be designed.

The movies and TV shows advocated in the first three chapters all use human actors. In these films programs, the end product has all the complexity of human behavior and has many unplanned qualities. Animated material is quite different because everything that appears before the camera is a deliberate and planned act by the film or program makers. In doing so, the originators of the product choose what to include, what to highlight, and what to omit. And, these choices are rarely masked by 'irrelevant' human behavior. When the choices coincide with the management educator's requirements, this makes animated material particularly clear in illustrating the key issues. In the fourth chapter, Joe Champoux looks at animated feature films as a serious and credible source of film scene materials for teaching various organizational behavior and management topics. He discusses several animated films that have not appeared before in the management education literature. These films range from 1930s hand drawn and hand painted "cel" animation, through molded Plasticine popularly called 'claymation,' to contemporary computer-animated films. The topics he illustrates include strategic planning, problem solving, organizational socialization, and personality.

The fifth chapter by Janet Sutherland takes a completely different approach again. Here, a single film, *Freedom Writers* (LaGravenese, 2007), is used as a motif throughout the length of an organizational behavior course as the basis for explaining key concepts. This particular film contains an example of inspirational teaching. It shows how students can think beyond the concrete example and expand their learning to make it much more experiential and value-driven. Janet encourages her own students to do this within their organizational behavior course, revealing how medium and message can combine to tremendous effect.

In the sixth chapter, Craig Webber considers how different forms of moving image, from cinema to television, from fiction to non-fiction, can help teachers elucidate difficult ideas and provide more immediate knowledge than can be achieved through words alone. He demonstrates the utility of using moving images by using real examples from his own teaching. He notes that different cohorts of students experience different challenges and he demonstrates how moving images can help students at different stages of their academic career. In addition, he shows how moving images can be used as a metaphor or shortcut for more complex ideas, to help students develop their understanding of a culture, and to challenge cultural indoctrination that has distorted students' impression of an occupation.

The seventh chapter offers an example of a feature film, namely *Twelve O'Clock High* (King, 1949), used as a case study. Steve Sloane uses this film to help his students analyze the complexity of human behavior and to get to the "So what?" question; i.e., helping them to understand the meaning of the knowledge they acquire. His goal is to improve the thinking skills of his students and to help them develop as individuals with their own goals, not as slaves to organizational managers. Here then is another example of a scholar using film for the development of ethics amongst his students.

Part Two: Critical Issues

The second section of the book picks out some key issues that may concern management educators who are thinking of using films and TV in their teaching. The first two focus on the nature of reality and drama in films. The third looks at films from the audience's perspective. The final one addresses issues of technology and copyright; something that seems to terrify everyone thinking of using movies and TV programs in their teaching!

One of the most intriguing qualities of feature films is the way they lend themselves to multiple readings. Although there may be some general themes that every viewer is aware of, there are an infinitive number of subtleties (and combination of subtleties) that viewers notice to create their impression of the movie. With a film like *The Company Men* (Wells, 2010), the themes of redundancy, outplacement, recruitment, and stockholder focus will be clear to all viewers, but each viewer will interpret the events slightly differently influenced by their own values. This encourages discussion and debate and, in the process, helps students understand their own values and that people always have different perspectives. This ability of feature films to generate different and often critical readings is one of the loci of Pauline Leonard in the eighth chapter in the book. In addition, she considers the nature of reality in films and suggests a structured way for educators to incorporate this media into their teaching.

These issues are developed further in the chapter by Emma Bell. She looks at film from the perspective of the audience and considers how they absorb the images of management and organization contained within feature films. Do they do so passively or actively, uncritically or critically? She also looks at whether these reactions differ according to demographic and psychological differences such as gender, age, ethnicity, personality, social position, values and beliefs, and life experiences. When management educators use feature films in the classroom they typically choose to use ones that mean a lot to them; you will see these selection decisions displayed in almost every chapter of this book. What are the implications of this behavior? Emma Bell argues that films are like books and lend themselves to many different readings and that management educators should resist the temptation to impose their own interpretations on their student audiences.

Andres Fortino's interest is in the drama in feature films. He argues that it is important to discover the basic principles under which successful drama is crafted and to use it appropriately as a basis for management education. When orchestrated carefully, the use of drama can provide a powerful, transformative experience for the student. He suggests that this practice should extend to all aspects of management including subjects rarely discussed in connection with feature films such as innovation management. He illustrates the power of drama to influence students' learning by showing how the motion picture *Shadow Magic* (Hu, 2000) can be used to in a technology management class to teach innovation management, technology adoption patterns, and barriers to adoption.

The final chapter in this section offers some practical advice on two issues that, judging by questions asked at workshops, worry many people new to using feature films and television programs in their teaching. The first of these issues is technology. What is the best way to show feature films in the management classroom? The authors, Joe Champoux and Jon Billsberry, take a historical perspective and show that the technology for showing video material is continually evolving. Despite this, the authors argue that that DVD is a particularly useful medium given its quality, transportability, and the ubiquity of DVD drives on students' computers. Future media such as digital copies are less likely to be as amenable. The second issue the authors explore is the legal issues surrounding the use of copyrighted materials in the management classroom. The legal framework in every country is different and could not be covered in this book. To give readers a flavor of the various issues, the authors discuss the relevant legislation in the USA and the UK.

Part Three: Imagining Inclusion

The final section of the book contains five chapters where the authors have imagined how video material might be used to teach particular subject areas. In most cases, these 'imaginings' are a blend of material and approaches that the authors have tried and tested combined with some new thinking. Hence, they do not contain random 'blue sky' thinking, but instead represent an extension by people already working with this material. The purpose of this section of the book is to illustrate the exciting range of possibilities that exist with video material.

Julie Charlesworth's focus is on teaching public sector management exploring the extent to which the state involves citizens in political, policy, and management processes. Although nothing new, the notion of engaging with the public has gained in importance in recent years, and discourses of community, civil society, social capital, co-production, active citizenship, and so on are often mobilized by politicians and other commentators as the means by which governance can be improved, communities revived, and complex issues tackled, such as poverty, social exclusion, and health improvement. To enliven her teaching, Julie advocates the use of visual media as 'real-life' case studies. She draws upon a rich mixture of media including photographs, documentary film, organizational promotional film, movies, and television series. In this chapter though, she focuses on how whole feature films or clips could be used to illustrate key themes in public involvement.

Bringing 'the real world' into the strategic management classroom is the concern of Véronique Ambrosini, Jon Billsberry and Nardine Collier. They note that strategic management is about practice and analysis, and strategic problems are generally complex, often with multiple answers. Hence, it is difficult for students lacking managerial experience to relate to and comprehend many strategy principles. They argue that the analysis of feature films can help students understand, remember, and apply concepts.

To illustrate how feature films could be employed, they review the strategy curriculum, highlighting some concepts that are particularly difficult to teach with students lacking managerial experience and present examples of feature films, the analysis of which may help students get to grips with the subject.

The first of the two chapters by Peter Galvin and Troy Hendrickson focuses on the teaching of strategic decision-making. This is a subject traditionally taught with somewhat sterile written case studies. To help 'attach' students to the relevant issues, the authors substitute a feature film, *Thirteen Days* (Donaldson, 2000), which brings the additional benefits of showing human cognitive limits, bias, irrationality, political influence, and uncertainty. In doing so, these authors illustrate a valuable quality of feature films; the ability to show micro-level behavior and the way that the theoretical is influenced by all manner of 'human' limitations.

As noted by Jon Billsberry, recruitment and selection has long been a subject that has incorporated video methods to support teaching. For example, mock interviews have been videotaped and played back to both interviewees and interviewers to help them identify their strengths and weaknesses, and make suitable adjustments. In his chapter, Jon thinks very broadly about the use of different forms of visual media to aid the teaching of recruitment and selection subjects. This ranges from the practical use of self-shot video for practical purposes, through the use of feature films for illustrative purposes, to the use of whole movies to analyze and critique important recruitment and selection issues. Along the way, Jon identifies a large number of potential resources for use in the management classroom.

In the final chapter of the book, Troy Hendrickson and Peter Galvin return to mainstream topics in business and management and develop a full pedagogic approach including teaching resources. They explore how three well-known Hollywood films, *Alive* (Marshall, 1993), *Braveheart* (Gibson, 1995) and *Coach Carter* (Carter, 2005), can be used to illustrate course ideas. The authors argue that well made feature films are thought-provoking and make viewers empathize with the characters thereby making them engaging. When the movies illustrate relevant material, these qualities help instructors embed and reinforce their teaching.

FINAL THOUGHT

In a book of this kind there are bound to be a range of different voices and perspectives about both the theory and the practice of using visual media in teaching and learning contexts. Indeed, as editors we wanted very much to bring together authors whose work crosses a range of disciplinary boundaries as well as national and theoretical traditions. When we take all the contributions in the volume together however, it is clear that they all share a passion for the value of using visual culture in the classroom. We very much hope that this book will extend this to encourage not only the more widespread use of this approach, but also further debate and reflection on different forms of good practice in teaching with film and television in management education.

REFERENCES

Alvarez, J. L., Miller, P., Levy, J., & Svejenova, S. (2004). Journeys to the self: Using movie directors in the classroom. *Journal of Management Education, 28*(3), 335–355.

Billsberry, J. (2009). The social construction of leadership education. *Journal of Leadership Education, 8*(2), 1–9.

Billsberry, J., & Gilbert, L. H. (2008). Using Roald Dahl's *Charlie and the Chocolate Factory* to teach different recruitment and selection paradigms. *Journal of Management Education, 32*(2), 228–247.

Birnik, A., & Billsberry, J. (2008). Re-orienting the business school agenda: The case for relevance, rigor and righteousness. *Journal of Business Ethics, 82*(4), 985–999.

Bluestone, C. (2000). Feature films as a teaching tool. *College Teaching, 48*(4), 141–143.

Bonwell, C., & Eison, J. (1991). *Active Learning: Creating Excitement in the Classroom AEHE-ERIC Higher Education Report No. 1.* Washington, DC: Jossey-Bass.

Buchanan, D., & Huczinski, A. A. (2004). Images of influence: *12 Angry Men* and *Thirteen Days. Journal of Management Inquiry, 13*(4), 312–323.

Bumpus, M. (2005). Using motion pictures to teach management: Refocusing the camera lens through the infusion approach to diversity. *Journal of Management Education, 29*(6), 792–815.

Champoux, J. E. (1999). Film as a teaching resource. *Journal of Management Inquiry, 8*(2), 206–217.

Champoux, J. E. (2001). Animated films as a teaching resource. *Journal of Management Education, 25*(1), 79–100.

Champoux, J. E. (2004). Commentary on "Filmmaking and Research" and "Images of Influence." *Journal of Management Inquiry, 13*(4), 336–340.

Champoux, J. (2005). Comparative analyses of live-action and animated film remake scenes: finding alternative film-based teaching resources. *Educational Media International, 42*(1), 49–69.

Champoux, J. E. (2006). At the cinema: Aspiring to a higher ethical standard. *Academy of Management Learning & Education, 5*(3), 386–390.

Chandler, R. C., & Adams, B. A. K. (1997). Let's go to the movies! Using film to illustrate basic concepts in public administration. *Public Voices, 8*(2), 9–26.

Comer, D. R. (2001). Not just a Mickey Mouse exercise: Using Disney's *The Lion King* to teach leadership. *Journal of Management Education, 25*(4), 430–436.

Comer, D. R., & Holbrook, R. L. (2005). All I really need to know I learned in kindergarten: How Dr. Seuss reinforces management concepts and promotes community citizenship. *Journal of Management Education, 29*(6), 870–887.

Dunphy, S. (2007). Using Hollywood's greatest film scenes to illustrate concepts of organisational behaviour and management. *Behaviour & Information Technology, 26*(2), 179–185.

Engert, S., & Spencer, A. (2009). International relations at the movies: Teaching and learning about international politics through film. *International Relations, 17*(1), 83–104.

Gallos, J. V. (1993). Teaching about reframing with films and videos. *Journal of Management Education, 17*(1), 127–132.

Giacalone, R. A. (2007). Taking a red pill to disempower unethical students: Creating ethical sentinels in business schools. *Academy of Management Learning & Education, 6*(4), 534–542.

Hassard, J., & Holliday, R. (Eds.) (1998). *Organization representation: Work and organization in popular culture.* London, UK: Sage.

Holbrook, R. L. (2009). OB in a video box: Using *Remember the Titans* as a microcosm for the organizational behavior course. *Journal of Management Education, 33*(4), 490–513.

Honey, P., & Mumford, A. (2000). *The learning styles helper's guide.* Maidenhead, UK: Peter Honey Publications.

Hunt, C. S. (2001). Must see TV: The timelessness of television as a teaching tool. *Journal of Management Education, 25*(6), 631–647.

Huczynski, A., & Buchanan, D. A. (2004). Theory from fiction: A narrative process perspective on the pedagogical use of feature film. *Journal of Management Education, 28*(6), 707–726.

Kenworthy-U'Ren, A., & Erickson, A. (2009). Adventure racing and organizational behavior: Using Eco Challenge video clips to stimulate learning. *Journal of Management Education, 33*(4), 420–443.

Kirschner, P. A., Sweller, J., & Clark, R. E. (2006). Why minimal guidance during instruction does not work: an analysis of the failure of constructivist, discovery, problem-based, experiential, and inquiry-based teaching. *Educational Psychologist, 41*(2), 75–86.

Kolb, D. A. (1976). Management and learning process. *California Management Review, 15*(3), 20–31.

Kuzma, L. M., & Haney, P. J. (2001). And . . . Action ! Using film to learn about foreign policy. *International Studies Perspectives, 2*(1), 33–50.

Leavitt, H. J. (2007). Big organizations are unhealthy environments for human beings. *Academy of Management Learning & Education, 6*(2), 253–263.

Leet, D., & Houser, S. (2003). Economics goes to Hollywood: Using classic films and documentaries to create an undergraduate economics course. *The Journal of Economic Education, 34*(4), 326–332.

Liedtka, J. (2001). The promise and peril of video cases: Reflections on their Creation and use. *Journal of Management Education, 25*(4), 409–424.

Mallinger, M., & Rossy, G. (2003). Film as a lens for teaching culture: Balancing concepts, ambiguity, and paradox. *Journal of Management Education, 27*(5), 608–624.

McCambridge, J. (2003). *12 Angry Men*: A study in dialogue. *Journal of Management Education, 27*(3), 384–401.

Mayer, R. (2004). Should there be a three-strikes rule against pure discovery learning? The case for guided methods of instruction. *American Psychologist, 59*(1), 14–19.

Mintzberg, H. (2004). *Managers, not MBAs.* Harlow, UK: Pearson Education.

Mintzberg, H., & Lampel, J. (2001). Matter of degrees: Do MBAs make better CEOs? *Fortune, 143*(4), 244.

Pfeffer, J., & Fong, C. T. (2002). The end of business schools? Less success than meets the eye. *Academy of Management Learning and Education, 1*(1), 78–95.

Scherer, R. F., & Baker, B. (1999). Exploring social institutions through the films of Frederick Wiseman. *Journal of Management Education, 23*(2), 143–153.

Serey, T. T. (1992). Carpe diem: Lessons about life and management from *Dead Poets Society. Journal of Management Education, 16*(3), 374–381.

Serva, M. A., & Fuller, M. A. (2004). Aligning what we do and what we measure in business schools: Incorporating active learning and effective media use in the assessment of instruction. *Journal of Management Education, 28*(1), 19–38.

Sesonske, A. (1974). Aesthetics of film, or A funny thing happened on the way to the movies. *Journal of Aesthetics and Art Criticism, 31*(1), 51–57.

Sexton, R. (2006). Using short movie and television clips in the economics principles class. *The Journal of Economic Education, 37*(4), 406–417.

Smith, G. W. (2009). Using feature films as the primary instructional medium to teach organizational behavior. *Journal of Management Education, 33*(4), 462–489.

Spender, J. C. (2007). Management as a regulated profession: An essay. *Journal of Management Inquiry, 16*(1), 32–42.

Tyler, C. L., Anderson, M. H., & Tyler, J. M. (2007). Giving students new eyes: The benefits of having students find media clips to illustrate management concepts. *Journal of Management Education, 33*(4), 444–461.

Ventura, S. A. B., & Onsman, A. (2009). The use of popular movies during lectures to aid the teaching and learning of undergraduate pharmacology. *Studies in Language*, 662–664.

Waddock, S. (2007). Leadership integrity in a fractured knowledge world. *Academy of Management Learning & Education, 6*(4), 543–557.

Films

Burton, T. (Director). (2005). *Charlie and the chocolate factory* [Motion picture]. United States: Warner Bros.

Carter, T. (Director). (2005). *Coach Carter* [Motion picture]. United States & Germany: Paramount Pictures.

Donaldson, R. (Director). (2000). *Thirteen days* [Motion picture]. United States: New Line Cinema.

Gibson, M. (Director). (1985). *Braveheart* (Motion picture). United States: Icon Productions & Ladd Company.

Hu, A. (Director). (2000). *Shadow magic* [Motion picture]. China, Germany, Taiwan, & United States: Beijing Film Studio, C & A Productions, Central Motion Pictures Corporation, China Film, Filmstiftung Nordrhein-Westfalen, Post Production Playground, Road Movies Vierte Produktionen, Schulberg Productions, & Taiwan Central Motion Picture Corporation.

King, H. (Director). (1949). *Twelve o'clock high* [Motion Picture]. United States: Twentieth Century Fox.

Kurosawa, A. (Director). (1950). *Rashômon* [Motion picture]. Japan: Daiei Motion Picture Company.

LaGravenese, R. (Director). (2007). *Freedom writers* [Motion picture]. Germany/United States: Paramount Pictures.

Marshall, F. (Director). (1993). *Alive* [Motion picture]. United States: Paramount Pictures

Rocha, G. (Director). (1967). *Terra em transe* [Motion picture]. Brazil: Mapa Filmes.

Wells, J. (Director). (2010). *The company men* [Motion picture]. United Kingdom & United States: The Weinstein Company.

Welles, O. (Director). (1941). *Citizen Kane* [Motion picture]. United States: Mercury Productions & RKO Radio Pictures.

SECTION ONE

INSPIRATIONAL EXEMPLARS

CHAPTER 1

VIEWING ORGANIZATIONAL BEHAVIOR, MANAGEMENT CONCEPTS, AND THEORIES THROUGH FILM

Joseph E. Champoux

FILM AS A TEACHING RESOURCE: A SUMMARY[1]

Film theorists view film as a different way of seeing and experiencing the world. Close-up shots, long shots, and various focusing techniques, for example, can create a unique viewer experience. Film serves many functions in its teaching role. It works well as a case or the target of an experiential exercise. It also can illustrate or show abstract theories and concepts, bringing them to life for the viewer. The opening scenes of *Top Gun* (Scott, 1986) show U.S. Naval aviation culture artifacts (people, aircraft, hand signals) so clearly that a viewer cannot fail to see them.

---

[1] Please see Champoux (1999) for a more detailed discussion of this section's summary.

Moving Images: Effective Teaching with Film and Television in Higher Education,
pages 3–17

Instructors can also use film in different ways. Showing film scenes before presenting concepts lets the instructor link to specific moments in the scenes that show the concepts discussed. The opening scenes from *Top Gun* also work well in this mode. Comparing film scenes from film remakes can give a viewer the experience of different times in a country's culture. The two versions of *Sabrina* (Wilder, 1954) offer a comparative view of American culture. Key differences appear in cultural values and gender roles. The 1995 version also shows the increased diversity in society and organizations.

Some advantages of using film follow from the fact that contemporary students see film as a comfortable, familiar experience. Careful instructor guidance can help connect students to the theories and concepts under discussion and the cinematic examples on the screen. Other advantages include the substitution of film for a field trip and the honing of students' analytical skills through cinema analysis. Viewer responses play a key role in student reactions to film scenes. Film editing techniques such as the shot/reverse-shot that is used to convey conversation between two or more people help a director create a unique cinematic experience. The *Broadcast News* (Brooks, 1987) editing booth scene vividly shows stress responses because of this technique.

Some disadvantages also exist. Showing film scenes during class, of course, absorbs some time. The careful selection of film scenes that best show the theories and concepts under discussion will make good use of that time. In most countries, copyright law prevents one from copying selected scenes to a single source, so there is some time used to position a DVD to a desired scene. I propose that the advantages of film in one's teaching program greatly outweigh the disadvantages. The rest of this chapter describes how to use film scenes in your lecture theatre and discusses useful film scenes in the four primary areas noted at the beginning of this chapter.

USING FILM SCENES IN THE LECTURE THEATRE

Applicable copyright laws always guide the use of film scenes in the lecture theatre. Under U.S. copyright law an educator can use no more than 10 percent of the running time of a film from a legal copy of that film in a non-profit educational environment. "Legal copy" refers to a DVD that the educator owns, rents, or borrows from a library of films at his or her institution. You should check your country's copyright law to determine fair use and legal use of film in your teaching environment.

You will have some unavoidable setup time when using film scenes in your teaching program. The setup time includes positioning the DVD at the desired scene either on a classroom DVD player or a laptop computer. Tables later in this chapter give scene position information for the scenes presented and discussed. The positioning information includes the DVD chapter and scene start and stop positions, if these occur within a chapter. Some scenes occur within a complete DVD chapter; others are parts of chapters. The setup time is not a burden and becomes easier with practice. I typically show two film scenes in a three hour class meeting or one scene each in classes that meet for one and one-half hours twice a week.

I start by briefly describing the film followed by a description of the scene that I will show. The latter includes what has happened in the film before the selected scene. I also present some discussion questions that students should consider while viewing the scene. All of this information appears in a handout that I give students before showing the film scene. The information also appears in available film teaching resources such as the *Our Feature Presentation* film work books from South-Western & Cengage Learning (Champoux, 2004, 2005, 2006, 2007). *BizFlix* is another resource from this publisher which appears in many of their organizational behavior and principles of management textbooks.

I noted earlier that there are several ways of using film in your classes. They include showing film scenes after presenting theories or concepts. You can also show the scenes before that presentation and link to the film scenes during your discussion. Further, you can repeat the film scenes to re-inforce some points, especially subtle or difficult ones for your students. In each instance, I give the information described in the previous paragraph.

I also assign entire films to student groups or teams for their outside-the-lecture-theatre viewing, analysis, and discussion. Each team receives a DVD of the assigned film. They work on this assignment over a specified time as part of the course requirements. Each team makes an in-class presentation of their project, accompanied by showing the class about 10 percent of the film's running time. The teams prepare and submit a written report as part of the class requirements.

FILM RESOURCES FOR TEACHING: SOME EXAMPLES

This section describes and discusses films and film scenes in each of the four teaching areas. Each section has an accompanying table with information that will help you locate the film scene on a DVD. All settings and timings are for Area 1 DVDs but likely vary only a little in the other five DVD regional domains.

Principles of Management

Table 1 shows films and selected film scenes that will work well for a principles of management course. The table gives film publication information and scene position information for the scenes discussed here.

Charlie Wilson's War (Nichols, 2007) showcases East Texas Congressman Wilson (Tom Hanks) in his effort to support Afghanistan rebels in their opposition to the 1980s Soviet invasion. Wilson's role in two major congres-

TABLE 1. Film Resources for Principles of Management Courses

Film Title	Year of Release	Rating	Director	Film Running Time	Distributor	Scene Position
Charlie Wilson's War	2007	R	Mike Nichols	1 hour, 42 minutes	Universal Studios Home Entertainment	Chapter 3, "Bigger Budget" (Stop: 0:10:15)
In Bruges	2008	R	Martin McDonagh	1 hour, 47 minutes	Universal Studios Home Entertainment	1. Chapter 1, "Medieval Town" (Start: 0:01:43—Stop: 0:02:13) 2. Start Chapter 1, "Medieval Town" 0:03:30—Stop: Chapter 2, "Terrible Tourist" 0:05:18
Inside Man	2006	R	Spike Lee	2 hours, 9 minutes	Universal Studios Home Entertainment	Chapter 5, "A Small Problem" (Start 0:28:57—Stop 0:30:25)
Baby Mama	2008	PG-13	Michael McCullers	1 hour, 39 minutes	Universal Studios Home Entertainment	Chapter 14, "First Date" (Stop 1:05:46)
Friday Night Lights	2004	PG-13	Peter Berg	1 hour, 58 minutes	Universal Studios Home Entertainment	Chapter 12, "Get the Job Done" (Start: 0:40:46—Stop: 0:43:14)

sional committees helps him champion the Afghan cause. The sequence noted in Table 1 looks at an organization's culture; in this case a piece of the U.S. Congress. Physical artifacts quickly appear in the form of business attire, pictures and other wall decorations, and social interaction patterns. One also can infer values and basic assumptions. The latter are second nature to veteran organizational members while the former are more visible. Social deference and the importance of social status clearly appear in the deferential behavior shown in the scenes. The importance of knowledge and taking action shows toward the end of the sequence, when Wilson reads the teletype and commits to taking some action.

In Bruges (McDonagh, 2008) is a fast-paced crime/action film set in the beautiful medieval Flemish city of Bruges, Belgium. Fellow hit men, Ray (Colin Ferrell) and Ken (Brendan Gleeson), are ordered by their London boss, Harry Waters (Ralph Fiennes), to go to Bruges for several weeks after Ray had botched a murder of a priest by also killing a young boy. Ken enjoys the Bruges scenery and culture and Ray pouts with boredom. The film's first two DVD chapters have useful sequences. The first sequence shows Ray and Ken walking along a street. A second sequence begins with a panning shot of a tower down to the boat carrying Ray and Ken. These combined sequences show entry into a foreign culture (from Ireland and England to Belgium) and differences in cultural sensitivity of Ray and Ken. The cultural differences do not impress Ray while Ken enjoys the Flemish architecture and history. Ray longs for his Irish culture but must endure the Flemish culture.

Inside Man (Lee, 2006), an action-packed film, presents a challenge to Detective Keith Frazier (Denzel Washington). The challenge is to remove Dalton Russell (Clive Owen) from a New York bank without injuring the hostages. The recommended sequence shows Captain John Darius (Willem Dafoe) describing his plan to Detectives Frazier and Bill Mitchell (Chiwetlel Ejiofor). His plan includes:

- Engaging four "perps" (perpetrators)
- Download the security video
- Close the city block
- Put men (armed) in the windows
- Check sewers
- Divert telephone calls
- Jam cellular telephones if Detective Frazier requests it
- Route 911 calls

Detective Frazier adds his element to Captain Darius' surprise; not calling them yet. All of these pieces are part of a plan for a course of action.

Baby Mama (McCullers, 2008) stars Tina Fey as Kate Holbrook who is career-oriented, childless, and in her late thirties. She wants a child but not the pregnancy risks at her age. Enter Angie Ostrowiski (Amy Poehler), whom Kate recruits to bear her child. Rob Ackerman (Greg Kinnear), owner of Super Fruity, begins dating Kate, adding another social dimension to already complex relationships. The vegan restaurant scene shows many aspects of diversity in the differences among Kate, Rob, and Chet the Vegan Waiter (Jon Glaser). They include basic personality difference and food preferences. You can see the sharp contrast in the latter by comparing the Vegan Waiter's reaction to vegan food as compared to Kate and Rob's reaction. The two quickly leave for a non-vegan dining experience. Kate's other diversity dimension clearly shows obsessive compulsive behavior about food preparation.

Friday Night Lights (Berg, 2004) has several useful scenes for aspects of management. This film focuses on the Permian High Panthers football team in Odessa, Texas. The town's Friday night passion for football shines in many places. Coach Gary Gaines (Billy Bob Thornton) leads the team to the 1988 semi-finals. Some slow introspective sequences combine with fast-moving playing sequences to make an engaging cinematic experience. The selected sequence features Coach Gaines trying to motivate quarterback Mike Winchell (Lucas Black). Gaines asks whether Mike can get the job done. The coach tries to focus Mike on his self-actualization needs while Mike has a greater focus on security needs because of his ailing mother. This sequence closes with a goal-setting emphasis by Coach Gaines which helps Mike play in later parts of the film.

Organizational Behavior

Table 2 lists films and selected film scenes that will work well for organizational behavior theories and concepts. The table gives film publication information and scene position information for the scenes discussed here.

The Breakfast Club (Hughes, 1985) has an exceptional sequence that shows the personalities of the five club members. One can see the Big Five personality dimensions in these scenes, as well as Type A or B, and Machiavellian personalities. The following are the five distinct personalities that appear in this sequence:

John Bender (Judd Nelson): A Machiavellian personality with high negative affectivity and extroversion. He shows low conscientiousness, agreeableness, and emotional stability.

Brian Ralph Johnson (Anthony Michael Hall): An example of a Type B personality. Brian is high on almost all the Big-Five personality dimensions except extroversion where he appears moderate.

Allison Reynolds (Ally Sheedy): A Type A personality with high extroversion and openness to experience. Low on the other Big Five personality dimensions.

TABLE 2. Film Resources for Organizational Behavior Courses

Film Title	Year of Release	Rating	Director	Film Running Time	Distributor	Scene Position
The Breakfast Club	1985	R	John Hughes	1 hour, 32 minutes	Universal Home Video, Inc.	Chapter 8, "Lunchtime" (Stop: 0:40:01)
The Emperor's Club	2002	PG-13	Michael Hoffman	1 hour, 49 minutes	Universal Studios	Chapter 18, "The Candidate" (Start: 1:32:23—Stop: 1:36:09)
Seabiscuit	2003	PG-13	Gary Ross	2 hours, 21 minutes	Universal Studios and DreamWorks LLC	Chapter 21
Dr. Seuss' How the Grinch Stole Christmas	2000	PG	Ron Howard	1 hour, 42 minutes	Universal Studios	Chapter 9, "Second Thoughts"
Scarface	1983	R	Brian DePalma	2 hours, 50 minutes	Universal Studios	Chapter 17, "Shakedown" (Start: 1:19:08—Stop: 1:22:04)

Claire Standish (Molly Ringwald): A strong Type A personality; the strongest of the five characters shown. She also is a complex mix of the Big Five dimensions. Claire shows high conscientiousness and extroversion; she is moderate on the other three dimensions.

Andrew Clark (Emilio Estevez): A Type B who is moderate on the Big Five dimensions. Andrew shows no Machiavellian characteristics here and elsewhere in the film.

The Emperor's Club (McCullers, 2002) stars Kevin Kline as Professor William Hundert of the Saint Benedict's Academy for Boys. He believes in living a principled life that is strongly guided by an ethics system. Former student Sedgewick Bell (Joel Gretsch) has shown an inability to lead a principled life. Professor Hundert twice observed his unethical behavior earlier in the film. This scene follows the banquet for Professor Hundert at Bell's estate. The essence of Bell's ethical system appears in his response to Professor Hundert's observations on ethics: "I live in the real world ... where people do what they need to do to get what they want. And if it's lying and it's cheating, then so be it." His son Robert (Jimmy Walsh) also heard what he said, making the result even more damning for Bell.

Seabiscuit (2003, Gary Ross) tells the story of the legendary horse who captivated people during the American depression. Seabiscuit's jockey Red Pollard (Tobey Maguire) suffered a severe leg injury and cannot ride Seabiscuit against War Admiral. Pollard recommends George Wolff (Gary Stevens) as his substitute. Samuel Riddle (Eddie Jones), War Admiral's owner, believes a new rider will not affect the race's result. Pollard carefully shapes Wolff's behavior. He clearly describes the steps Wolff should follow for behavioral success. An example: "Now. Show him the stick at the quarter pole. And he'll give you a whole new gear." Pollard positively reinforces Wolff's behavior with simple feedback such as "Great!"

Dr. Seuss' How the Grinch Stole Christmas (aka *How the Grinch Stole Christmas*; Howard, 2000) shows the Whoville Whos as great lovers of Christmas and the Grinch (Jim Carrey) as one who hates Christmas. Cindy Lou Who (Taylor Momsen) has invited the Grinch to return to the celebrations. He now faces a serious round of decision making. The Grinch follows the decision-making process in assessing his many choices:

- Wallow in self-pity at one o'clock.
- Stare into the abyss at four thirty.
- Solve world hunger at five o'clock.
- Jazzercise at Five thirty.
- Dinner alone at six thirty.
- Wrestle with his self-loathing at seven o'clock.

His biggest decision centers on a proper outfit for the occasion. The presence of the unfortunate Yodeler (Gavin Grazer) solves that problem for him. The scene clearly shows the Grinch's decision criteria; make only selfish choices.

Scarface (De Palma, 1983) portrays Antonio "Tony" Montana (Al Pacino), a Cuban refugee, as trying to pursue the American dream in Miami. He quickly becomes a powerful leader within Miami's drug world. His interaction with Narcotics Chief Detective Mel Bernstein (Harris Yulin) in this sequence shows the dimensions of a power relationship. The relational dimension appears when Bernstein describes Montana as public property. Both the dependency and sanctioning dimensions appear for each of them. They need each other but for different reasons. Tony needs protection by Mel's officers and Mel needs Tony for financial resources. Mel also has coercive, expert, and information power over Tony. He can arrest him at any time and has full knowledge of Miami's drug operations.

Human Resource Management

Table 3 shows films and selected film scenes that will work well in a human resource management course. The table gives film publication information and scene position information for the scenes discussed here.

Intolerable Cruelty (2003, Joel and Ethan Coen) pits Miles Massey (George Clooney), a brilliant divorce attorney, against the ruthless Marilyn Rexroth (Catherine Zeta-Jones). She caught her husband Rex Rexroth (George Herrmann) having an affair with a young woman (Kristen Dattilo). Rex now desperately needs some legal advice. The successful performance of Massey's job requires certain knowledge, skills, and abilities (KSAs). They include his legal knowledge about divorce and domestic relations. An example of this knowledge appears when he asks Rex about a prenuptial agreement. Skills and abilities include capable analysis of a case and court presentation. Some of Massey's job activities and tasks also appear in this scene. He must represent his clients and ensure confidentiality of that relationship. One primary job task is data gathering as he does in this first meeting. Client meetings and court representation are examples of some of Massey's job activities.

Backdraft (Howard, 1991) has exquisite special effects that show Chicago fire-fighters in action. Sibling rivalry hovers over the relationship between Lieutenant Stephen "Bull" McCaffrey (Kurt Russell) and his younger brother Brian (William Baldwin). Brian has just joined Bull's Engine Company 17. This sequence shows his first day on the job. Brian is a new fire-fighter in Engine Company 17 (a "probie" or probationary fire-fighter), a point made clear at the beginning and later in these scenes. Bull views his role as the training and development of his brother. He arranges his fire-fighting gear directly and instructs him to stay by his side. The closing scene of this

TABLE 3. Film Resources for Human Resources Management Courses

Film Title	Year of Release	Rating	Director	Film Running Time	Distributor	Scene Position
Intolerable Cruelty	2003	PG-13	Joel Coen	1 hour, 40 minutes	Universal Studios	Chapter 5, "The War Room"
Backdraft	1991	R	Ron Howard	2 hours, 15 minutes	Universal Home Video, Inc.	Chapter 4, "The First Day" (Stop: 0:30:47)
The Wedding Date	2005	PG-13	Clare Kilner	1 hour, 30 minutes	Universal Studios Home Entertainment	Chapter 3, "Trying too hard" to Chapter 4, A simple business transaction (Stop: 0:13:35)
Scent of a Woman	1992	R	Martin Brest	2 hours, 37 minutes	MCA Universal Home Video	Chapter 9, "Tango Lessons" (Start: 1:37:04)
Erin Brockovich	2000	R	Steven Soderbergh	2 hours, 11 minutes	Universal Studios	Chapter 17, "Ed comes over" (Stop: 0:45:47)

sequence shows Bull's anger with his brother about deviating from his pre-scribed pattern.

The Wedding Date (Kilner, 2005) stars Debra Messing as Kat Ellis who needs a date to travel with her to London for the wedding of her sister Amy (Amy Adams). She frantically searches the classifieds for a male escort. Nick Mercer (Dermot Mulroney) emerges as a good choice. He also exceeds Kat's expectations for his charm and dash. Fairness of Nick's pay is a major compensation issue that emerges in these scenes. Nick has travelled with her to London. He worked with Kat while she tried on several dresses in the pub because her first choice too closely matches Nick's tie. Nick also must stay with her for several days during the wedding. Kat pays him $6,000 which Nick appears to accept as fair. He does not even want to count the cash but Kat insists that he count it, which he does quickly while she looks on carefully.

Scent of a Woman (Brest, 1992) presents Charlie Simms (Chris O'Donnell) as the young caretaker and guide for Lt. Col. Frank Slade (Al Pacino) who is blind, retired, and ill-tempered. Charlie took the job to earn some money for airfare to return home during his school's Christmas break. This scene shows some negotiations with Ferrari salesman Freddie Bisco (Leonard Gaines). Frank Slade wants to enjoy the ride while Charlie Simms drives the Ferrari. One can assume that money motivates Freddie and that any use of an incentive could shape and change his behavior. Frank Slade offers Freddie $2,000 to let them have access to a car. The reward works! Freddie lets them take the car. Moments later the film shows Charlie driving a Ferrari with Frank as the passenger.

Erin Brockovich (Soderbergh, 2000) shows Julia Roberts in her Academy Award winning title role. She convinces Ed Masry (Albert Finney), a skeptical attorney, to hire her. She quickly discovers that Pacific Gas & Electric Company (PG&E) has some major pollution problems. Unfortunately, some earlier events led to her termination at Masry's firm. Now Masry needs her back and Erin is able to negotiate for higher pay and some important fringe benefits. The scene's opening establishes the importance with the shots of past due bills and Erin looking through the newspaper want ads.

Strategy

Table 4 shows films and selected film scenes that will work well for a strategy or strategic management course. The table gives film publication information and scene position information for the scenes discussed here.

U-571 (Mostow, 2000) stars Matthew McConaughey as Lt. Andrew Tyler. He is now the commander of the submarine after the drowning of its former commander Lt. Commander Mike Dahlgren (Bill Paxton). He and his crew have retrieved an Enigma encryption device from a German submarine. That disabled submarine now becomes their way of escaping from the

TABLE 4. Film Resources for Strategy Courses

Film Title	Year of Release	Rating	Director	Film Running Time	Distributor	Scene Position
U-571	2000	PG-13	Jonathan Mostow	1 hour, 57 minutes	Universal Studios	Chapter 16, "160 Meters" (Stop: 1:25:21)
Ray	2004	PG-13	Taylor Hackford	2 hours, 58 minutes (extended version)	Universal Studios	Chapter 8, "Messing Around" (Start: 0:40:07—Stop: 0:45:58)
About a Boy	2002	PG-13	Paul Weitz, Chris Weitz	1 hour, 42 minutes	Universal Studios	Chapter 4, "s.p.a.t." (Stop: 0:16:55)
Meet the Parents	2000	R	Jay Roach	1 hour, 48 minutes	Universal Studios	Chapter 18, "No More Lies"
Erin Brockovich	2000	R	Steven Soderbergh	2 hours, 11 minutes	Universal Studios	Chapter 34, Erin and Ed meet with Kurt and Theresa (Stop: 1:38:00)

enemy. Lt. Tyler goes through many of the recommended steps for forming a strategy or strategic plan:

- External environment assessment which includes the state of his submarine and the German destroyer.
- Create a new part of the external environment with the debris field.
- Resources: Mazzola's (Erik Palladino) body and the buoyancy of his submarine.
- Threats: his submarine's slow speed.
- Opportunities: the debris field and a fast rise to periscope depth.

Ray (Hackford, 2004) tells the story of Ray Charles' fast rise in music despite some impossible odds. Jamie Foxx plays Ray Charles. Ahmet Ertugen (Curtis Armstrong) has told Charles that Atlantic Records has bought Charles' Swingtime contract. It is now time for Charles to show his talents, but he falls short of everyone's expectations. In much the same way a manager would analyze a company, Ahmet analyses Charles. He sounds too much like Nat Cole or Charles Brown (weaknesses). But, his energy, virtuosity, and voice timbre are his strengths, along with his Pete Johnson style of stride piano playing. Ray Charles shows his capabilities in a moving rendition of "The Mess Around," following Ahmet's strong guidance.

About a Boy (Weitz & Weitz, 2002) takes you along an adventurous path as Will Lightman (Hugh Grant) learns to reframe his life as a wealthy bachelor. He succeeds in having no responsibilities and forming short-term relationships with no guilt feelings. Will gets the idea that he should date single mothers. He attends a meeting of Single Parents Alone Together (SPAT) where he describes his son Ned (fictional). Will uses focused differentiation as part of his strategy to make himself (the product) appeal to this group (the customers or market). He further builds his differentiation by focusing on psychological factors, those that are hard for strangers to see. Ned plays an important role in this product's differentiation. Few two year olds, for example, would likely say to their father, "You hang in there, Dad."

Meet the Parents (Roach, 2000) offers an engaging sequence that emphasizes the important strategic move of assessing an acquisition. The "acquisition" in this case is Greg Focker (Ben Stiller). He comes to girlfriend Pam's (Teri Polo) home for a weekend visit to leave a positive impression on her parents. Pam's father Jack Byrnes (Robert De Niro) dislikes him immediately. Jack Byrnes, an ex-CIA psychological profiler, uses his many talents in this area to assess this potential acquisition. He holds Greg's wrists to assess his pulse during questioning (simulating a lie detector test). Jack focuses on emotional issues first, such as smoking marijuana. He then moves to serious issues such Greg's love of Pam and his desire to marry her. Jack closes the acquisition assessment by saying, "Gaylord Focker, will you be my son-in-law?" and presents the engagement ring.

Erin Brockovich offers another sequence that shows some issues in creating and maintaining alliances. This sequence appears much later in the film, about 30 percent from the film's end. Kurt Potter (Peter Coyote), an attorney with toxic litigation experience, and Ed Masry have entered into a partnership. Masry wants to share resources with Potter by forming a horizontal strategic alliance. It is also a business-level partnership that combines their resources for the litigation success they finally get. The conflict in this scene between Erin and Theresa (Veanne Cox) is an often unfortunate result of such alliances.

SUMMARY

This chapter opened with a brief discussion of using film as a teaching resource. It described various features of cinema that make it a powerful teaching tool. The chapter included examples from various well-known films. A discussion of guidelines for using film in the lecture theatre followed along with a discussion of copyright issues. Separate sections focused on film resources for teaching principles of management, organizational behavior, human resource management, and strategy.

REFERENCES

Champoux, J. E. (1999). Film as a teaching resource. *Journal of Management Inquiry, 8*(2), 206–217.

Champoux, J. E. (2004). *Our feature presentation: Management.* Mason, Ohio: South-Western, Thomson Learning.

Champoux, J. E. (2005). *Our feature presentation: Organizational Behavior.* Mason, Ohio: South-Western, Thomson Learning.

Champoux, J. E. (2006). *Our feature presentation: Strategy.* Mason, Ohio: Thomson South-Western.

Champoux, J. E. (2007). *Our feature presentation: Human Resource Management.* Mason, Ohio: Thomson South-Western.

Films

Berg, P. (Director). (2004). *Friday night lights* [Motion picture]. United States: Universal Studios.

Brest, M. (Director). (1992). *Scent of a woman* [Motion picture]. United States: City Light Films & Universal Studios.

Coen, J. (Director). (2003). *Intolerable cruelty* [Motion picture]. United States: Universal Pictures.

DePalma, B. (Director). (1983). *Scarface* [Motion picture]. United States: Universal Pictures.

Hackford, T. (Director). (2004). *Ray* [Motion picture]. United States: Universal Pictures.

Hoffman, M. (Director). (2002). *The emperor's club* [Motion picture]. United States: Beacon Communications.

Howard, R. (Director). (1991). *Backdraft* [Motion picture]. United States: Imagine Films Entertainment.

Howard, R. (Director). (2000). *Dr. Seuss' how the Grinch stole Christmas* [Motion picture]. United States/Germany: Universal Pictures & Imagine Entertainment.

Hughes, J. (Director). (1985). *The breakfast club* [Motion picture]. United States: A&M Films & Channel Productions.

Kilner, C. (Director). (2005). *The wedding date* [Motion picture]. United States: Gold Circle Films.

Lee, S. (Director). (2006). *Inside man* [Motion picture]. United States: Universal Pictures.

McCullers, M. (Director). (2008). *Baby mama* [Motion picture]. United States: Michaels Goldwyn.

McDonagh, M. (Director). (2008). *In Bruges* [Motion picture]. United Kingdom/ United States: Blueprint Pictures, Film4, Focus Features, & Scion Films.

Mostow, J. (Director). (2000). *U-571* [Motion picture]. France/United States: Universal Pictures, Canal+ Image, & Dino De Laurentiis.

Nichols, M. (Director). (2007). *Charlie Wilson's war* [Motion picture]. United States/ Germany: Universal Pictures.

Roach, J. (Director). (2000). *Meet the parents* [Motion picture]. United States: Universal Pictures & Dreamworks.

Ross, G. (Director). (2003). *Seabiscuit* [Motion picture]. United States: Universal Pictures, DreamWorks, & Spyglass Entertainment.

Soderbergh, S. (Director). (2000). *Erin Brockovich* [Motion picture]. United States: Jersey Films.

Weitz, P., & Weitz, C. (Directors). (2002). *About a boy* [Motion picture]. United Kingdom: Universal Pictures, Studio Canal, Tribeca Productions, & Working Title Films.

CHAPTER 2

ART MOVIES IN THE CLASSROOM

Thomaz Wood Jr.

In an article published a few years ago at New York Times, Van Ness (2005) reveals the apparent paradox between the generous offer of vacancies in college cinema courses, the great interest of students and the scarcity of openings in the labor market. The reason, Van Ness writes, is that cinema studies courses develop skills in understanding power structures in organizations. Perhaps in the future, Van Ness proposes, cinema, literature, and arts programs may supersede MBAs. Although this may seem like an exaggeration, her suggestion is backed up by the increasing use of full-feature films in business school classrooms (e.g., Buchanan & Huczynski, 2004; Bugos, 1996; Champoux, 1999, 2001a, 2001b, 2001c; Comer, 2001; Comer & Cooper, 1998; Harrington & Griffin, 1989; Huczynski, 1994; Huczynski & Buchanan, 2004; Roth, 2001); a practice that may be regarded as part of a broader trend that involves the use of fictional works in management learning and teaching (e.g., Czarniawaska-Jorges & Guillet de Monthoux, 1994).

On examination, this literature exhibits a certain conservativism. Despite their remarkable contribution, a significant portion of the studies advocate the use of industrially-produced Hollywood feature films (e.g.,

Moving Images: Effective Teaching with Film and Television in Higher Education,
pages 19–35

Champoux, 2001a, 2001b) to illustrate traditional concepts as defined in popular management handbooks. But movies comprehend a vast span of manifestations, with different styles and dramatic content, just as organization studies include perspectives beyond functionalism-positivism and managerialism, which are the field's more central and disseminated schools of thought. In fact, the field of management is broad and contains varied disciplines, research activities, practical activities, learning activities and application environments (Mingers, 2000).

The purpose of this chapter is to argue for the use of 'art films' in organization studies. In particular, this chapter focuses on how these 'art films' can be used in teaching *Critical Management Education* (CME). For Perriton and Reynolds (2004), CME has its roots in Paulo Freire's work on critical pedagogy, but with great influence on critical reflection as conceived of by Jurgen Habermas. CME questions the assumptions and practices that characterize managerial education. For authors allied with this movement, management activities must be perceived in terms of their social, moral and political meanings. Education must, therefore, challenge managerial practice rather than support it (Grey & Mitev, 1995). Perriton and Reynolds (2004, p. 65) point out four pedagogical assumptions that drive CME practices:

- a commitment to the moral questioning of the fundamentals of theory and practice;
- an emphasis on analyzing the power and ideology processes that underlie structures and interact with issues of race, class, age and gender;
- an appreciation of a social and communal perspective instead of an individualistic one; and,
- an appreciation of emancipation and the pursuit of a more just and equitable society.

Before proceeding, it is important to define the term 'art film' as it is central to what follows. In everyday use, it refers to productions whose goals include aesthetic and social concerns beyond entertainment and box-office sales. They are, therefore, different to commercial films, where production is based on value chains similar to those typical of other business activities.

This chapter is divided into three sections. In the first section I look at the use of films in management classes and the pedagogical implications thereof. The second section offers an example of how I have used two art films in my CME teaching. In the final section, I discuss the use of full-feature films in management education.

THE USE OF FILMS IN THE CLASSROOM

In recent years, management education has assimilated assorted methods and media. Concerning the former, exercises, case studies and group dynamics were gradually incorporated. As for the latter, technological progress has led to successive waves of change: From blackboards to overhead projectors, and then to micro-computers, projectors, VCRs, DVDs and now online streaming from the internet. From the pedagogical viewpoint, reasonable consensus exists about the benefit of using varied methods and media in the pursuit of an optimal alignment between teaching method and the goals, subjects and audience profile of the course. For example, Champoux (1999) notes that no instructional medium stands above others, and that the use of different media, in order to present a single concept, has positive cumulative effects.

Furthermore, the use of visual media helps students learn and remember new and abstract concepts. Films, for instance, allow students to access realities other than their own. They may also offer the audience new explanations and perspectives and stimulate new world-views and new ways of perceiving specific phenomena. Films may catch students' attention, give rise to interesting discussions, and "help draw connections between classroom lectures and today's cultural world" (Hobbs, 1998, p. 262).

Most of the advocates of using films as teaching tools focus on the more superficial traits of the management education narrative (Buchanan & Huczynski, 2004). This misses an excellent opportunity because films can explore complex organizational phenomena and processes—such as politics and leadership—where outcomes are not the direct result of actions intended to produce them, but the result of events taking place in specific contexts (Huczynski & Buchanan, 2004). Full-feature films can also provide more dramatic, intense and dynamic depictions of organizational life than management texts (Hassard & Holliday, 1998).

Roth (2001) notes that action films allow students to become immersed in the story and see things from a different perspective; an experience starkly different from reading and memorizing theories from a textbook. Dramatic films are actually very effective in showing how the social and organizational context can have impact on personal experience at work and on decision-making. By watching the interaction among characters and as a plot unfolds, students can absorb a high level of complexity and develop greater tolerance to the ambiguity of real-life situations.

Matheus and Fornaciari (1999) argue that feature films, by their very narrative nature and their affective and metaphorical roots, are presented in such a manner as to stimulate our system for processing information acquired through experience. As a result, the content bypasses the rational system and is unconsciously stored. This explains why we can easily recall films or scenes from films, even many years after watching them. While the rational system is analytical, logical, requires justifications and evidence, the experiential system is integrative, affective, and represents reality by means of narrative, metaphor, and imagery.

Essentially, the process of reading a textbook is no different from the process of "reading" a film: they are both pervasively filled with symbolical codes that demand a certain mastery of the language from readers. Hobbs (1998, p. 260) argues that "films and TV are easily decoded because they use pre-existing cognitive and visual skills." Unlike written language, which requires a lengthy initiation, image interpretation is quickly learned.

For this to happen in the classroom, however, the professor must have a solid base of information on the film's production, director, plot, and connection with the subject's topics. For students to be able to understand and appreciate the medium in a critical manner, they must develop awareness of its constructed character, know how content is generated and by whom, and understand how the audience interacts with it, rebuilding meaning from the perceived messages (Hobbs, 1998, p. 265). It is also important to provide guidance on how and what to watch and how to interpret what they will see. In addition, the instructor must make sure that the selected clips are necessary and sufficient to address the intended concepts. A clip that is shorter than it should be may generate frustration and a sense of disconnection from the addressed topics. On the other hand, too lengthy a clip may introduce excessive elements and overwhelm the group's capacity for analysis.

At the same time, it is important to understand the fact that the perception that watching films is a leisure activity has a negative effect on using the medium for educational purposes. This happens because:

- students tend to behave like a "relaxed audience" without the discipline they might display on studying from a textbook;
- students do not always have available information on the economic, social and cultural contexts that concern the film and this may result in a limited capacity to understand it;
- the audience is not necessarily capable of decoding and understanding the messages provided; and,
- the practice may subject those using it to suspicion from colleagues, thereby discouraging its use.

Learning requires specific discipline. Developing the ability for structured, rigorous thought on organizational phenomena requires a systematic effort. An attitude of trying to develop a critical and broad vision does not come naturally to many students. Students, often managers in pursuit of career improvement, usually expect models and tools that can be directly applied to facilitate successful adaptation to everyday professional situations. Therefore, the use of films in the classroom must come after an initiation into the medium.

Films can be "windows into the world," but are not neutral or naive artifacts. Instead, they are the product of certain historical, cultural, and commercial conditions, developed, in most cases, with commercial purposes in mind and intended for certain audiences. Films, or film clips, must be presented after a general explanation of the industry's reasoning, including its history, production and distribution process, and a discussion of the culture industry. Furthermore, students must prepare to analyze films shown in class by reading basic texts on film reviews (Leet & Houser, 2003) that provide the perspective, vocabulary and some frames of reference required to appropriately read films. Otherwise, the students may be induced to act as an uncritical audience, unable to uncover deep meanings in the scenes being watched.

In this chapter, I argue for the use of art films in the classroom. Cinema is a broad, variegated cultural manifestation. Many movements marked its history. Art films include movies from German expressionism, the Soviet school, classic American cinema, Italian neo-realism, the French *nouvelle vague* and more contemporary independent movies (for an extensive review, see Bordwell & Thompson, 1993). Despite this incredible diversity, most documented uses of films in the classroom mentions only one archetypical style: the Hollywood movie. This is indeed a shame.

A cinephile can easily identify an art movie, when he or she watches one, but the term 'art film' itself is difficult to define. In general, it refers to productions whose main concerns are aesthetic achievement and/or a critical reflection on social problems. Therefore, art films oppose the so-called commercial films, whose main concerns relates to financial outcomes. While commercial films are produced mainly for business reasons, art films seek to address deep human questions. While commercial films reflect and fictionalize reality in conventional and often standardized ways, art films seek to discover and uncover the human reality. Art films and CME can be associated because both seek to nurture critical thinking and to question assumptions and practices taken for granted. Besides, art movies commonly present a strong authorial voice, emphasize meaning, and, properly introduced by the instructor, can surprise audiences more used to commercial movies.

DESCRIPTION OF THE 'EXPERIMENT'

This section presents an experiment in the use of images, still and moving, in an CME course entitled 'Post-Industrial Organizations', that was offered to masters' and PhD students in a Brazilian business school. The course was taken by fifteen students and a few guests.

The course was divided into thirteen weekly gatherings, each of three hours. In the first stage, I introduced the debate of modernity versus post-modernity. I used texts by Goffman (1959), Boorstin (1962), Debord (1994), Eco (1975), Baudrillard (1994; 1995), Harvey (1993), Alvesson (1990), and Denzin (1995) to locate the "post-industrial scenery"; and texts by Chia (1995), Burrell (1988, 1994), Cooper and Burrell (1988), Cooper (1989), and Wood (2001, 2002) to show how the field of Organization Studies approaches the debate.

I based the second stage of the course on the Weberian concept of 'ideal type' and explored a genealogy of ideal organizational types that included the bureaucratic machine, the professional bureaucracy, the virtual organization, the matrix organization, the knowledge intensive firm, and the symbol-intensive organization, among others. This last ideal type was emphasized due to its relevance to the contents of the discipline. According to the definition proposed by Leikola and Wood (1999), symbol intensive organizations are environments where (1) symbolic leadership prevails as a managerial style (Smircich & Morgan, 1982); (2) leaders and led consciously or unconsciously apply impression-management techniques (Giacalone & Rosenfeld, 1991); (3) managerial innovations are treated as dramatic events (Lampel, 1994); and (4) symbolic analysts prevail among the workforce (Reich, 1992).[1] The component elements of the definition were used as topics for classes.

The third portion of the course was dedicated to an analysis of the 'management industry.' Classes focused on the following topics: (1) the business media and its influence on managerial imaginary (Wood & Paes de Paula, 2002a); (2) management consultancies and the dissemination of managerial knowledge and fads (Wood & Paes de Paula, 2004); (3) business schools and the dissemination of knowledge and values (Wood & Paes de Paula, 2002b); and (4) the phenomenon of management gurus (Clark & Salaman, 1996; Paes de Paula & Wood, 2002).

Methodological Approach

All sessions were similarly conducted. I began with a general introduction supported with a PowerPoint presentation. These were followed by presentations given by students and, on occasion, special group activities, such as group discussions, content analysis and image analysis. There was intensive use of visual resources like images, photographs and film stills. The concepts of symbolic analysis and symbolic analyst (Reich, 1992) were introduced by means of a discussion of the work of Dutch painter Piet Mondrian. Concepts of identity and image were introduced by means of an analysis of the work of photographer Cindy Sherman and Woody Allen's

---

[1] According to Reich (1992), symbolic analysts' abilities comprehend by manipulating a broad range of tools; from mathematical algorithms to psychology concepts. Their chief task is to translate reality into abstract images that can be communicated to other specialists, manipulated and, eventually translated back into reality. Symbolic analysts, working in complex and chaotic environments, cannot put their focus solely on the existing stock of knowledge. They must deal creatively with this stock, but must also face the fragmentation of information and the obsolescence of known solutions.

film, *Zelig* (Allen, 1993). When feature films were used in the teaching, clips of approximately 10 minutes were shown. When film clips were unavailable, film stills were provided, with comments on the film's director, characters and plot.

Discussion of the Concept of Leadership

Two consecutive sessions included a specific activity whose purpose was to verify students' comparative perception when faced with different ways (for instance, textbooks, photos and films) of addressing a certain theme. The selected theme was leadership, one of the fetish-topics in organizations, in popular management books and in organizations studies, as well as a recurring subject in movies. In all, five different approaches were tried sequentially:

1. We discussed leadership from the 'mainstream' perspective based on organizational behavior handbooks. We presented the concepts and then discussed these in seminars.

2. We used references from CMS (Alvesson & Willmott, 1992) and from organizational symbolism and culture studies literatures to focus on the concepts of symbolic leadership and meaning manipulation as developed by Smircich and Morgan (1982) and also on the view of leadership as a fetish concept proposed by Sievers (1994). As in the first approach, concepts were introduced by presentation prior to discussion in seminars.

3. The third approach used a news story from the American magazine *The Atlantic Monthly* featuring a profile of President George W. Bush. This session, too, began with a presentation followed by discussion. The purpose of the approach was to compare the journalistic and academic perspectives.

4. Then, we used a series of photographs of business leaders taken for a special edition of a local (Brazilian) business magazine. This session had the following format: The photographs were shown for 3–4 minutes each, and students were asked to take notes on the impressions and notions of leadership the images conveyed. There was no stimulus for them to establish links with prior readings or concepts. The ensuing discussion was free-form. This was intended to surface each individual's and the group's repertoire and interpretations of the images. After the presentation, the group discussed the images, first individually, then taken together.

5. Finally, we used clips from two films: the documentary on the rise and fall of Charles F. Kane from *Citizen Kane* (Welles, 1941), and a selection of clips containing the main characters of Terra em Transe (commonly translated into English as *Land in Anguish* or

Entranced Earth; 1967, Rocha, 1967). Before the 10-minute clips, a brief introduction was given on the film makers, their *oeuvre*, and the general context of each film (summarized ahead). After the projection, there was an non-directed discussion of perceptions.

CITIZEN KANE

Citizen Kane is a unique work in the history of cinema. Orson Welles created it when he was only 25 years old. Whereas Welles had been regarded as an *enfant terrible* before the film, *Citizen Kane* helped make him one of the movie industry's greatest directors, albeit, a director shrouded in mystery and mystique. Shown in film clubs and cinema schools, it became a cult item. For decades it has appeared in lists of the best films of all time, and often in top slot. The film has generated countless books and articles over sixty years. Specialists describe it as a portrait of a powerful personality of our time, as an in-depth study of the life of a great character that ends in tragedy, or as a classic tragedy that takes place in the 20th Century (see Maxfield, 1986).

The idea that *Citizen Kane* can be regarded as a tragedy is controversial. One argument offered against a tragic reading of the film is that its comical elements would be impeditive. Another is that a tragedy requires a tragic, noble hero. Kane, however, is pathetic. For Maxfield (1986), none of these arguments invalidate a tragic reading. The first counter-argument is that comic elements are not foreign to the tragic system. The second is that many classic tragedies feature heroes as pathetic as Kane, which does not make them any less tragic.

According to Boal (1975), the first essential aspect of Aristotle's tragic scheme is the presence of a hero. At the beginning of the show, the audience is led to establish a relationship of empathy with this hero. But the hero has had a serious flaw and the plot reveals that this fault is the reason for the happiness and privilege the hero enjoys. Suddenly, something happens to jeopardize the hero's happiness and risk turning his existence into tragedy. As a result, the audience, in its empathy with the hero, suffers with his misfortune and experiences his terror. Following the Aristotelian schema, the hero accepts and confesses to his error. But this is not enough. Aristotle requires tragedies to have terrible endings. The catastrophe is a *catharsis* that cleanses the hero and the audience of their errors.

From this perspective, *Citizen Kane* may be seen as a tragedy, an ethical fable about the divide between substance and image (Alvesson, 1990). Kane's path is the construction of an illusory character, a public persona based on an equation that makes success and personal grandeur equal. Kane cannot possibly be regarded as a model of righteousness, nor as evil incarnate. He is a character that lies somewhere between the two opposite ends. He is cruel at times, but this is the result of his insensitivity, of his drive to attain success and grandness, rather than of an inherently evil nature (Maxfield, 1986).

The imagery in *Citizen Kane* is crucial. This becomes particularly clear in the sequences depicting Kane as he builds his news empire. On releasing the *Inquirer,* the first page of the paper features a statement of principles where he proclaims that his two main goals as editor are "to tell the news with honesty" and "to be a relentless fighter for the rights of citizens." His words are sincere in their rhetoric. Kane does not appear to deliberately deceive his audience. But his intent is challenged when one realizes that all he wants, his true goal, is to increase circulation and popularize his image as champion of a cause.

Kane has great personal aspirations. He wants to please readers and voters and to pave his way to the Presidency with popularity. Along this path, even his personal life becomes an instrument. Kane marries the niece of a former president. His emotional involvement with his wife is minimal, but the marriage amounts to something like a lordship, something that supposedly enables him to fulfill his dreams of becoming president by releasing him from his humble roots.

In a remarkable sequence we see Kane standing behind a podium. Behind him is a giant blow-up of his face. The real-life character tries to give life to the character in the picture. They both have the same look in their eyes. The Kane in the photograph glares intently at a distant point. The candidate behind the pulpit glares through the crowd. For candidate Kane, the audience is a mirage, an idealized projection, a faceless crowd of voters who only matter for their ability to help him attain his personal objectives. The turnaround happens during the campaign, when the papers publish a story about a scandal in Kane's private life; a relationship with a singer. It is the beginning of the end; the point where the divide between image and substance enters the public eye.

As noted earlier, a basic element in the Aristotelian tragic scheme is the audience's identification with the hero. In the case of *Citizen Kane* it is hard to tell whether such identification existed, even at the time of the film's release. The character may be a stereotype, an intentionally built cliché. On the other hand, it seems perfectly plausible to regard him as a post-modern hero, a character that seeks to build himself and his public image with help from the media. The public persona cannot stand, however. Creature turns against creator. Image and self are inseparable to him. But there is a price to pay. There are limits to the divide between substance and image. The disruption of the public image's coherence caused by the advent of the mistress reveals the farce and destroys both the public persona and the man behind it.

Kane dies alone in the castle of Xanadu, a *kitsch* scenario he set up in Florida, surrounded by symbols of greatness and power; a forlorn stage sentenced to decay. For Maxfield (1986), reading the death of Kane as punishment for his errors, for his dreams of power, is a moralistic, reductionistic view of the film. The author believes that the tragic ending does not reflect the evil Kane may have caused. Kane dies whispering the emblematic word *rosebud,* the name of a sled, a favorite childhood toy he was separated from much too soon. His lonely death would then be, in fact, the reflection of a universal human tragedy.

TERRA EM TRANSE

Terra em Transe is a classic among Brazilian films. Produced in 1967, it is generally regarded Glauber Rocha's best work. The film is an allegorical depiction of a historical moment in the transformation of Brazilian identity. In the fictional republic of Eldorado, a sense of urgency sets in as great changes are imminent. Socially representative characters—the intellectual, the populist and the businessman—carry the narrative. These are archetypical figures with roots in the country's historical and cultural processes.

Terra em Transe is a typical product of Cinema Novo (New Cinema), the Brazilian equivalent of the French *Nouvelle Vague* or the Italian Neo-realism. In Brazil in the 1950s, film production was divided between two extremes: On one extreme, comedies intended for the popular audience; on the other, the productions of the Vera Cruz Studios, that attempted to emulate European 'high quality cinema' and American melodrama. Cinema Novo marked the Brazilian cultural elite's discovery of a new way to express their political and aesthetic concerns (Bernadet, 1991, p. 101).

The movement lasted for about twenty years, from 1955 to 1975, and was characterized by five central traits: First, a fundamental concern with reflection about the country and its reality; secondly, an ideal of making films that cause the audience to think about social issues; thirdly, developing a distinctive film language; fourthly, practicing authorial cinema; and fifthly, simple productions with relatively low budgets. "A camera in hand and an idea in mind": this was how Rocha described the working conditions under Cinema Novo. Rocha was one of the movement's main theorists and greatest film directors (Thomas, 1990, p. 705).

Terra em Transe unfolds in the Republic of Eldorado and is narrated in flash-back by journalist and poet, Paulo Martins. In the opening scenes, Paulo Martins remembers his political trajectory and his relationship with right-wing coup-master Porfírio Diaz, with populist left-wing governor Felipe Vieira, and with nationalist businessman Júlio Fuentes. Paulo Martins had been an ally and protégé of Porfírio Diaz, but left him to join Felipe Vieira's campaign to be elected governor of the Province of Alecrim. The campaign gains momentum and moves forward through rallies, samba and repression. Once elected, Felipe Vieira is unable to overcome the contradictions that exist among his campaign promises, his supporters' expectations, and objective conditions. He sees himself assailed by increasing pressures and is eventually overcome by Diaz's coup.

According to Johnson and Stam (1982, p. 150) "the narrative in [*Terra em Transe*] is a lucid recitation of a life overwhelmed by political illusion" and is aligned with a "Quixotesque formula of systematic disenchantment." In the film, the characters' ideals and purity "rot in the tropical gardens" (Johnson & Stam, 1982, p. 156). The disenchantment of Paulo Martins, his farewell to illusion, is marked by his political and personal relationships. Porfírio Diaz is the "god of his youth." Felipe Vieira is the leader, "our great leader," who fails by refusing to resist Porfírio Diaz's coup.

Rocha's treatment of themes like power, leadership and change exposes the complexity and ambiguity of the characters. Porfírio Diaz, the right-wing dictator-to-be, and Felipe Vieira, the left-wing populist, are located at extreme sides of the political scene. Furthermore, they are enemies at a personal level. But the film's comparison of their political campaigns exposes similarities rather than differentiating them. Porfírio Dias and Felipe Vieira are a single character playing different roles and separated by circumstance alone. The same happens with nationalist businessman Júlio Fuentes and Porfírio Diaz, supported by foreign interests. Instead of the expected conflict, their characters converge. Even protagonist Paulo Martins, in his profound commitment to his role as a liberating agent sometimes takes on a repressive stance. In his poetic speeches, when he makes reference to the people, he does so in a detached, idealized manner. Paulo Martins is the confluence of several political and social forces at a turbulent moment; he is a complex character; "a stage where society's contradictions manifest" (Johnson & Stam, 1982, p. 156).

Eldorado's leaders are weak, anti-heroic, and powerless in playing their roles. Their grandeur is ephemeral, lonely and selfish. Their acts correspond neither to their self-image nor to their followers' expectations. Felipe Vieira is a 'stage' that might represent many Brazilian left-wing populists. His discourse assimilates popular symbols, communicates the illusion of equality and hides paradoxes and ambiguities. Vieira, like Paulo Martins, is a leader that lacks self-determination; a charismatic image built on massive contradictions. Vieira embodies many of our (Brazilian) most striking traits: Authoritarianism, paternalism, indecisiveness, plasticity and ambiguity.

After victoriously staging his coup, Porfírio Diaz is finally crowned. He represents the country's colonial past and bears the symbols of the Portuguese conqueror and the black flag of the Holy Inquisition. His gaze and solitude are regal. During his coronation, his speech exclaims,

> They shall learn! They shall learn! I shall rule this land, and set these historical traditions in proper order! By force, by the love of force, by the universal harmony of Hell we shall become a civilization! (Rocha, 1985, p. 324)

Porfírio Diaz wears a bureaucratic black suit to his coronation. Over the suit, clasped about the neck is a white mantle that will give him special powers and turn him into a great leader, the leader that will cause Eldorado to attain civilization. As Diaz looks directly ahead, several possibilities come to mind. The first impression is that he might be looking at the crowd watching his coronation. But his gaze seems to be lost, fixed on something ethereal. Maybe there is no crowd. Or maybe he just can't see it, and is replacing it with an imagined entity. His raised, clenched fists are supposed to indicate power, but the position of his arms shows that this power may be limited, even empty, perhaps. Body language shows Diaz as a leader uncertain of his victory. In Eldorado, there are no true victors, as there are no true leaders.

Characters in *Terra em Transe* are archetypical in Brazilian history. The director deals harshly with leaders. They are not heroic leaders. Rocha demystifies them through the traits of the characters, inevitably ambiguous, contradictory, complex, and deeply real. Rocha does not allow empathy or identification with his characters; he demands a reflective, critical attitude from viewers.

Assessment

The multimedia experiment appears to have been stimulating and effective. Many students offered comments on how the two approaches were complementary and on the richness of the reflections caused by the tension between different outlooks and media.

The first two sessions were more traditional in nature. Concepts were introduced in the same order as they appeared in texts, with support from charts and diagrams. The class was interested, but unenthusiastic. In comparison with the view found in management handbooks, the perspective of CMS and organizational culture and symbolism generated stronger reactions and more debate.

The presentation based on a news article had ambiguous results: On the one hand, the text's richness in terms of locating the topic in relation to its historical, economic, social and psychological connections was clearly displayed; on the other hand, the character the article dealt with—President George W. Bush—engendered reactions and emotions that led to sidetracked discussions and made it difficult to objectively analyze the concept of leadership.

The presentation with photographs was quite stimulating. Each image generated rich and unique interpretations. The power of images to draw connections and cause complex analyses was clear. Students were able to make sophisticated deductions and draw hypotheses on complex characteristics of the depicted leaders and how they related with the role.

The presentation that involved showing film clips was equally rich in terms of comments and discussion. Comparatively, *Citizen Kane* generated less open interpretations than *Terra em Transe*. The first clip was perceived by many as a rather faithful depiction of the concept of symbolic leadership. *Terra em Transe*, in turn, generated open-ended, richer reflections. First, students took note of the film's unique aesthetic traits. Second, there were several reflections on its ability to depict Brazil's social and cultural situation. Finally, there was speculation on the characters' instability, lack of linearity and frailty, and on the fact that these characteristics accurately describe Brazilian reality while, at the same time, challenge ordinary views of leadership. The film clip elicited a suspicion that the concept of leadership as discussed in management handbooks would probably "melt down in the tropical heat."

At the end of the course I carried out a survey with students, using open-ended questions to assess their general perception of the use of visual resources and to determine what images had generated the most impact. All students responded to the questions. When asked about the image that had left the greatest impression on them, they were divided. This, taken together with how they expressed their reaction, leads to the inference that individuals with different life experiences and different cultural repertoires react differently. The images they mentioned were: The documentary about the life of Charles F. Kane, telling of his rise and fall; the film clip from *Citizen Kane* illustrating the concepts of symbolic leadership and manipulation of meanings; the selected clips featuring characters from *Terra em Transe* used to add a critical and local dimension to the debate about the concept of leadership; and the series of photographic portraits of Brazilian businessmen that was used to encourage a relational and complex reading of the leadership phenomenon. Glauber Rocha's film was also mentioned as the one that generated the most reflection and unease.

Students took well to the use of visual props, such as images, film clips, and photos. Among other aspects, they mentioned the following: The ability to illustrate and memorize subjective and complex concepts ("an image is worth a thousand words"), the enriched learning process, and the fact that it makes classes more interesting, sparking debate and catching participants' attention. One student highlighted the ability films have of bringing out emotion-related elements with nuances of intensity and diversity that other media cannot achieve. Others indicated that the use of visual resources helped broaden discussions and generating greater depth of analysis, reflection, and learning. It was also noted that the selected method would probably cause students to watch movies with new eyes, searching for connections with organizational themes, and that the course was eye training to spot symbols and meanings that might previously be hidden.

On the other hand, one student noted that audiovisual resources must be used with care. As finished works, they tend to generate lengthy and occasionally unfocused discussions, which the student considered "a dangerous distraction." Furthermore, there were comments relating to the interpretation of the relevant works, which were seen as highly dependent on the instructor's frame of reference, creating a risk of biased treatment of concepts. Another participant noted that, in his case, previous reading of the text was crucial as preparation for class, so that the audiovisual material seen in class acted as more of a complement.

Concerning the use of films as opposed to merely mentioning them (with the use of film stills), responses were polarized. Some participants said they preferred film clips, as long as preceded by a general explanation of the work, as they favored a more open understanding of concepts. Others declared their preference for film stills because they provide for more objective discussions and better management of the time spent in class.

CLOSING COMMENTS

The use of films in management education is no trivial task. Films are artifacts loaded with symbols and meaning, and surrounded by the cultural and economic context in which they were generated. One must, therefore, master the language and be knowledgeable about the films and directors that are going to be used. A specific pedagogical approach is also required, as visual resources foster particular reflections and lead to discussions that are often difficult to guide. There is a substantial risk of losing focus.

Another point worth mentioning has to do with the profile of students. In the case of this experiment, I had quite a heterogeneous group in terms of professional backgrounds, lines of research and cultural repertoires. This occasionally led to 'naïve' discussions. Significantly, one student mentioned trouble assimilating all of the concepts and interpretations the course addressed. The same participant declared himself "frustrated with his own ignorance." Again, it is the instructor's job to make sure, by means of appointed readings and well-prepared introductions, that all participants are equipped to understand and interpret the films.

Finally, the introduction of films is an additional opportunity to review the pedagogical approach and contents. Art films are not resources that can be easily used by management instructors. On the other hand, they stand as an element capable of bringing fresh perspectives and dynamics into the classroom.

In an essay addressing the so called 'relevance gap', the distance between academic research and practitioners' needs, Weick (2001, p. 72) argues that what managers really need and want to see is the 'big picture', the 'big story', one about 'beginnings and restarts, consequences both anticipated and unanticipated, dynamics, sequences and small origins with large consequences'. Weick alerts that many practitioners would like academics to see their world as the 'real world'. Indeed, many common uses of feature films in the classroom do exactly this, as they reinforce accepted notions of leadership, team-work, strategy etc. But that is not the academic's job. According to Weick (2001, p. 74), the academic's job 'is to understand how an idiosyncratic individual world comes to be seen as a universal world and how vested interests work to convey this definition of universality'. That's precisely where CME and art films can help, i.e., jolting the audience, bringing new meanings, questioning taken for granted notions of reality, and even putting into question the very language that we use to describe reality.

REFERENCES

Alvesson, M. (1990). Organization: From substance to image? *Organization Studies*, *11*(3), 373–394.

Alvesson, M., & Willmott, H. (1992). *Critical management studies*. London, United Kingdom: Sage.

Baudrillard, J. (1994). *Simulacra and simulation*. Ann Arbor, MI: The University of Michigan Press.

Baudrillard, J. (1995). The virtual illusion: Or the automatic writing of the world. *Theory, Culture and Society*, *12*(4), 97–107.

Bernadet, J. C. (1991). *O que é Cinema*. São Paulo: Brasiliense.

Boal, A. (1975). *Teatro do Oprimido e Outras Poéticas Políticas*. Rio de Janeiro, Brazil: Civilização Brasileira.

Boorstin, D. J. (1962). *The image: A guide to pseudo-events in America*. New York, NY: Atheneum.

Bordwell, D., & Thompson, K. (1993). *Film art: An introduction*. New York, NY: McGraw-Hill.

Buchanan, D., & Huczynski, A. (2004). Images of influence: *12 Angry Men* and *Thirteen Days*. *Journal of Management Inquiry*, *13*(4), 312–323.

Bugos, G. E. (1996). Organizing stories of organizational life: Four films on American business. *Studies in Cultures, Organizations and Societies*, *2*, 111–128.

Burrell, G. (1988). Modernism, postmodernism and organizational analysis: The contribution of Michel Foucault. *Organization Studies*, *9*(2), 221–235.

Burrell, G. (1994). Modernism, postmodernism and organizational analysis: The contribution of Jurgen Habermas. *Organization Studies*, *15*(1), 1–45.

Champoux, J. E. (1999). Film as a teaching resource. *Journal of Management Inquiry*, *8*(2), 206–217.

Champoux, J. E. (2001a). *Management: Using film to visualize principles and practices*. New York, NY: South-Western College Publishing.

Champoux, J. E. (2001b). *Organizational behavior: Using film to visualize principles and practices*. New York, NY: South-Western College Publishing.

Champoux, J. E. (2001c). Animated films as a teaching resource. *Journal of Management Education*, *25*(1), 79–100.

Chia, R. (1995). From modern to postmodern organizational analysis. *Organization Studies*, *16*(4), 579–604.

Clark, T., & Salaman, G. (1996). The management guru as organizational witchdoctor. *Organization, 3*(1), 85–107.

Comer, D. R. (2001). Not just a Mickey Mouse exercise: Using Disney's *The Lion King* to teach leadership. *Journal of Management Education, 25*(4), 430–436.

Comer, D. R., & Cooper, E. A. (1998). Gender relations and sexual harassment in the workplace: Michael Crichton's *Disclosure* as a teaching tool. *Journal of Management Education, 22*(2), 227–241.

Cooper, R. (1989). Modernism, postmodernism and organizational analysis: The contribution of Jacques Derrida. *Organization Studies, 10*(4), 479–50.

Cooper, R., & Burrell, G. (1988). Modernism, postmodernism and organizational analysis: An introduction. *Organization Studies, 9*(1), 91–112.

Czarniawska-Jorges, B., & Guillet de Monthoux, P. (Eds.) (1994). *Good novels, better management: Reading organizational realities in fiction.* Switzerland: Hardwood Academic Publishers.

Debord, G. (1994). *The society of spectacle.* New York, NY: Zone Books.

Denzin, N. K. (1995). *The cinematic society: The voyeur's gaze.* London, United Kingdom: Sage.

Eco, U. (1975). *Travels in hyperreality.* San Diego, CA: Harvest Book.

Giacalone, R. A., & Rosenfeld, P. (Eds.) (1991). *Applied impression management: How image-making affects managerial decisions.* Newbury Park, CA: Sage.

Goffman, E. (1959). *The presentation of self in everyday life.* New York, NY: Anchor Books.

Grey, C., & Mitev, N. (1995). Management education: A polemic. *Management Learning, 26*(1), 73–90.

Harrington, K. V., & Griffin, R. W. (1989). Ripley, Burke, Gorman and friends: Using the film, *Aliens,* to teach leadership and power. *Organizational Behavior Teaching Review, 14*(3), 79–86.

Harvey, D. (1993). *Condição Pós-moderna.* São Paulo, Brazil: Edições Loyola.

Hassard, J., & Holliday, R. (Eds.) (1998). *Organization representation: Work and organization in popular culture.* London, United Kingdom: Sage.

Hobbs, R. (1998). Teaching with and about film and television: Integrating media literacy into management education. *Journal of Management Development, 17*(4), 259–272.

Huczynski, A. (1994). Teaching motivation and influencing strategies using *The Magnificent Seven. Journal of Management Education, 18*(2), 273–278.

Huczynski, A., & Buchanan, D. (2004). Theory from fiction: A narrative process perspective on the pedagogical use of feature film. *Journal of Management Education, 28*(6), 707–726.

Johnson, R., & Stam, R. (1982). *Brazilian cinema.* East Brunswick, NJ: Associated University Presses.

Lampel, J. (1994). *Innovation as spectacle: Dramaturgical construction of technological change.* Paper presented at conference on the Social Construction of Industries and Markets, Chicago, IL.

Leet, D., & Houser, S. (2003). Economics goes to Hollywood: Using classic films and documentaries to create an undergraduate economics course. *Journal of Economic Education, 34*(4), 326–332.

Leikola, V., & Wood Jr., T. (1999). Symbol intensive organizations: Management in the age of metaphor and rhetoric. In R. Goodman (Ed.) *Modern organizations and emerging conundrums*. Lanham, MD: Lexington Books.

Matheus, C. S., & Fornaciari, C. J. (1999). *Understanding the use of feature film in the classroom learning*. Paper presented at the annual meeting of the Academy of Management.

Maxfield, M. (1986). A man like ourselves: Citizen Kane as an Aristotelian tragedy. *Film Literature Quarterly, 14* (3), 195–203.

Minger, J. (2000). What is to be critical ? Teaching a critical approach to management undergraduates. *Management Learning, 31*(2), 219–237.

Paes de Paula, A. P., & Wood Jr., T. (2002). Pop-management. *Revista Ciência Empresarial, 2,* 17–31.

Perriton, L., & Reynolds, M. (2004). Critical management education: From pedagogy of possibility to pedagogy of refusal? *Management Learning, 35*(1), 61–77.

Reich, R. (1992). *The work of nations.* New York, NY: Vintage Books

Rocha, G. (1985). Land in Anguish. In O. Senna (Org.) *Glauber Rocha: Roteiros do Terceyro Mundo.* Rio de Janeiro, Brazil: Alhambra/Embrafilme.

Roth, L. (2001). Introducing students to 'The Big Picture.' *Journal of Management Education, 25*(1), 21–31.

Sievers, B. (1994). *Work, death and life itself: Essays on management and organization.* Berlin, Germany: Walter de Gruyter.

Smircich, L., & Morgan, G. (1982). Leadership: The management of meaning. *The Journal of Applied Behavioral Science, 18*(3), 257–273.

Thomas, N. (Ed.) (1990). *International dictionary of films and filmakers 2—Directors.* Chicago, IL/London, United Kingdom: St. James Press.

Van Ness, E. (2005). Is a cinema studies degree the new MBA. *The New York Times,* nytimes.com, March 6.

Weick, K. (2001). Gapping the relevance bridge: Fashions meet fundamentals in management research. *British Journal of Management, 12*(special issue), S71–S75.

Wood Jr., T. (2001). *Organizações Espetaculares.* Rio de Janeiro, Brazil: Editora FGV.

Wood Jr., T. (2002). Spectacular metaphors: From theatre to cinema. *Journal of Organizational Change Management, 15*(1), 11–20.

Wood Jr., T., & Paes de Paula, A. (2002a). *Pop-management: A literatura popular de gestão no Brasil.* Relatório de pesquisa, GV-Pesquisa, FGV-EAESP.

Wood Jr., T., & Paes de Paula, A. (2002b). *Pop-management: MBAs no Brasil. Relatório de pesquisa.* GV-Pesquisa, FGV-EAESP.

Wood Jr., T., & Paes de Paula, A. (2004). *Pop-management: Grandes empresas de consultoria no Brasil.* Relatório de pesquisa, GV-Pesquisa, FGV-EAESP.

Films

Allen, W. (Director). (1993). *Zelig* [Motion picture]. United States: Orion Pictures.

Rocha, G. (Director). (1967). *Terra em transe* [Motion picture]. Brazil: Mapa Filmes.

Welles, O. (Director). (1941). *Citizen Kane* [Motion picture]. United States: Mercury Productions & RKO Radio Pictures.

CHAPTER 3

RESEARCH AS DETECTIVE WORK

Using Film With Postgraduate Students

Richard Thorpe and Mark Easterby-Smith

We have been working together for over 20 years on the development and dissemination of management research methods. During this time, we have maintained a keen interest in translating ideas and methodologies from the social sciences into the management domain; we have also sought to understand the unique challenges of management research such as the political and ethical issues of working with large and powerful organizations.[1] We have looked for novel ways of introducing research ideas and methodologies to doctoral students. In this context, film and video can be very useful in bringing alive the issues that researchers need to tackle whether at the postgraduate stage or later in their academic careers.

One of the areas where we have found films to be useful is in bringing to life the dusty subject of research philosophy. The method we have developed over the years uses the analogy between the crime detective and the

---

[1] The idea of using detectives was an idea originally developed and published in French by Jean Moscarola (1991). A version of the idea was published in English (Thorpe & Moscarola, 1991) following Richard's sabbatical in France, and subsequently developed into teaching material by both Richard and Mark

Moving Images: Effective Teaching with Film and Television in Higher Education, pages 37–47

37

role of the researcher. We believe that, apart from the intrinsic interest in the subject, there are credible similarities between the two roles. In both cases the person is inquiring into something, whether it be a crime or an organizational process, where the perpetrator or the underlying causes are currently unknown. The job of the researcher/detective is therefore to peel back the layers in order to identify what has, or is, taking place. In some respects, the job of the (fictional) detective is simpler than that of the researcher, because there is usually a body, or some other physical evidence, and the crime usually has to be solved within the allotted hour or two allowed by the program makers; whereas, the researcher may be examining more nebulous and vague processes such as decision-making, strategy, or productivity which do not have clear starting and ending points and usually involve a greater degree of complexity.

Television drama can be a powerful vehicle, because it provides clear and memorable images. On the surface, research seems quite simple: it is largely a matter of defining research questions or hypotheses, gathering data through questionnaires or interviews, and finding answers which will satisfy the majority of the interested parties in the research. But underneath there are many complex assumptions and choices to be made: about the nature of the phenomena being investigated (ontology), the best ways of conducting the enquiry process (epistemology), and the ways of configuring data so that it relates directly to the research questions. And there are compromises to be made between the interests of different stakeholders including the researchers, funders, employing organizations, journal editors, and so on. An important feature of film is that it can provide some clear markers against which this myriad of choices can be mapped.

So, for some years now our method of demystifying these alternative approaches and styles has been to see what might be learnt from the methods adopted by the characters in fictional detective stories. The key thing is to choose fictional characters from television and films who represent distinct styles that are theoretically relevant. We will come back to the issue of relevance at the end of the chapter, but in the meantime we will explain how we use four distinct styles as 'anchors' to make sense of management research choices. Here we discuss the use of brief extracts from episodes of Hercule Poirot, Sherlock Holmes, Miss Marple and Dirty Harry.

USING FICTIONAL CHARACTERS
FROM FILM AND TELEVISION

The four fictional characters discussed here represent distinct styles and methods of investigation. In each case we show a clip or vignette that exemplifies the essence of their approach and we use it as a trigger film. The incorporation of this short film clip within the classroom leads to discussion and debate around the way in which the detectives set about their investigations and this is then linked to common management research methods and to the students' own research plans.

Hercule Poirot: The Theorist

Poirot adopts a theoretical, rational approach; he is the model armchair detective. For instance, in the majority of his cases, whether it is behind closed doors in *Ten Little Nigger Boys* (Christie, 1939) or in the sleeping compartment of the *Orient Express* (Christie, 1934), he proceeds by logical deduction. His approach is to listen to witnesses of the crime and then to withdraw and reflect. During his reflection, he goes over their behavior, their routines and habits and motives, and within these he searches for patterns and contradictions. By reconstructing events, and through a process of deductive reasoning, Hercule Poirot discovers the guilty party. Of course in order to make for good television the viewer is also nearly always offered the majority of the details of the crime and invited to play the detective and work out for themselves (using the same information as Poirot) who is the guilty party.

An understanding of Poirot's character therefore enables us to illustrate to students a style and method of investigation that can be used in management research. Such an approach would have a strong theoretic underpinning and involve the student:

- collecting all sources of relevant information;
- remaining detached from the events or processes being studied;
- applying his/her own knowledge and expertise; and
- analyzing the findings in order to deduce answers.

Here there is a need to combine theories with different forms of data. For example, students might use models and estimations of market size in marketing simulations. Or they might deduce the size of a new market by simply calculating and extrapolating from existing data about populations and customer buying habits. Similarly this approach might be used to model or predict the movements in financial markets, or economic models will be used to predict the effect of changes in fiscal policy on buying behavior. In all these cases the researcher uses existing data, and is personally independent and distanced from its creation.

Sherlock Holmes: The Scientist

Sherlock Holmes adopts a classic scientific approach in his work. We therefore use clips of film which show him with a magnifying glass or scientific instruments. He is a master of detail, but a very different kind of detail is observed to that of ethnography. Holmes takes a reductionist approach, and from samples or fragments builds up an understanding of the whole. So, armed with a scalpel and magnifying glass, he uncovers the tiniest fragment of dried mud which he then proceeds to examine. Knowing how to extract *significant* information from the most insignificant detail, he fashions the overwhelming proof. So the clay or mud extracted from a person's shoes offers irrefutable evidence that the person was present at the scene of the crime.

We link Sherlock Holmes' observations of details to how quantitative researchers collect and analyze samples of data—often also in great detail. Holmes arrives at his understanding by elaborate, technical and often mysterious research methods, and his use of observation and instruments provide a starting point for analysis. It is interesting to note that the significance of Sherlock Holmes' observations almost always escape Dr Watson. Watson complains when invited to draw some conclusions from an object, a hat, or a walking stick that *he can see nothing!* Exasperated, Holmes declares *that on the contrary you can see everything but fail to reason from what you see!* Holmes then helpfully explains to Watson (and the viewer) how he forms his deductions. The key point is that he uses external theories to make his deductions: from the observation of sweat around the inner lining of a hat he uses 'medical' knowledge to deduce that the owner is out of condition; from the observation that the hat has not been brushed for weeks he uses 'social' knowledge about marital responsibilities in 19th Century London to deduce that the owner's wife has ceased to love him! The key point is that scientific method as portrayed here requires both detailed observations and interpretative theories.

We can use Holmes' method to create an analogy with the use of methods where samples are selected in order that features of the whole population can be determined. A method similar to that used by Sherlock Holmes would require students to:

- collect purposeful samples of data through questionnaires or closed interviews;
- use robust methods of both collection and analysis; and
- develop appropriate theories in advance in order to organize and interpret the data.

This 'scientific' method may be the beginning of new knowledge and real discoveries if it produces information about unknown phenomena. But it also has advantages because it bases its conclusions on highly rigorous observation, quantification, and formalized procedures. The results look more objective than many other methods and are therefore considered sound by stakeholders, such as managers, funders, and research colleagues.

Tutors might point out that quantitative methods still have a huge attraction with students and employers as it offers an element of science and a semblance of rigor. Even if the findings don't really surprise anyone, the fact that the proof offered has been achieved and produced with supporting figures can often on its own justify the use of the magnifying glass! In terms of research the students need to know that surveys can cost a great deal of time and money and may not yield conclusive findings. Moreover they may collect large mounds of data, but they will not be able to make much use of it without some kind of theoretical framework which is tested against the data.

Miss Marple: The Ethnographer

The approach of Miss Marple is to get close to the scene of the crime and immerse herself in the setting where the murder took place. This often takes her to unfamiliar worlds and in order to understand them she needs to be able to understand the perspectives of local inhabitants. As she tries to reconstruct their reality she may appear to be wandering about simply gaining impressions, but her aim is to understand the whole in its cultural and historical context, as opposed to individual fragments. She drifts around meeting people in hotels or cafés, and she gradually gains their trust and cooperation; she is interested in the jobs people do, the way they live, their habits, fears and pleasures. Steeping herself in the local atmosphere, she often visits the scene of the crime and tries to imagine why the victims might have gone there on that particular evening, and at that particular time.

Much of this seems to be determined by chance,[2] but following her *intuition* she advances towards a full understanding of the motives of the different actors. In one of the video clips, a famous Scotland Yard detective explains how she is so successful—it is because she is able to draw parallels—she lives in the small village of Saint Mary Mead and it is from a deep understanding of the individuals in that village that she appears to know the world. The skills required for this approach are to be able to integrate oneself into the surroundings with the minimum of fuss, to listen, and become accepted. When asking questions, watch for doors to open and spot the opportunities that a *prepared mind*[3] will give you.

This example of Miss Marple illustrates the importance of skills such as knowing how to be accepted and being able to empathize with others, but they are not suited to everyone. Nevertheless, many of the significant findings in the management field have come from such approaches, and we believe that students should receive some exposure to constructionist ap-

---

[2] '*Chance*' is a concept in research that relates to the attitude of mind that researchers might adopt. This concept is dealt with in Easterby-Smith, Thorpe and Jackson (2012).

[3] A prepared mind is one of the ingredients in creativity identified by Austin (1978).

proaches to the collection and the analysis of data. Vignettes from films are useful for spelling out the requirements of such an approach, suggesting that researchers should be able to:

- have physical contact with the field in question;
- accept the need to listen to others and see things from their perspective;
- understand things in depth, and within their cultural historical context;
- remain open-minded and trust one's intuition and instinct; and
- know how to identify and win the confidence and help of the real experts.

This approach can offer great savings in time and can lead to original findings. It is through empathy, good questioning and observation that facts are revealed which would otherwise have escaped the logical reasoning approach of Poirot, or the more scientific approach of Sherlock Holmes. We suggest to students that this approach is particularly useful when little is known about the field—the researcher's role might be likened to that of an explorer, discovering new and interesting paths. It is also valuable when the research is seeking to understand things that cannot easily be quantified, such as politics, or the motives and feelings of participants.

This method can give significant insights into a range of topics. For example, it has been used in apparently quantitative disciplines such as accounting to show how budgets are used to control subordinates (Otley, 1987), or the resulting behavior from bonus schemes designed to increase output (Bowey & Thorpe, 1986) or how consumers develop protocols when making buying decisions (O'Shaughnessy, 1987). The various methods and approaches to observation and analysis are explained by Easterby-Smith et al. (2012).

Dirty Harry: Action Researcher

Clint Eastwood plays this maverick detective (Eastwood, 1983; Fargo, 1976; Post, 1973; Siegel, 1971; Van Horn, 1988). He is a man of action, and hence contrasts sharply with the intellectual detectives. Dirty Harry also brings about solutions and resolves problems by provoking a reaction often when the reaction of the opponent cannot be simulated or otherwise predicted in advance. So what we get across to students through clips from these films is that it might be necessary sometimes to try (or provoke) something in order to get a reaction, and through action to remove uncertainty. There are many ways in which interaction with respondents can take place but the classical detectives almost always use this approach when they wish to confirm their suspicions. They do this by laying a fateful trap into which the guilty individuals fall, and when they do take the bait the detective has their suspicions verified and their hunches confirmed.

This approach to research has its appeal in management as it often links organizational objectives with those of the research and education community. For example, in areas such as marketing, the approach could be used to test the market reaction to a new product, or to assess the effectiveness of a new process.

Action research, as a research design is now used a great deal in studies of management and organization, and is based on this type of philosophy. Its three premises being:

- that the best way of learning about an organization or social system is through attempting to change it, and this should be the objective of the action researcher to some extent;
- that those people most likely to be affected by, or involved in, implementing these changes should as far as possible become involved in the research process itself (Lewin, 1948); and
- that the researcher must be considered part of the thing being studied.

So the Dirty Harry example helps us to explain how attempts to change the organization might reveal, for example, where the power lies, or whether the change strategy is appropriate, and the conditions under which it ought to be modified. Because of the multiple outcomes now expected from research an understanding of interaction and engagement is an essential ingredient in doctoral training. Of course it is also the case that many researchers might also be managers researching into their own organizational practices, and understanding of this perspective for them is of even more importance.

DISCUSSION

We have illustrated above how four fictional characters can be used to illustrate quite different styles and strategies for research (see Figure 1). Although each character evokes a certain style, there are possible areas of overlap. Sherlock Holmes not only needs to be able to handle his magnifying glass, he also needs to know how to use both reason and instinct. Although intuition guides Hercule Poirot, he still needs to confirm his suspicions and also therefore needs facts and to know how to collect them.

This leads to three kinds of issue which we discuss in this concluding section. These cover the choice of film/video clips, ways of handling the teaching/learning process when using video, and questions about different interpretations of the material that we have presented here.

As indicated above, most of the video clips that we use are fairly short (3–4 minutes on average), and we use them as trigger films. In other words, they provide clear and memorable images around which members of the class can discuss what is taking place. Consequently, when choosing video clips it helps if characters can be chosen who are familiar to most students, and they also need to provide contrasts which are theoretically relevant. Hence, Hercule Poirot the intellectual can be seen as contrasting with Dirty Harry the action man; Sherlock Holmes who observes precise details and draws conclusions from them can be seen to contrast with the more intuitive and holistic approach of Miss Marple. In discussion with students the two dimensions in Figure 1 can be developed further. For example, the Poirot-Dirty Harry dimension is a matter of research style demonstrating the distinction between a detached style and a highly engaged style. The horizontal dimension can also be shown to be underpinned by different ontologies. Whereas Sherlock Holmes is looking for facts and hard evidence in order to form his deductions, Miss Marple is more interested in feelings and relationships in order to resolve the puzzle.

In some respects it does not matter particularly which characters are used, provided an appropriate set of contrasts can be established. This particular set of contrasts works equally well if Maigret or Agent Cooper from *Twin Peaks* (Frost & Lynch, 1990) is substituted for Miss Marple; similarly, instead of Dirty Harry we sometimes use Rambo (Cosmatos, 1985; Kotcheff,

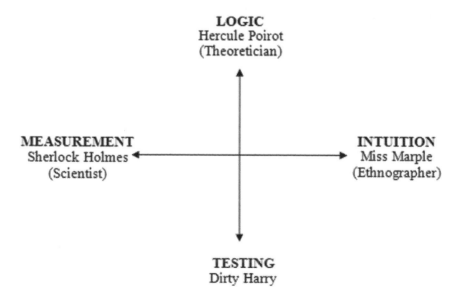

FIGURE 1.   Mapping Different Styles

1982; MacDonald, 1988; Stallone, 2008) who, although not technically a detective, still provides a very vivid image of someone taking action as a way to understand how to resolve a problem.

An important element in using these video images is the interaction with the class. The tutor needs to be able to pose appropriate questions which gets members of the class to derive (and largely from what has been seen on the clip) the principles that each of the characters demonstrates in terms of research methods. The map that is displayed in Figure 1 can therefore be built up on a whiteboard in stages after each of the video clips is shown. We do not use precisely the same labels every time, because it is often better to make use of words and concepts generated by members of the class. Thus it is best to portray this as a map which helps people understand differences, and to acknowledge that this is not the only way of representing or projecting these differences. With regard to timing, although the four video clips may take no more than 12 minutes in total, it is quite easy to spend 30 or 40 minutes discussing the examples and constructing the map.

Once the map has been constructed it is important to link it to students' experience. Thus, if it is introduced at a time when students are starting to think of their research projects or dissertations, it is usually quite easy to get a few people to identify where they fit on the map, and to explain what it is about their proposed research methods which would locate them in that particular spot or quadrant. If the class includes people from different disciplines it is usually very easy to identify examples which can be located in each of the four quadrants, and this is often the case even when students are working in similar disciplines.

The realization that people can conceptualize and research the same problem from different perspectives is usually quite an important insight for students. This often leads naturally to discussions about whether any of the positions are better than others (answer: no, they all have their place, and the most appropriate position may depend on individual preferences, institutional norms, the subject matter, or the interests of stakeholders/ funders); whether it is possible to combine different positions (answer: generally it is possible to combine adjacent positions, but this gets difficult when one tries to combine solutions that are directly opposite, especially along the horizontal ontological dimension); whether it is possible for a researcher to move around the map at different stages in the research (answer: generally yes, and there is not necessarily an ideal route, although it may be best for the researcher eventually to focus on one area); whether all researchers need to develop skills in all four areas (answer: we think it is important that all management researchers should be able to understand and appreciate each of these positions, although we would expect that in most cases people would specialize for their own dissertations on one particular area).

CONCLUSION

We hope that this chapter has provided some ideas and principles about the use of video, particularly when developing theoretical understanding among students. As indicated above, we are not trying to prescribe any particular method or framework, and indeed the two of us have our own distinct ways of handling this material. But we do think that there are general principles indicated here which can be applied when people seek to develop teaching materials for other kinds of subject or purpose.

REFERENCES

Austin, J. H. (1978). *Chase, chance and creativity*. New York, NY: Columbia University Press.

Bowey, A. M., & Thorpe, R., with Hellier, P. (1986). *Payment systems and productivity*. London, United Kingdom: Macmillan.

Christie, A. (1934). *Murder on the Orient Express*. London, United Kingdom: Collins Crime Club.

Christie, A. (1939). *Ten little nigger boys*. London, United Kingdom: Collins Crime Club.

Easterby-Smith, M., Thorpe, R., & Jackson, P. (2012). *Management research*, (4th Ed.). London, United Kingdom: Sage.

Lewin, K. (1948). *Resolving social conflict*. New York, NY: Harper &Row.

Moscarola, J. (1991). *Enquêtes et Analyse de Données*. Paris, Paris: Vuibert Gestion.

O'Shaughnessy, J. (1987). *Why people buy*. Oxford, United Kingdom: Oxford University Press.

Otley, D. T. (1987). *Accounting control and organisational behaviour*. London, United Kingdom: Heinemann.

Thorpe, R., & Moscarola, J. (1991). Detecting your research strategy. *Management Education and Development*, 22(2), 127–133.

Films and Television Series

Cosmatos, G. P. (Director). (1985) *Rambo: First blood part II* [Motion picture]. United States: Anabasis.

Eastwood, C. (Director). (1983). *Sudden impact* [Motion picture]. United States: Warner Bros.

Fargo, J. (Director). (1976). *The enforcer* [Motion picture]. United States: Warner Bros.

Frost, M., & Lynch, D. (Producers). (1990). *Twin peaks* [Television series]. New York, NY: ABC.

Kotcheff, T. (Director). (1982). *First blood* [Motion picture]. United States: Anabasis & Elcajo Productions.

MacDonald, P. (Director). (1988) *Rambo III* [Motion picture]. United States: Carolco Pictures.

Post, T. (Director). (1973). *Magnum force* [Motion picture]. United States: Warner Bros.

Siegel, D. (Director). (1971). *Dirty Harry* [Motion picture]. United States: Warner Bros.

Stallone, S. (Director). (2008) *Rambo* [Motion picture]. United States/Germany: Lionsgate, The Weinstein Company, Millennium Films, & Nu Image.

Van Horn, B. (Director). (1988). *The dead pool* [Motion picture]. United States: Warner Bros.

CHAPTER 4

THE UNIQUE EFFECTS
OF ANIMATED FILM IN
TEACHING AND LEARNING
ENVIRONMENTS

Joseph E. Champoux

Are animated films a credible source of film teaching resources for various management courses? Wegner (1977), an early user of film in teaching, recommended using animated film. Present day users of film in teaching also have argued for using animated film and pressed for their serious consideration (Champoux, 2001; Comer, 2000). Many cinema scholars view animated film as a serious cinematic art form, one that deserves the careful attention of adults (Barrier, 1999; Bendazzi, 1994; Kanfer, 1997; Moritz, 1996). The potentially serious quality of animated film positions it as a resource with several important functions in one's teaching program.

Sadly, some students, and perhaps some colleagues, will dismiss animated film as silly children's cartoons. They might view animated film as "just entertainment," a source of pleasure, fantasy, and escape, not a serious source of teaching and learning examples (Rockler, 2002). Perhaps anticipating objections to accepting animated films as serious teaching resources, Com-

Moving Images: Effective Teaching with Film and Television in Higher Education,
pages 49–62
49

er's main title of a thoughtful, detailed analysis of *The Lion King* (Allers & Minkoff, 1994) reads, "Not Just a Mickey Mouse Exercise" (Comer, 2000).

This chapter continues that theme and proposes further serious consideration of animated films as teaching resources. I review and discuss animated films not published before in the management education literature. They range from the hand drawn and hand painted "cel" animation of the 1930s to contemporary computer-animated films. I present the film scenes in the context of different functions of film in a teaching environment and different ways of using animated film scenes (Champoux, 1999b).

Animation differs greatly from live-action film making. It features a form of stop motion photography which creates a series of related images. The images can come from any source. They include classical hand drawn images, hand painting directly on film, and modern computer generated animation. Hand-drawn images are individually photographed and then played back as a continuous stream. Painting directly on film creates a series of images for continuous playback. Computer generated animation creates a series of images with each differing slightly from the previous to get the desired movement (Bendazzi, 1994; Crafton, 1996; Laybourne, 1998).

Cinema historians differ in their accounts of animated film's roots. Some say it started with *Matches: An Appeal* (Cooper, 1899), a British appeal for match donations to soldiers fighting the Boer war (Bendazzi, 1994). Other historians credit *Humorous Phases of Funny Faces* (Blackton, 1906) as the beginning of animation (Bendazzi, 1994; Crafton, 1996). Some credit its invention to Emile Reynaud's Théatre Optique in Paris, France, 1892, three years before the Lumière Brothers showed their first live-action film. Or was it the French cartoonist Emile Cohl's work beginning in 1908 (Bendazzi, 1994)? Still other historians trace it to Lucretius' description in *De Rerum Natura* (70 BC) of a machine that projected hand-drawn moving images (Hoffer, 1981). The unquestionable consensus: serious animated cinema creation has existed for more than 100 years around the world.

Like modern day live-action cinema, animated films have widely dispersed international sources and appeal. Bendazzi's comprehensive history of animation documents examples of serious animated cinema from each of the world's continents.[1] The largest animation sources are Japan, Europe, and North America. Japanese animation ("Animé") has carved a special place in the hearts of animation lovers worldwide, with its extraordinary quantity and quality of animated film (Bendazzi, 1994, chap. 15; Napier, 2001).

[1] Bendazzi's work is comprehensive in coverage. I highly recommend it as a readable extension to this brief animated film history. See also Moritz (1996).

ANIMATED FILM'S UNIQUE CHARACTERISTICS

Animated film gives its directors many mesmerizing features. The director tightly controls all aspects of presentation. Such control includes defining images, staging scenes, color saturation, color tonality, defining a character's personality, timing actions, and music. (Adamson, 1974). Animation's history shows the extraordinary creativity of people in this industry (Barrier, 1999; Bendazzi, 1994; Kanfer, 1997; Klein, 1993).

Animation's unique qualities make it an especially effective teaching tool. Here are the main reasons for this assertion:

- Animation's extraordinary visualization creates lasting images of concepts. The scene from *Chicken Run* (Lord & Park, 2000) discussed later shows several strategic planning efforts that should remain with viewers.
- Animated film's strong caricature powerfully shows concepts. The exaggerated performance of the Genie (Robin Williams) in *Aladdin* (Clements & Musker, 1992) described later offers a stunning metamorphosis experience.
- Often animated films' deliberate exaggeration helps associate visual symbols with abstract concepts. Any abstractness about problem-solving disappears in three minutes with the scene described later from *Toy Story 2* (Lasseter, 1992).

ANIMATED FILM TEACHING RESOURCES

Table 1 lists animated films with scenes showing many organizational behavior and management theories and concepts. They add to a growing set of teaching resources built from animated film (Champoux, 2001; Comer, 2000). The films listed in Table 1 have film scenes that will work well for the following topics:

- Strategic planning
- Personality and personality change
- Problem-solving
- Organizational socialization
- Cross-cultural experience

Table 1 gives distributor information and scene locations on an Area 1 DVD. Film scene descriptions in this section use a bracketing method, describing what occurs before and after a scene. This scene description method lets you easily locate the scene on a recorded source from another

TABLE 1.   Animated Film Scene Teaching Resources

Aladdin

Color, 1992   Running Time: 1 hour, 30 minutes   Rating: G

Director: Ron Clements, John Musker   Distributor: Walt Disney Home Video

Scenes: DVD Chapter 10, Trapped! through Chapter 11, "Friend Like Me"

Chicken Run

Color, 2000   Running Time: 1 hour, 24 minutes   Rating: G

Director: Peter Lord, Nick Park   Distributor: DreamWorks Home Entertainment

Scenes: DVD Chapter 1, No Chicken Escapes From Tweedy's Farm (Start: 0:00:46) to DVD Chapter 3, Eggless Edwina (Stop: 0:07:33)

The Emperor's New Groove

Color, 2000   Running Time: 1 hour, 18 minutes   Rating: G

Director: Mark Dindal   Distributor: Walt Disney Home Video

Scenes: (1) DVD Chapter 17, An Apparent Change Of Heart, and (2) DVD Chapter 18, Battle At The Bridge

Lilo & Stitch

Color, 2002   Running Time: 1 hour, 25 minutes   Rating: PG

Director: Dean DeBlois, Christopher   Distributor: Buena Vista Home Entertainment, Inc.
Sanders

Scenes: (1) DVD Chapter 1, Jumba's Trial through Chapter 2, Stitch Escapes, and (2) Chapter 29, "This Is My Family" to Chapter 30, Hawaii Forever/End Credits (Stop: 01:19:05)

Princess Mononoke (Dubbed in English)

Color, 1997   Running Time: 2 hours, 14 minutes   Rating: PG-13

Director: Hayao Miyazaki   Distributor: Miramax Home Entertainment

Scenes: DVD Chapter 2, Prince Ashitaka's Fate (Stop: 0:10:50)

Ratatouille

Color, 2007   Running Time: 1 hour, 51 minutes   Rating: G

Director: Brad Bird   Distributor: Buena Vista Home Entertainment, Inc.

Scenes: DVD Chapter 14, Cooking With Colette

Snow White and the Seven Dwarfs

Color, 1937   Running Time: 1 hour 24 minutes   Rating: G

Director: David Hand   Distributor: Walt Disney Home Video

Scenes: DVD Chapter 11, "Heigh-Ho" (Start: 0:23:35) to Chapter 14, Snow White Washes Up (Stop: 0:42:46)

Toy Story 2

Color, 1999   Running Time: 1 hour, 32 minutes   Rating: G

Director: John Lasseter   Distributor: Walt Disney Home Video

Scene: DVD Chapter 16, Crossing the Road

distributor or format. The rest of this section discusses films and film scenes for several conceptual areas in organizational behavior and management.

Strategic Planning: Chicken Run

Some early scenes from *Chicken Run* show several aspects of strategic planning and carrying out the plan. The stunning claymation of this film will captivate almost any viewer. Set on Tweedy's Farm, a failing 1950s Yorkshire, England chicken farm, the chickens fear for their necks. Rocky Rhodes, a Rhode Island Red rooster voiced by Mel Gibson, suddenly arrives. The resident chickens turn to Rocky as their savior and hero to help them escape from the farm. The selected scenes pay homage to World War Two prisoner of war films such as *The Great Escape* (Sturges, 1963) and *The Wooden Horse* (Lee, 1950).

These scenes start after some opening credits. They follow the black title screen, "a AARDMAN production." The camera pans from the moon to chicken barns 15 and 17. They follow a failed escape effort at the beginning of the film. These scenes end after Ginger (voiced by Julia Sawalha) returns from her solitary confinement. Babs (voiced by Jane Horrocks) asks her if she is back from holiday (vacation). Ginger says she was in solitary confinement. The film cuts to a ringing bell on a post.

None of Ginger's plans work. She also does not involve the other chickens in developing the plan, producing flawed, incomplete plans. Ginger presents the plan and expects no failures in carrying it out. She and the other chickens do not consider possible situations they could meet when carrying out the plan. Each effort fails with Ginger paying the price of time in solitary confinement.

Personality: Snow White and the Seven Dwarfs (Hand, 1937)

Walt Disney's first feature-length animated film offers a strong example of personality and differences among personalities. This film adapts the famous Brothers Grimm fairy tale. The studio developed new animation techniques to get smooth character movement. To get further realism, Disney hired live actors as models. Marge Belcher (later Marge Champion), a local dancer, modeled for Snow White (Culhane, 1986; Kanfer, 1997).

The jealous Queen (voiced by Lucille La Verne), Snow White's stepmother, fears Snow White's beauty. She transforms herself into an old hag and convinces Snow White (Adriana Caselotti) to eat a poisoned apple. Snow White falls into the Sleeping Death. Her seven dwarf friends try to protect her in their forest house and stand watch over her sleep.

These scenes start as the dwarfs' shadows fall onto a hillside. They follow the end of the workday and after Dopey locks the storeroom door. The dwarfs march from their diamond mine singing the famous "Heigh-Ho" song. The seven dwarfs in the line are Doc (voiced by Roy Atwell), Grumpy (voiced by Pinto Colvig), Happy (voiced by Otis Harlin), Sleepy (voiced by Pinto Colvig), Sneezy (voiced by Billy Gilbert), Bashful (voiced by Scotty Mattraw), and Dopey (voiced by Eddie Collins). These scenes end as Grumpy angrily leaves the house after Snow White insists he wash for dinner. The film continues with Grumpy complaining about women and the other dwarfs start to wash their hands.

The Seven Dwarfs share some *Big-Five* personality dimensions (McCrae & Costa, 1999). Each is high in conscientiousness. They are hard workers who toil in their diamond mine each day. They also are high in agreeableness with Grumpy as an exception. Although overtly a grouch, he always goes with the whole group.

Each dwarf has the following distinctive personality characteristics:

Doc: High on extroversion, moderate on emotional stability. He becomes easily agitated and confuses his words. Moderate to low on openness to experience.

Grumpy: Low on emotional stability as shown by his bursts of anger. Moderate to low on extroversion. Grumpy does not extend himself out to other people, especially strangers and women. Low on openness to experience. He does not enjoy the new and unusual as shown by his reaction to Snow White.

Happy: Although all the dwarfs are high on agreeableness, Happy symbolically represents this dimension. He also is high on the extroversion dimension as he enjoys other people and reacts warmly to Snow White. Happy is moderate on the emotional stability dimension as shown by his lack of depression and anxiety.

Sleepy: Low on extroversion, Sleepy is a visual symbol of introversion. He is not outgoing and takes time to catch up with everyone else. Sleepy is high on emotional stability and low on openness to experience. He is not curious about anything and leads a simple, unimaginative life.

Sneezy: He is high on extroversion and emotional stability. He interacts freely with other people, when he is not sneezing. He is secure, relaxed and has some curiosity, suggesting he is moderate on openness to experience.

Bashful: He is low on the extroversion dimension, another visual symbol of an introvert. Bashful is also low on the emotional stability dimension. His low self-esteem contributes to his insecurities in new situations. He is moderate on openness to experience. Although he embarrasses easily, Bashful accepts the newness of Snow White.

Dopey: He is high on extroversion, a person who loves the company of other people. He also is high on the emotional stability dimension. Although he does not talk (Happy says, "He don't know. He never tried."), Dopey shows no insecurity about it. He is the highest of the dwarfs on the openness to experience dimension. Dopey has unbounded curiosity that constantly gets him into trouble.

These are clearly fictional characters. In the great tradition of personality animation, the Disney studio created a distinctive set of standout personalities.

Problem-Solving: Toy Story 2

Animated film directors often insert strong symbolism into their films. Whether intentional or not, a three minute sequence from *Toy Story 2* has a memorable symbolic look at the essence of problem-solving.

Greedy toy collector Al McWhiggen (voiced by Wayne Knight) kidnaps Sheriff Woody (voiced by Tom Hanks), setting off an adventurous search by all his toy friends. All of Woody's toy friends engage in a frantic search for him. This scene follows Woody's conflict with Jessie (voiced by Joan Kusack) over who turned on Al's television set. The scene begins as Buzz Lightyear (voiced by Tim Allen) slashes his way through some brush. Hamm (voiced by John Ratzenberger) and the others follow him through the bushes. This scene ends after they successfully cross the street. Buzz says, "Good job troops. We're that much closer to Woody." The camera pans to the top of an apartment building and the film cuts to the toy cleaner arriving at Al's apartment.

These scenes are a visual metaphor of problem-solving. The problem: cross the street to get to Al's Toy Barn. Innovation in problem-solving often requires using items immediately available. The traffic likely would not stop for them to cross the street, nor were they at a light-controlled pedestrian crossing. Problem solution: use the traffic cones. Of course, the humor from the scenes follows from the unintended effects of their problem solution: enormous traffic accidents.

Metamorphosis: Aladdin

The abstract quality of socialization theory's metamorphosis concept (Van Maanen & Schein, 1979) quickly disappears in the lightening fast blue Genie transformation scenes in Disney's *Aladdin*. Academy Award® winning songs, Robin Williams' blue Genie, and wisecracking parrot Iago (voiced by Gilbert Gottfried), offer smart entertainment and stunning symbolism.

Aladdin (voiced by Scott Weinger) wants to marry Princess Jasmine (voiced by Linda Larkin). Her society's law says she must marry a member of royalty. Genie can grant many of Aladdin's wishes but not the one most important to win Jasmine; learning to be himself. Pay close attention to Genie's changes and quick dialogue or you will miss many satirical allusions. Watch closely for Ed Sullivan, Groucho Marx, and many others.

These scenes start with Aladdin lying on the ground knocked out by the fall down the shaft. Abu the monkey (voiced by Frank Welker) tries to awaken him. The scenes follow the old prisoner's efforts (disguised evil sorcerer Jafar, voiced by Jonathan Freeman) to steal the magic lantern and kill Aladdin. These scenes end as the three fly off on the magic carpet with Genie saying, "Weeeeeee're outa here." The film cuts to the Sultan (voiced by Douglas Seale) telling Jafar that he must discuss prisoner sentencing with him before beheading them.

The rapid-fire animation matches Genie's lightening fast dialogue. These scenes offer unquestionable symbolism of the "metamorphosis" concept from organizational socialization theory (Van Maanen & Schein, 1979). Derived from a Greek word meaning "transformation" or change in form, Genie alters in shape and number. Along the way, he mimics and characterizes Ed Sullivan, Groucho Marx, Peter Lorre, and many other well-known figures.

Trust, Problem-Solving: The Emperor's New Groove (Dindal, 2000)

Only describing management and organizational behavior concepts, even with clear definitions, can leave students searching for a concept's meaning. Animated film's unique qualities described earlier help it give strong meaning to concepts that stay in a student's memory. *The Emperor's New Groove* offers back-to-back scenes that bring meaning to trust and problem-solving.

Self-centered, arrogant Emperor Kusco (voiced by David Spade) becomes a llama at the hands of sorceress Yzma (voiced by Eartha Kitt). Yzma's clumsy, distracted henchman Kronk (voiced by Patrick Warburton) and she want to take over the emperor's kingdom. A hilarious adventure unfolds after Kusco becomes a partner with peasant Pacha (voiced by John Goodman).

You can use two sets of scenes that appear one after the other to show aspects of trust and problem-solving. Watch the first set and decide whether Pacha should trust Kuzco. Watch the second set to see their interdependence to reach a mutually desired result.

These scenes follow Tipo's (voiced by Ed Russell Linnette) bad dream and ChiCha (voiced by Wendie Malick) putting Tipo and his sister Chaca (voiced by Kellyann Kelso) back to bed. They each repeatedly say "Yah uh" to each other. The scenes start after a black screen and a swarm of flying bats. Pacha approaches a pond, stretching after awakening from his night's sleep. These scenes end as Kuzco and Pacha walk up a hill. The film cuts to a shot of the hilltop palace.

The second set of scenes starts with the shot of the hilltop palace. The camera pans to Pacha and Kuzco crossing the bridge. The scene ends after Kuzco says, "What are the chances of you carrying me?" Pacha replies, "Not good." The film cuts to Yzma scratching lines across some symbols while searching for Kuzco. Kronk has her carrier on his back.

Kuzco clearly deceives Pacha in the first set of scenes. Pacha trusts Kuzco to keep his word because of their handshake. The viewer easily develops a sense of distrust from Kuzco's aside to the camera toward the end of the first set of scenes.

A problem develops soon after they start across the bridge. The problem forces Kuzco and Pacha into an interdependent relationship to solve their problem. Questions of trust quickly evaporate as they discover they likely will die if they do not depend on each other to solve their problem.

Cross-cultural Experience: Princess Mononoke (Mononoke-hime[2]; Miyazaki, 1999)

Live-action films can give viewers a vicarious visit to another time or another culture (Champoux, 1999a; Summerfield, 1993; Summerfield & Lee, 2001). Animated film does the same as shown in an opening scene of the Japanese animated film *Princess Mononoke*.

Prince Ashitaka (voiced by Billy Crudup) kills an injured boar taken over by a *tatarigami*, a violent god (Napier, 2001). Now inflicted with a curse that will kill him, he goes to the forests of the west to find a cure. His adventures and challenges unfold when he discovers Iron Town and its continuous intrusion on the surrounding forest. San or Princess Mononoke (voiced by Claire Danes), a human raised by wolves, leads the forest animals against the proud Iron Town residents. Lady Eboshi (voiced by Minnie Driver), Iron Town's cold ruler, becomes San's arch-enemy. This exquisitely animated film is definitely not targeted at small children but should delight worldwide fans of Japanese anime.

These scenes appear early in the film following Prince Ashitaka's encounter with the wild boar. They open at the Emishi tribe's village with a panning shot up to a lighted room where Prince Ashitaka sits in front of a village elder (voice uncredited). These scenes end after the elder says their laws do not let them watch him leave. The Prince leaves the room and the film cuts to him dressed in a helmet and an animal skin cape, approaching his red elk, Yakul.

These scenes offer an animated vicarious visit to another culture. Although set in the fourteenth century Muromachi period (Napier, 2001), these scenes help one observe behaviors in a culture different from one's own. People sit on the floor. The village elder reads her stones to predict Prince Ashitaka's fate. Traditions are a strong part of this culture. The

---

[2] The following are the original Japanese voices for the referenced characters: Prince Ashitaka (Yôji Matsuda), San (Yuriko Ishida), and Eboshi-gozen (Yûko Tanaka). The English subtitles likely do not capture the nuances of spoken Japanese.

Prince must cut his hair before leaving and the village people present cannot watch him leave. He is dead forever. Napier (2001) presents a more detailed analysis of *Princess Mononoke*.

Personality Change: Lilo & Stitch (DeBlois & Sanders, 2002)

People's personalities typically are stable over the life course, but can change in adulthood from direct efforts to modify personality (Bandura, 1969; Costa & McCrae, 1994). Personality change is a dynamic concept presented in personality theory but often appears static in classroom lectures or discussions. Comparing scenes showing the same character in different parts of a film can return dynamism to the personality change concept. Animation's typically strong characterization, as in *Lilo & Stitch*, humorously shows personality change.

Nani (voiced by Tia Carrere) tries hard to raise sister Lilo (voiced by Daveigh Chase) to become a well-behaved child without their parents. Despite Nani's efforts, Lilo engages in socially unacceptable behavior causing other children at school to reject her. Stitch (voiced by Christopher Michael Sanders) arrives in Hawaii from planet Turo with socially unacceptable behavior that over shadows Lilo's behavior. Lilo adopts Stitch from the animal shelter, tries to reshape his behavior, and integrate him into their small family.

Two sequences at different places in the film allow personality observations and comparisons. View the first set of scenes and note aspects of Stitch's personality. View the second set of scenes to see if Stitch develops a different personality after Lilo's behavior shaping efforts.

The first sequence has the establishing scenes before the opening credits. They begin after the Walt Disney Pictures logo lifts off the screen. Text on a purple screen reads, "GALACTIC FEDERATION HEADQUARTERS PLANET TURO." It is the start of Jumba's (voiced by David Ogden Stiers) trial. The sequence ends after Stitch flies away in the red police cruiser. Captain Gantu (voiced by Kevin Michael Richardson) scratches his head while saying, "Get me Galactic Control." The film cuts to the Grand Councilwoman (voiced by Zoe Caldwell) entering the control room while asking about Stitch's location.

The second sequence appears near the film's end. It follows Stitch rescuing Lilo from Captain Gantu's spaceship. The sequence starts with a shot of the surf and Stitch arriving on a surfboard with Nani and David Kawena (voiced by Jason Scott Lee). One of Grand Councilwoman's guards puts Stitch in arm cuffs. This sequence ends after the performance of the song "With Burning Love" as the camera pans away from the photograph at Graceland. The end credits come onto the screen.

The first set of scenes shows the original Stitch, Jumba's creation from experiment #6–2–6. Stitch has a mean, aggressive personality with a singular focus and instinct: focus on self and destroy anything that prevents him from reaching a desired goal. Stitch is so foul mouthed that he offends the observers during Jumba's trial.

The second set of scenes shows a more mellow Stitch. He moves more slowly and without the aggression shown in the first set of scenes. His new personality is perhaps the product of socialization in Lilo's family and Lilo's endless behavior shaping from the moment she got him at the animal shelter.

Organizational Socialization: Ratatouille (Bird & Pinkava, 2007)

Discussions of organizational socialization introduce potentially complex and interdependent concepts. Animated film's unique qualities discussed earlier can let well-chosen scenes efficiently represent the concepts.

Remy (voiced by Patton Oswalt), a French gourmand rat, differs from his relatives. He prefers to forage for food in Paris' finest restaurants, while his father and others forage elsewhere. Remy aspires to become a great chef, especially in the late Auguste Gusteau's (voice by Brad Garrett) restaurant. Linguini (voiced by Lou Romano) comes to the restaurant and starts working as a garbage boy. He joins forces with Remy to contribute to the restaurant's world-class reputation. This beautifully animated film has many captivating moments for viewers of all ages.

A 3¼ minute sequence wonderfully shows several aspects of the organizational socialization process. It follows Chef Skinner's (voiced by Ian Holm) discussion with his lawyer Talon Labarthe (voiced by Teddy Newton) about Gusteau's will and the effect of Linguini's presence in the restaurant. This sequence opens with Linguini cutting vegetables. Colette (voiced by Janeane Garofalo) immediately corrects his behavior. Remy sits atop Linguini's head inside his toque and observes Colette's behavior with disbelief. This sequence ends as they thank each other for giving and receiving advice. The film cuts to a close-up of Chef Skinner driving his car.

The following socialization process concepts appear in the scenes (Bauer, Morrison & Callister, 1998; Katz & Kahn, 1966; Powell, 1998; Schein, 1992; Van Maanen & Schein, 1979):

- Role: duties and behavior required for success in this kitchen.
- Pivotal role behavior: essential behaviors for success; these are not optional.
- Role sender: person or persons who define a role.
- Focal person: receives the defined role.
- Role episode: a sequence of interactions between the role sender and focal person.
- Entry/Encounter socialization stage: the stage within which a person learns his or her role in the organization.

- Apprenticeship or mentoring socialization process: assignment to an experienced person who defines pivotal role behavior.

The entire film sequence occurs within the entry/encounter stage of socialization and is a role episode. Colette is the role sender and mentor. Linguini is the focal person and apprentice. He quickly learns the efficient way of cutting vegetables and the pivotal role behavior of keeping your work area well organized. Colette says, "Keep your station clear, or I will kill you!" She then emphasizes other pivotal role behavior such as proper arm position, following Gusteau's recipes, and how to tell good bread. Colette also describes some characteristics of each co-worker so that Linguini can understand his future interactions with them. The sequence closes with her observation that he is now one of them. This socialization process also works on Remy who listens and observes from within Linguini's toque.

CONCLUSIONS

Animated film's unique qualities give it uncommon power to induce positive learning responses. Tight directorial control keeps animated scenes efficiently focused on a central theme. The scenes from *Toy Story 2* that metaphorically show problem-solving are an example of this efficiency. Similar efficiency appears in the organizational socialization scenes from *Ratatouille*. Character development can create riveting images that fully engage a viewer's mind. *The Emperor's New Groove* scenes have this quality for showing examples of trust and problem-solving. Careful staging of scenes helps deliver complex concepts in an unambiguous way. Such staging often happens with more focus in animated film than in live-action film. The strategic planning and execution scenes from *Chicken Run* have this effect. Animation's potentially strong caricature shows clearly in the scenes from *Lilo & Stitch*. I propose that students will well remember what you mean by personality change, after you compare the two recommended scenes described earlier.

REFERENCES

Adamson, J. (1974). Suspended animation. In G. Mast & M. Cohen (Eds.), *Film theory and criticism: Introductory readings* (pp. 391–400). New York: Oxford University Press.

Bandura, A. (1969). *Principles of behavior modification.* New York, NY: Holt, Rinehart, and Winston.

Barrier, M. (1999). *Hollywood cartoons: American animation in its golden age.* New York: Oxford University Press.

Bauer, T. N., Morrison, E. W., & Callister, R. R. (1998). Organizational socialization: A review and directions for future research. In G. R. Ferris (Ed.), *Research in personnel and human resources management* (Vol. 16, pp. 149–214). Stamford, CT: JAI Press.

Bendazzi, G. (Ed.) (1994). *Cartoons: One hundred years of cinema animation* (A. Taraboletti-Segre, Trans.). Bloomington, IN: Indiana University Press.

Champoux, J. E. (1999a). Film remakes as a comparative view of time. *Educational Media International, 36*(3), 210–217.

Champoux, J. E. (1999b). Film as a teaching resource. *Journal of Management Inquiry, 8*(2), 240–251.

Champoux, J. E. (2001). Animated films as a teaching resource. *Journal of Management Education, 25*(1), 78–99.

Comer, D. R. (2000). Not just a Mickey Mouse exercise: Using Disney's "The Lion King" to teach leadership. *Journal of Management Education, 25*(4), 430–436.

Costa, P. T., Jr., & McCrae, R. R. (1994). Set like plaster? Evidence for the stability of adult personality. In T. Heatherton & J. Weinberger (Eds.), *Can personality change?* (pp. 21–40). Washington, DC: American Psychological Association.

Crafton, D. (1996). Tricks and animation. In G. Nowell-Smith (Ed.), *The Oxford history of world cinema* (pp. 71–78). Oxford, United Kingdom: Oxford University Press.

Culhane, S. (1986). *Talking animals and other people*. New York: St. Martin's Press.

Hoffer, T. W. (1981). *Animation: A reference guide*. Westport, CT: Greenwood Press.

Kanfer, S. (1997). *Serious business: The art and commerce of animation in America from Betty Boop to Toy Story*. New York: Scribner.

Katz, D., & Kahn, R. (1966). *The social psychology of organizations*. New York: John Wiley.

Klein, N. M. (1993). *Seven minutes: The life and death of the American animated cartoon*. New York: Verso.

Laybourne, K. (1998). *The animation book: A complete guide to animated filmmaking— From flip-books to sound cartoons to 3-D animation*. New York: Three Rivers Press.

McCrae, R. R., & Costa, P. T., Jr. (1999). A five-factor theory of personality. In L. A. Pervin & O. P. John (Eds.), *Handbook of personality: Theory and research* (2nd ed.). New York: Guilford Press.

Moritz, W. (1996). Animation in the post-industrial era. In G. Nowell-Smith (Ed.). *The Oxford history of world cinema* (pp. 551–558). Oxford, United Kingdom: Oxford University Press.

Napier, S. J. (2001). *Anime from* Akira *to* Princess Mononoke: *Experiencing contemporary japanese animation*. New York: Palgrave.

Powell, G. N. (1998). Reinforcing and extending today's organizations: The simultaneous pursuit of person-organization fit and diversity. *Organizational Dynamics* (Winter), 50–61.

Rockler, N. R. (2002). Overcoming "It's just entertainment": Perspective by incongruity as strategy for media literacy. *Journal of Popular Film and Television, 30*(1), 16–22.

Schein, E. H. (1992). *Organizational culture and leadership*. San Francisco, CA: Jossey-Bass.

Summerfield, E. (1993). *Crossing cultures through film.* Yarmouth, ME: Intercultural Press, Inc.
Summerfield, E., & Lee, S. (2001). *Seeing the big picture: Exploring American cultures on film.* Yarmouth, ME: Intercultural Press, Inc.
Van Maanen, J., & Schein, E. H. (1979). Toward a theory of organizational socialization. In B. M. Staw (Ed.), *Research in organizational behavior,* (Vol. 1, pp. 209–264). Greenwich, CT: JAI Press.
Wegner, H. (1977). *Teaching with film.* Bloomington, IN: The Phi Delta Kappa Educational Foundation.

Films

Allers, R., & Minkoff, R. (Director). (1994). *The lion king* [Motion picture]. United States: Walt Disney Pictures.
Bird, B. (Director). (2007). *Ratatouille* [Motion picture]. United States: Pixar Animation Studios & Walt Disney Pictures.
Blackton, J. S. (Director). (1906). *Humorous phases of funny faces* [Motion picture]. United States: Vitagraph Company of America.
Clements, R., & Musker, J. (Directors). (1992). *Aladdin* [Motion picture]. United States: Walt Disney Pictures.
Cooper, A. M. (Director). (1899). *Matches: An appeal* [Motion picture]. United Kingdom: Birt Acres.
DeBlois, D., & Sanders, C. (Directors). (2002). *Lilo & Stitch* [Motion picture]. United States: Walt Disney Pictures.
Dindal, M. (Director). (2000). *The emperor's new groove* [Motion picture]. United States: Walt Disney Pictures.
Hand, D. (Director). (1937). *Snow White and the seven dwarfs* [Motion picture]. United States: Walt Disney Productions.
Lasseter, J. (Director). (1999). *Toy story 2* [Motion picture]. United States: Walt Disney Pictures & Pixar Animation Studios.
Lee, J. (Director). (1950). *The wooden horse* [Motion picture]. United Kingdom: Ian Dalrymple's Wessex Film Production, British Lion Film Corporation, & London Films.
Lord, P., & Park, N. (Directors). (2000). *Chicken run* [Motion picture]. United Kingdom: DreamWorks, Pathé, & Aardman Animations.
Miyazaki, H. (Director). (1999). *Princess Mononoke* [Motion picture]. Japan: Studio Ghibli.
Sturges, J. (Director). (1963). *The great escape* [Motion picture]. United States: The Mirisch Company.

CHAPTER 5

EXPECT THE UNEXPECTED

Janet Sutherland

I like nothing better than coming home on a Friday evening and flopping onto the couch with a DVD and the ubiquitous take out meal. Movies allow me to suspend my own reality—to live someone else's life for a time. This particular Friday night was no different. Browsing the shelves in my dingily-lit local video store, I was attracted to a new release, *Freedom Writers* (LaGravenese, 2007), starring two-time best actress Oscar winner, Hilary Swank.

I had expected to be entertained and moved by *Freedom Writers*. I'd also been prepared for another movie about an idealistic teacher who takes on a tough class and wins against the odds, in the league of films like *Stand and Deliver* (Menéndez, 1988), *Lean on Me* (Avildsen, 1989) and *Dangerous Minds* (Smith, 1995). However, what I had not expected to find encapsulated in one film, was a wealth of case studies for teaching a broad spectrum of organizational behavior concepts, such as: leadership, organizational structure, organizational culture, organizational change, workplace power and politics, conflict and negotiation, motivation, communication, values, attitudes, and personality.

I had not consciously considered this film as a teaching tool when I picked it off the shelf. However, during the preceding week I had started exploring the possibility of using film in my organizational behavior teach-

Moving Images: Effective Teaching with Film and Television in Higher Education,
pages 63–76
Copyright © 2012 by Information Age Publishing
All rights of reproduction in any form reserved.

63

ing. Articles by Huczynski and Buchanan (2004) and Champoux (1999) had been particularly helpful and inspirational. What I was experiencing, as I watched *Freedom Writers,* confirmed what the literature was telling me about the benefits of using film to teach organizational behavior and management theories and concepts. The manner in which film records the complexity and situational context of physical reality suggests that it has the ability to provide role models and referents for the abstract theories and concepts taught in organizational behavior and management (Champoux, 1999; Huczynski & Buchanan, 2004).

I will explore why I fell in love with *Freedom Writers* as a film and how I used it as the basis for teaching multiple concepts across an entire organizational behavior unit. In the "why to" aspects of this articles, I will discuss how the rationale for using film, as outlined in the literature, aligns with the contingency based approach to organizational behavior I use. In the "how to" aspects of the article, I will discuss how techniques and resources align with the pedagogy used in our school, and my desire to further democratize the teaching and learning process.

FREEDOM WRITERS: FROM IDEALISM TO ACTION

This 2007 film, directed by Richard LaGravenese and based on the book *The Freedom Writers Diary: How a teacher and 150 teens used writing to change themselves and the world around them,* is the 'true' story of teacher Erin Gruwell and her students. Students dubbed themselves "The Freedom Writers," a play on words expressing how writing becomes a vehicle for change as powerfully transforming as the Freedom Riders of the 1960s civil rights movement.

Swank worked closely with Gruwell and the Freedom Writers to bring the characters to life on screen. Set again the backdrop of the 1992 race riots in Los Angeles, the film tells the story of an idealistic new teacher who chooses teaching over law because she believes that she can make a difference where it counts. She elects to teach at Woodrow Wilson High School, which has undergone voluntary integration, i.e. an affirmative action plan to represent minorities more equitably.

Dressed in pearls and a neat suit, Gruwell comes face-to-face with inner city kids from a broad array of ethnic backgrounds, including African-American ("The Ghetto"), Hispanic ("South of the Border"), and Cambodian ("Little Cambodia"). Groups are segregated and fight for their territory. Many students have firsthand experience of the juvenile justice system and gang violence. The film explores how Gruwell's determination to make a difference wins against all odds, as she finds a way to give her students their own voice and a purpose to transcend their situation. These students had been branded as unteachable by the school system and marginalized. Gruwell battles the hierarchical and uncaring system to make a difference in her students' lives, including making financial and personal sacrifices. Few of these students had expected to graduate from high school, let alone see their eighteenth birthdays, because of gang violence. However, all of Gruwell's students graduated and many have gone on to be teachers who have carried on her legacy.

The pivotal moment in the film is when a racial caricature of one of the African-American students, Jamal Hill, circulates the classroom and is intercepted by Gruwell. She compares the caricature to a Nazi exaggeration of Jews during the Holocaust. Her tirade is met with blank looks and she is appalled to discover that only one child (the only white student) in her class knows about the Holocaust. In contrast, Gruwell discovers that nearly all have been shot at in their own neighborhoods and lost someone they knew and loved to gang violence.

This prompts Gruwell to introduce her students to books like *Anne Frank: The Diary of a Young Girl* (Frank, 2007). The students go from reluctant readers to developing an intense connection with the texts. Gruwell then encourages each student to keep his or her own anonymous diary. The students' diary entries, which document the horrors of gang violence, domestic violence, drugs, and neglect, became the book on which the film is based and the foundation for a life-changing journey and a strong voice for acceptance and change.

TEACHING MULTIPLE
ORGANIZATIONAL BEHAVIOR CONCEPTS

As the story unfolds, Gruwell emerges as a role model for transformational leadership. She is an idealistic, skilled and committed teacher who believes in her students. She is juxtaposed against a hierarchical organizational structure, where people are promoted on seniority and not merit and command and control leadership is the order of the day. Within this context, Gruwell's students are seen as "unteachable" and not worth expending any effort or resources. She fights to change this perception within her own school and then use upward influence to take her fight to more senior figures in the district school system.

The essence of Gruwell's character aligns with Bass' (1995) definition of transformational leadership. He defines the transformational leader

> as someone who raised their [followers] awareness about issues of consequence, shifted them to higher-level needs, influenced them to transcend their own self-interests for the good of the group or organization, and to work harder than they originally had expected they would. (Bass, 1995, p. 467)

While the focus is on the good of the group, this is achieved through the building blocks of the transformational leader which are: idealized influ-

TABLE 1. Scenes Which Demonstrate Gruwell's Transformational Leadership Attributes

Transformational Leadership Attributes*	Film Clip
Idealized influence, i.e. leader as role model with high standards of moral and ethical conduct.	Ch 1 (00:05:00–00:06:08): Gruwell meets with Margaret Campbell, head of the English Department. She expresses her vision that teachers can make a difference and explains that she has been influenced by her father a former civil rights activist. Campbell attempts to temper her enthusiasm but Gruwell shows her willingness to lead by example by saying: "I know I have a lot to learn as a teacher, but I'm a really good student."
Inspirational motivation, i.e. leaders inspires followers to reach higher levels of expectation and shared vision.	Toast for change (Ch 10: 00:01:00) is when Gruwell outlines a vision for a better future and invites her students to articulate their own vision.
Intellectual stimulation, i.e. leaders encourages followers to be creative and innovative and challenge their own beliefs	Ch 5–6: (from 00:07:55) Gruwell discovers a caricature of an African-American student with exaggerated lips. She likens this to Nazi caricatures of Jews but realizes that her students do not know about the Holocaust. In contrast, virtually every student has been shot at or has lost someone to gang violence. She uses this situation to develop the Line Game to get students to begin challenging their stereotypical views. Other examples are: Toast for Change (Ch 10: 00:01:00); visit to the Simon Wiesenthal Center (Museum of Tolerance) and dinner with Holocaust survivors (Ch 9: 00:03:24–00:07:05), reading Anne Frank's Diary; and inspiring the students to write their own anonymous diaries (Ch 6 00:07:45–00:09:24).
Individualized consideration, i.e. leader creates a supportive climate for followers and listens to individual needs	• Room 203 is seen by the students as a home, a haven from the chaos of their lives outside of school (see Ch 10). See also Ch 15 where Eva Benitez says: "This is our kicking spot … everyone is cool with everyone … this is where we get to be ourselves … there is no place out there like this." • Gruwell chooses books in response to personal experiences of students, e.g. several students speak of living through a war. In response, Gruwell chose books by teenagers who had lived through war, e.g. *The Diary of Anne Frank*. Gruwell says that the books she has chosen remind her in some way of her students (Ch 10: 00:01:29–00:05:45) and she acknowledges each students' individual voice and creates a safe space for them to express their individuality. • Gruwell says to Andre Bryant (Ch 15): "I won't let you fail even if it means coming to your home every night. I won't let you fail."

Note: *Based on Bass, 1985, 1995, Northouse, 2004 and Rosser, 2007.
All references are for the 2007 Australian (Pal Region 4) DVD version.

ence, inspirational motivation, intellectual stimulation, and individualized consideration. Moreover, transformational leaders should be charismatic, visionary, and strategic. It is critical that they are a change champion, with the ability to neutralize resistance and induce people to change (Eisenbach, Watson, & Pillai, 1999). All of these attributes define Gruwell's character and practice in the film. The authentic transformational nature of her leadership is demonstrated in the changes which manifest in her students and in the actions they take as a result (Bass & Steidlmeier, 1999). Her students are motivated to rise above their circumstances and become agents of change and transformational leaders in their own right. One student says: "I am willing to step forward, unafraid of who or what lies ahead. After all, history tells me that I am not alone (The Freedom Writers, 1999, p. 27)." Table 1 outlines scenes from the film which demonstrate how Gruwell epitomizes the role of transformational leader through her actions.

ON THE LOOKOUT FOR A NEW WAY...

All organizational behaviors have a context, and the motivation for using film as a teaching medium is its ability to replicate this context. Film gives students the opportunity to explore abstract concepts by viewing observable behaviors. It demonstrates the complexity of interrelated concepts and introduces "students to themes and ideas that approximate real-world untidiness more closely than fragmented and oversimplified textbook models" (Huczynski & Buchanan 2004, p. 709). Furthermore, by using film, all participants would have access to a common context, although they may still have very differing perspectives or interpretations (Huczynski & Buchanan, 2004).

The use of film as common context is supported by film being a familiar medium (Champoux, 1999, Huczynski & Buchanan, 2004) or "popular culture artifact" (Callahan, Whitener, & Sandlin, 2007). Films not only shape and constitute our understanding of social and organizational life (Huczynski & Buchanan, 2004) but have become a substantial, if not the primary, educational force influencing norms and values (Giroux, 1999). These factors create the perfect platform for learners to develop theory-to-practice thinking (Callahan, Whitener, & Sandlin, 2007). As learners make sense of the theory through the context of the film, they may develop the critical thinking required to do so in their work context. Films encode processes rather than neatly linking antecedents to consequences and spelling out the relationships between independent and dependent variables. To understand the process flows, students have to analyze beneath the surface structures of 'what' and 'where' and consider the deep structures of 'how' and 'why' (Huczynski & Buchanan, 2004).

In choosing to use film, I accepted that the empathy and engagement generated by the film could not replace the kinesthetic imprint achieved through a truly experiential learning process. However, because we are not passive recipients of popular culture, film comes close. When we view film we live the experience and feel a wide range of emotions. Furthermore, because of film-making techniques, film is unequalled in its ability to capture and hold the attention of the viewer, while submerging them in the complexity of the detail (Champoux, 1999).

The transcendent and affective nature of this film was evident in the feedback I received from students. One student felt inspired by Gruwell's story and questioned whether her current job was meaningful. She expressed the desire to find a job where she felt she was making a difference.

> I thought the film was a great way to get the concept of leadership and all its intricacies across to the class. Just quietly between you and me, I found the film to be very powerful and I drove home feeling very emotional, yet strangely exhilarated that one woman could achieve so much. It made me question whether or not I was actually doing a meaningful enough job in my own life... I really enjoyed the film and I can definitely see how it is useful and something that we will remember down the track.

Some months later, this same student asked me to be a referee for her on a scholarship application to complete a higher diploma of education.

Films invite us to view them from the perspective of our own experiences and values. Not surprisingly, therefore, the film resonated differently with different students (Huczynski & Buchanan, 2004). In contrast to the experience of the student above, another student, while admiring what Gruwell's achievement, passion and commitment, was frightened by the personal sacrifices that often accompany such passion. In the film, Gruwell's marriage fails, as her husband is not longer prepared to play second fiddle to her passion for her career and the time commitment this requires. This student questioned whether she would personally be able to make these kinds of sacrifices in order to pursue a passion. In critiquing the film, Keltner (2008, p. 62), a professor of psychiatric nursing, who was asked to review the movie by a friend who had found it inspiring and full of mental health issues, picks up on Gruwell's "willingness to abandon her family in order to reach Maslow's highest rung" as his central reason for not liking the film. Keltner (2008) acknowledges that giving one's self to help the less fortunate is noble, but that when you are married or have children there needs to be a balance. Keltner's words echo those of Gruwell's husband, Scott, when he tells her that he is leaving her. He says that he feels like he is living a life he did not agree to. He says (see beginning Ch. 14) that what Gruwell is doing is noble and good and that he is proud of her, but he just wants to live his life and not feel bad about it. In this context, Keltner (2008) sees what Gruwell does, not as laudatory, but rather as selfish and a violation of the sacred vow to love, honor and obey.

TRANSLATING TRADITIONAL LEARNING AND TEACHING PRACTICES TO MATCH A NEW MEDIUM

In choosing *Freedom Writers,* I not only needed to develop the necessary learning and teaching resources to support the use of this new tool, but I needed to map these across to the traditional learning objectives. My key objective was to use the film as a central, common, and multifaceted case study, to foster students' analytical skills (Champoux, 1999). Furthermore, I was determined to foster the democratization of the teaching and learning process, as modeled in the film. Gruwell (The Freedom Writers, 1999, p. 28) believes that you should "[a]llow your students to teach you about what they know and where they come from. Make your curriculum relevant to their lives." This aspect of the film aligns with my constant striving to achieve meta-learning in all my learning and teaching strategies.

Freedom Writers has all the hallmarks required of a film to be an effective organizational behavior case study. While some have criticized the film for being formulaic (Smith, 2007), I believe it works as a case study because it shows a real and contemporary work environment, and contains universal themes and messages, hidden biases, transferability, and complexity (Callahan, Whitener, & Sandlin, 2007). The authenticity and credibility of the context is further enhanced by the film being based on a true character and the fact that Swank worked closely with Gruwell to bring her character to screen.

I used the film in conjunction with a text book (Robbins, Waters-Marsh, & Millett, 2004), which provides a sound overview of the organizational behavior theories, models and concepts. The text was used in conjunction with the film to support analysis and the development of theory-to-practice thinking.

The film was shown in its entirety in the first three hour lesson of a fourteen week trimester. It is critical that you understand how copyright governs the use of film in the classroom in your country. This will determine whether you will be able to show the film in class or whether students will need to view it in their own time. Time constraints will also play a role in the decision about when to show the film or whether to use a film in its entirety. The decision to show students the film ahead of any discussion or in-depth reading was an attempt to allow the students to experience the full emotional impact of the film. This technique gives students a quickly and easily recallable visual reference to which they can compare topics under discussion at a later date (Champoux, 1999).

Once students have watched the film in its entirety, they were asked to watch it again in their own time and complete a worksheet (see student example in appendix 1). Students had to choose scenes from the film which matched with organizational behavior concepts taught in the course and explain how these linked to the concept. This exercise had three goals. Firstly, it supported the desired democratization of the teaching process because it allowed students to select the scenes which were of interest to them and most relevant to their own experience and learning.

Secondly, as no detailed reading about the theories, models, and concepts had been undertaken, student responses would be intuitive, "gut feeling" responses. Robbins, Waters-Marsh, and Millett (2004) emphasize the importance of systematic study based on empirical evidence as the basis of making predictions about organizational behavior. They encourage practitioners to move from using intuition alone to a systematic approach to improve accuracy in explaining and predicting behavior. Capturing intuitive responses provides students with the opportunity to challenge their assumptions about concepts for accuracy once they have read the theory. However, whenever I teach theory I always encourage students to ask the big questions: "So what?" and "What does this mean for me?" By asking these questions I get students to challenge their personal assumptions and to challenge the relevance and applicability of theory based on their own personal experience and in this case, their analysis of the film.

Lastly, this method served as a barometer to determine the level of understanding and knowledge students may have of key concepts to be studied. This approach ensured that students were engaged in creating and monitoring the learning agenda, which is a key factor in encouraging the advocacy of the learner (Smith & Ragan, 1993).

The worksheet also contained prompts for reflective thinking. Reflective thinking and reflective journaling are extensively used in our school to assess students' critical thinking. Reflective processes are a key part of the experiential learning cycle (Kolb, 1984) and align with adult learning principles and the development of skills and competencies, such as emotional intelligence (Goleman, Boyatzis & McKee, 2002). In this case, reflective journaling was a good technique to assess students' ability to analyze the film, compare and contrast emerging themes with the theory in the text book, and then synthesize theory and apply it in practice in their personal lives and work environment.

For each week of the trimester, there was a specific theme. Students were required to read the necessary text book chapter ahead of the class. In class, the scenes identified by students to demonstrate specific theories or concepts were re-shown as mini case studies. In some instances scenes were used as the springboard for experiential activities. For example, students were shown the scene where Gruwell speaks with Andre Bryant about his evaluation assignment (Ch 15—00:06:00). Bryant gives himself an "F" and says that it is what he deserves. Gruwell challenges this with uncharacteristically strong language and says that his stance is an affront to everyone in the class. It is as if she chooses a register that she believes Bryant will understand. She refuses to let him fail. In this case, I asked students to work in groups. They needed to analyze the scene using the various motivational theories they had studied, for example goal-setting theory, reinforcement theory, flow and intrinsic motivation theory. They were then tasked with developing an alternative strategy to encourage Andre and explain how this might have delivered the desired outcome, that is, re-engagement in the learning process.

PLAY IT AGAIN... DEFINITELY

Using *Freedom Writers* reinvigorated my teaching and brought a new energy to the learning process for students. The achieved outcomes aligned with suggested outcomes in the literature and convinced me of the efficacy of using film in teaching organizational behavior concepts. The techniques I used involved students actively in the learning and teaching process. The outcomes of assessment, including reflective learning journals, indicated that students had developed a deep understanding of organizational behavior theories, models, and concepts and were able to apply these effectively in their own work context. It is clear to me that the film had a profound impact on many students. By linking their understanding of key theories, models, and concepts to their analysis of a film with which they have a connection, I believe that students will better retain their learning. Moreover, at a process or meta-learning level, students experimented with and developed a broad range of skills and competencies including: theory-to-practice thinking, critical and creative thinking, active listening and viewing, presentation, negotiation, and debating.

APPENDIX 1: VIEWING NOTES AND PROMPTS FOR REFLECTIVE THINKING (EXAMPLE OF STUDENT RESPONSES)

Exploring organizational behavior theories and concepts through a study of the film FREEDOM WRITERS

We will be using the film *Freedom Writers* to explore multiple organizational behavior concepts over the coming weeks. The concepts we will discuss are listed in the worksheet below. As you view the film please note scenes, in the space provided, which you think link to each of these concepts. Briefly explain how you think these link or demonstrate the OB concept. It is important to note the location of the scene so that we can easily find these later. These will act a prompts for discussion after we have viewed the film, but will also be used as mini case studies as the basis for exploring, understanding and challenging the theories we will investigate in this unit.

OB Concept	Description/Location of Scene (student examples)	How this Links to OB Concept (student examples)
Values and Attitudes	Ch 1; 00:05:00–00:06:08. Gruwell meets with head of English, Margaret Campbell and says that she specifically chose Wilson High because of its integration program and that she is excited.	Gruwell is idealistic and values social justice. She is influenced by her father who was active in the civil rights movement and chose teaching over law because she believes that teachers can make a difference. Her values are reflected in her positive attitude which is in contrast to the negative attitude expressed by Campbell.
Personality, emotions and perceptions	Ch 5: Eva's speech about hating white people.	Eva is an extrovert who is not afraid to speak her mind. She is also a product of her environment. She holds strong views, but these are stereotypical and polarized by a gang mentality which blames others for misfortune and draws borders along racial lines. Eva reflects a very strong external locus of control, i.e. what happens to her is controlled by outside forces and she does not have control over her own destiny. It is when she hears Miep Gies speak about ordinary people doing what is right that she can take control of her own destiny. She tells the truth at the trial in which she is the witness and in which she intends to lie to protect her own. For Eva, this means going against her family and community to stand up for the truth.
Communication at Work	Ch2: Welcome to Freshman English—Gruwell meets her class for the first time	From the very start, Gruwell works hard at connecting with her pupils although they are determined to make her life hell in the classroom. She models active listening, e.g. when she mispronounces Eva's name and is corrected, she repeats it in the correct way to reinforce that she has heard and understood. From the start she attempts to connect with the students by selecting material which they can relate to, e.g. using Tupac Shakur's hip hop lyrics as an example of internal rhyme and playing the music. She is vibrant and enthusiast despite the responses she gets. We see her make her breakthrough in Chs 5–6 when she challenges the caricature found in class and decides to play the Line Game.
Leadership	Ch 6: Encounter between Gruwell and Campbell in the book room. This scene and others in which these two speak can be used to compare and contrast leadership and management as concepts.	Gruwell epitomizes leadership and particularly transformational leadership, whereas Campbell is a manager (transactional). Her focus is on maintaining the system through command and control. She believes students cannot be trusted and should be taught discipline. Gruwell believes in her students and makes them believe that they can do anything that they put their minds to. She inspires them to achieve the previously unachievable in contrast to Campbell who believes that students must be disciplined and controlled.

Workplace Power and Politics	Ch 6: Gruwell's conversations with Campbell and Gelford about books. Both reinforce the chain of command in place in the school. Both are patronizing towards Gruwell. Gelford belittles Gruwell's idealism and reinforces the status quo.	Those in positions of formal power work to maintain the status quo. They use power tactics/ defensive behaviors to resist change/challenges to the status quo, e.g. belittle those who challenge the system.
	Ch 8: Gruwell meets with Dr Cohn, district school board head, to seek his support. He reinforces the system, but Gruwell is determined and mounts a sound argument to attempt to influence him.	Gruwell demonstrates the ability to influence upward which is a critical leadership competency. Later (Ch 10) Gruwell is perceived by Campbell and Gelford as having Cohn in her back pocket because she has been able to persuade him.
Conflict and Negotiation	Ch 15: Meeting between Gruwell, Campbell, Gelford, the Principal Banning and the Dr Carl Cohn to discuss whether Gruwell was able to take her class through into Junior year.	This meeting models negotiation, as well as the impact of affective or dysfunctional conflict. Campbell and Gelford hold a position based on the status quo and promotion based on seniority and not merit. They are not prepared to budge from their position. When they are confronted by good reasons why Gruwell should be allowed to continue to teach this class, Campbell in particular makes personal attacks on Gruwell's character. She suggests that if her students go on to fail in another teacher's class it will not be them who fails, but rather Gruwell who has failed. Dr Cohn functions as a mediator or conciliator at times.
Workplace Motivation	Ch 15—00:06:00. Gruwell speaks with Andre Bryant about his evaluation assignment after he returns to school of a prolonged absence due to his brother's trial and conviction.	Gruwell is able to motivate Bryant because she understands what motivates him and others in her class. Bryant gives himself an "F" and says that is what he deserves. Gruwell challenges this with uncharacteristically foul language and says that his stance is an affront against everyone in the class. It is as if she chooses a register that she believes Bryant will understand. She refuses to let him fail. In so doing, she is able to motivate him to re-engage in the learning process and in the group dynamic.

OB Concept	Description/Location of Scene (student examples)	How this Links to OB Concept (student examples)
Organizational Culture	Ch 6: 00:00:00–00:00:45. Gruwell has a conversation with Campbell about using books like *The Diary of Anne Frank* and *Romeo and Juliet* which are stored in the school's book room. Campbell objects on the basis of the students' reading scores and says that if she gives them the books she will never see them again and if she does they will be damaged.	Campbell's attitude to the students in Gruwell's class reflects an organizational culture in which students who do not conform are not valued. Her attitude reflects a culture which is conservative/risk-averse, values command and control and financial prudence over creativity and innovation.
Organizational Structure	Ch 2: 00:05:28. Gruwell is introduced to Brian Gelford, who teaches Junior English and the Distinguished Honors class. His advice to her is that if she puts in the time in a few years she will be able to teach Juniors.	Comments reflect a hierarchical organization where people are promoted on the basis of length of tenure as opposed to merit. See Ch 10 when Gelford is outraged because one of his Honors students has requested to transfer to Gruwell's class. He blames Gruwell, intimating that she cannot change the way the system works.
Organizational Change	Ch 15– 00:00:15. Students want Gruwell to continue to be their teacher into Junior year despite this being contrary to the school system.	Gruwell has modeled the way (Kouzes & Posner, 2002) for her students and shown them that anything is possible. They become agents of change and suggest that they challenge the hierarchical school system like the Freedom Riders challenged segregation and racism.

Note: All references are for the 2007 Australian (Pal Region 4) DVD version

Some Prompts for Reflection on the Film

Describe Erin Gruwell's personal leadership traits.
- Where do you think she learnt her initial leadership style and how appropriate is it for motivating her students and engaging/influencing her colleagues?
- How does her leadership style develop? What leadership theories are applicable to understanding, describing this?
- What are some of the other leadership styles in the film, e.g. the principal, the head of department? What leadership theories are applicable to understanding, describing these?
- How do these styles/attitudes impact on attitudes to class, cultural diversity and hierarchy?
- What does the film tell us about workplace power and politics? How does Erin handle this?

REFERENCES

Bass, B. M. (1985). *Leadership and performance beyond expectation*. New York, NY: Free Press.

Bass, B. M. (1995). Theory of transformational leadership redux. *Leadership Quarterly, 6*(4), 463–478.

Bass, B. M., & Steidlmeier, P. (1999). Ethics, character and authentic transformational leadership behavior. *Leadership Quarterly, 10*(2), 181–217.

Callahan, J. L., Whitener, J. K., & Sandlin, J. A. (2007). The art of creating leaders: Popular culture artifacts as pathways for development. *Advances in Developing Human Resources, 9*(2), 146–165.

Champoux, J. E. (1999). Film as a teaching resource. *Journal of Management Inquiry, 8*(2), 206–217.

Eisenbach, R., Watson, K., & Pillai, R. (1999). Transformational leadership in the context of organizational change. *Journal of Organizational Change Management, 12*(2), 80–89.

Frank, A. (2007). *Anne Frank: The diary of a young girl*. London, United Kingdom: Puffin.

Freedom Writers & Gruwell, E. (1999). *The Freedom Writers: How a teacher and 150 teens used writing to change themselves and the world around them*. New York, NY: Broadway Books.

Freedom Writers Foundation. (2006). www.freedomwritersfoundation.org.

Giroux, H. (1999). *The Mouse that Roared: Disney and the end of innocence*. Lanham, MD: Rowman & Littlefield.

Goleman, D., Boyatzis, R., & McKee, A. (2002). *Primal leadership: Realizing the power of emotional intelligence*. Boston, MA: Harvard Business School Press.

Huczynski, A., & Buchanan, D. (2004). Theory from fiction: A narrative process perspective on the pedagogical use of feature film. *Journal of Management Education, 28*(6), 707–726.

Keltner, N. L. (2008). Freedom Writers. *Perspectives on Psychiatric Care, 44*(1), 62–63.

Kolb, D. A. (1984). *Experiential learning: Experience as the source of learning and development.* Englewood Cliffs, NJ: Prentice Hall.

Kouzes, J. M. ,& Posner, B. Z. (2002). *The leadership challenge* (3rd ed.). San Francisco, CA: Jossey-Bass.

Northouse, P. G. (2004). *Leadership: Theory and practice* (3rd ed.) Thousand Oaks, CA: Sage.

Robbins, S. P., Waters-Marsh, T., & Millett, B. (2004). *Organizational behavior* (4th ed.). Frenchs Forest, Australia: Pearson Education.

Rosser, M. H. (2007). The magic of leadership: An exploration of *Harry Potter and the Goblet of Fire. Advances in Developing Human Resources, 9*(2), 236–250.

Smith, A. (2007). Freedom Writers. *Sight and Sound, 17*(4), 59.

Smith, P. L., & Ragan, T. J. (1993). *Instructional Design.* New York, NY: Macmillan.

The Freedom Writers (1999). *Instructor, 114*(4), 27–28.

Films

Avildsen, J. G. (Director). (1989). *Lean on me* [Motion picture]. United States: Norman Twain Productions & Warner Bros.

LaGravenese, R. (Director). (2007). *Freedom writers* [Motion picture]. Germany/United States: Paramount Pictures.

Menéndez, R. (Director). (1988). *Stand and deliver* [Motion picture]. United States: American Playhouse, Olmos Productions, & Warner Bros.

Smith, J. N. (Director). (1995). *Dangerous minds* [Motion picture]. United States: Hollywood Pictures, Don Simpson/Jerry Bruckheimer Films, & Via Rosa Productions.

CHAPTER 6

COPS, ROBBERS AND MASKED VIGILANTES

Teaching Through Representations of Crime

Craig Webber

NEW BEGINNINGS: THE CHALLENGES OF TEACHING STUDENTS NEW TO A SUBJECT AND HOW MOVING IMAGES CAN HELP

The masked vigilante is locked in a vicious fight to the death with Ras Al Ghul, the leader of a terrorist group whose aim is to destroy Gotham city, a symbol of decadence and crime. Hero and enemy are inside a train, on rails high in the air, like an airplane flying through the city's skyscrapers. Batman is fighting to stop his enemy from crashing the train into a huge tower. Inside the tower is nerve gas that will infect the population of Gotham with a crippling feeling of fear when it is unleashed by the exploding train.

Batman Begins (Nolan, 2005) was an attempt to reinvigorate the franchise of a comic book character that had undergone a transformation from a brooding vigilante in Tim Burton's two films to a cinematic approximation of the gaudy and camp 1960s television series in two films by Joel Schum-

Moving Images: Effective Teaching with Film and Television in Higher Education,
pages 77–85

acher. The director of *Batman Begins,* Christopher Nolan, envisioned a character that could believably exist in a contemporary setting. But, more than this, Nolan is an accomplished film-maker able to create an intelligent blockbuster with subtext and hidden themes. It is this that made me use the film to help first year social science undergraduates understand what social scientists do when they seek to go beyond the common-sense understanding of the world. *Batman Begins* is a Hollywood blockbuster, a comic book film, the epitome of a popcorn movie. But, it is also a metaphor for the terrorist attacks on America in 2001. The film is about fear and the crippling effect that can have on society. It is about terrorism and the fortress mentality that enveloped many countries after the terrorist attacks in the early 21st century such as New York, London, and Madrid. In the film, Gotham shares a similar geography as Manhattan, surrounded by a river. When the attack on the city begins the bridges and other access routes to the city are blocked. The barricades go up.

As a criminologist I am always struggling to make students, and academics from other disciplines, understand that criminology is an intellectual discipline that deals with many of the more troubling social science questions such as, why do we punish? What is justice? What is crime? It might be assumed that using a film such as *Batman Begins* undermines the seriousness of the discipline. However, the use of films such as this is useful for a number of reasons. In order to explain the utility of using a film such as this, it is best to start with the learning objectives for this particular lecture. The aim is to introduce students to what social scientists do, whilst also introducing them to a particular subject, in my case criminology. The problem with doing this with students new to the discipline is that they have not completed much social science reading. The other problem is that few people will ever be confronted by a crime in progress, and few are likely to be victims despite what the media might suggest. Consequently film and television, either fictional or factual, can provide visual images that are not accessible in any other way.

Batman Begins is a film that many students are familiar with, or they are familiar with the character. The character has been seen in comics since his creation in 1939 and appeared on television in the 1960s, various animated series and, since 1989, big budget Hollywood movies. Because of the familiarity with the film or character, revealing that the director and writers deliberately set out to make a political point amongst the action and mayhem becomes, for the majority, a revelation. I use this emotional reflection on a familiar film and character to explain the sense of discovery that social scientists routinely feel. The use of this film in a lecture encourages reflection on their assumptions about the world. This demonstrates to them that even in a film such as *Batman Begins* there is a subtext that can be appreciated beneath the pyrotechnics and melodrama. If a comic book film can have subtext, then what about our assumptions about the economy, politics, the workplace, gender etc.? The students are actively engaged in doing the discovery through seeing the film clip *and* realizing that our common-sense appreciation of the world is often wrong. *Batman Begins* is about a comic book hero. But, it is also a reflection of deeper anxieties in a post-9/11 world. The moving images in this instance become a metaphor for the real world. This method is fast and engaging, and lays a foundation for their further reading.

"WE ARE THE MODS, WE ARE THE MODS, WE ARE, WE ARE, WE ARE THE MODS": PROVIDING VISUAL CONTENT FOR THE BUILDING OF KNOWLEDGE

The use of moving images as a metaphor for more complex issues is one ob-vious use of film given that many filmmakers deliberately set out to accom-plish this. Another use of film is to provide visual information that might be difficult any other way. Many lecturers will find themselves staring at blank faces when alluding to some occasion in our recent history that we suddenly discover is akin to an alien world for many students. For example, where once the leadership of the UK by Margaret Thatcher and the US by Ronald Reagan were taken for granted cultural references, they are now distant memories at best. Most traditional students attending university for the first time were born after their respective terms of office. Consequently, we cannot take for granted that they will have this information as part of their cultural lexicon. It is common practice for lecturers to refer to major historical events without realizing that the audience may not be familiar with them. Of course, we could argue that students should bring themselves up to our level rather than academia regressing back to that of the student. It is a valid point, but there are occasions when we cannot expect our stu-dents to be aware of every event and where cultural practices may no longer be very relevant and you wish to raise awareness of the importance of them. Moving images are one method to provide such knowledge in the setting of a lecture or seminar.

One such example is a series of lectures I give on youth culture. It is very easy to say there were groups termed punks, hippies, or skinheads. But, the visceral quality and visual distinctiveness of these subcultures are not expressed merely by naming them. Moreover, these subcultures also rep-resent quite distinct historical moments and some would argue that their attitudes, music and fashion reflect the historical era of their existence (see e.g., Cohen, 1972; Cohen, 1973; Hall & Jefferson, 1976). The punks, spe-cifically The Sex Pistols, were formed in the UK in 1975 as the Labour gov-ernment began a series of pay caps to bring down soaring inflation. This resulted in massive industrial strikes that brought the nation's services to a standstill in the so-called 'winter of discontent' at the end of 1978. Clearly, it is difficult to explain the multitude of cultural factors that would help explain the genesis of this band and their impact on the fashions and music of contemporary times. More so when fashion and music has become, arguably, ever more sterile, manufactured and corporate (although some would say the same of The Sex Pistols, although without being sterile). Moving images help to show aspects of this period that by their very nature cannot be presented in any other way. The sneering venom of Johnny Rotten's vocals in the banned Sex Pistols' song *God Save the Queen* (Cook, Jones, Lydon, & Matlock, 1977) and the bare-chested, leering swagger of Sid Vicious cannot be expressed easily without the sound and images of a snippet of concert footage.

However, rarely is it possible to come up with a teaching plan and then find suitable footage to illustrate your learning objective. In my case, I was already familiar with the documentary film *The Filth and the Fury* (Temple, 2000) when I felt the need to better illustrate my lecture with footage of a variety of youth cultures. The film combines images from a country in the depth of an industrial dispute alongside the anarchic band and their fans as their short initial burst of fame began to self-destruct. If the film did not exist it might be necessary to find a variety of different sources to provide the same visual knowledge or punk might have to give way to another subculture if a film existed on that topic. Such serendipity also suggests the need for flexibility and opportunism when channel surfing or buying DVDs. One note of caution on the use of extended clips or entire films. Initially I showed the whole film during a two hour double lecture. I now show clips because 90 minutes of footage of The Sex Pistols was too much for some students. I suspect that Johnny Rotten would not be too displeased.

Another subculture that needs to be visually represented is the mods and rockers. Generally speaking, you need to be sure that the images you show are at least authentic and not misleading. Clearly documentary footage of a period in history that is captured at the time is less controversial than a fictional film if the intention is an accurate representation. However, footage from the film *Quadrophenia* (Roddam, 1979) made almost 15 years after the year in which it is set, 1965, represents a unique way to both visually present mod and rocker fashion styles whilst also demonstrating the problem with media accounts of these clashes. The film was produced by the British rock band The Who and tells the story of two friends as they grow up and become increasingly polarized into their respective youth subcultures of the mods and rockers. The film ends with a riot on Brighton beach. The fashions, music and era are faithfully recreated, but so are the media representations of the time. A famous sociological book by Stan Cohen called *Folk Devils and Moral Panics* (1973/2002) suggested that the clashes between the mods and rockers so widely reported after a bank holiday weekend in 1964 were largely the creation of media exaggeration rather than reality. Although violence did take place, it was sporadic and relatively trivial. Yet the newspapers reported a wholly different event to that which took place. The reporting often suggested an all out war rather than the occasional smashed window and bloody nose. Many students have come across this work in school and college before attending university. In a lecture, I show my students a clip from *Quadrophenia* in which great swathes of Brighton seafront are depicted as a war zone with police on horseback and the sharp-suited mods and leather-jacketed rockers engaging in a swirling riot of fighting and destruction. The film is both a visual representation of an era unknown to the majority of students *and* a representation of Cohen's point about exaggeration for dramatic effect. This one film clip helps demonstrate two points in no more that 5 minutes.

ILLUSTRATING THE PRACTICALITIES OF THE 'THIN BLUE LINE'

One of the problems in teaching criminology is that students choose the subject with very little understanding of what the subject entails. In much the same way that the media exaggerate the problem of crime, so they also exaggerate the responses to crime. For example, the police tend to be depicted in film and television dramas as being involved in action packed chases and the intuitive detection of criminals. They also tend to show teams of forensic scientists swarming over a crime scene, offender profilers with seemingly magical abilities for getting into the mind of the many serial killers that prowl the streets of small towns and cities and the resolution of a case in 45 minutes. 'Reality' television programs about the police over-dramatize the role played by the police when they use CCTV footage of car chases or fights. Moreover, the police are thought to be heroic and considerate. The majority are; but some are not and this is reflected in disproportionate stop and search rates for ethnic minority groups and distrust in allegations of rape reported by women. When students are told that the fictional police role is only a very small proportion of the police officer's job many seem not to believe me and would prefer to cling to the media depiction instead. Here moving images become support for difficult issues, rather than metaphor or the presentation of visual knowledge about fashion or culture.

I use several documentaries to demonstrate some of the problems in the criminal justice system. Again, to add visual images to the often dry descriptions of the history of the police in Britain, I use a documentary recorded several years ago called *Coppers* (Norman, 1999). Even though it is now several years old, its depiction of the history of women in the police, policing during wartime and the general development of the strategies of policing crowd disturbance are all still relevant. As the videos became increasingly worn, their transfer to DVD and then having them streamed online became essential. Obviously, this helps students to view the material from home, but unless the material is embargoed until after the lecture during which they are shown, it also means students tend to skip the lecture and therefore miss the attendant contextualization of the material. This is especially important where the film is controversial. In one of the editions of *Coppers*, a clip from an earlier documentary on the Thames Valley Police authority near London is shown. This was a highly controversial film by Roger Graef made in 1982 where he gained unprecedented access to an initial interview of a female victim of rape being questioned by three male police officers. The film caused controversy because it showed for the first time what women had been saying for many years. The police interview made them feel like liars and they were effectively put on trial and their character called into question. It is important to use the initial reaction to this scene and not allow it to be held over for another session. Such clips help in getting through to students brought up on a diet of Hollywood super cops such as the *Lethal Weapon* (Donner, 1987, 1989, 1992, 1998) or *Die Hard* (Harlin, 1990; McTiernan, 1988, 1995; Wiseman, 2007) films that the police can be corrupt and prejudiced in their everyday practice, not just when they are offered multi-million dollar bribes in fictional plots by drugs barons or gun runners. The prejudice felt by ethnic minorities, women and whoever has been deemed the current folk devil is an everyday occurrence and rarely motivated by anything as simple as greed.

This point is effectively made in a documentary wherein a journalist managed to apply for, and be accepted into, the police where he secretly filmed the new recruits from training to their first weeks in the job. *The Secret Policeman* (Ford, 2003) showed undercover scenes of one recruit with a pillowcase on their head imitating the Ku Klux Klan. The recruit was demonstrating what he would do if he were to meet a 'Paki' by repeatedly performing a stabbing motion. Asking students if they found this behavior surprising elicits many different responses. It is often quite clear to see who has been following the suggested reading. Those who say they are shocked tend to be those who have not understood the implications of the Scarman report into the Brixton riots in 1981. This suggested the police had some bad apples in their ranks. In 1999, Sir William Macpherson reported on the failed murder investigation of black teenager Stephen Lawrence. Macpherson stated that the police were institutionally racist, the whole barrel was rotten, as were most of the other organizational 'barrels' in society. The point I try to get the students to consider is that such activity is integral to the police, and many other institutions. Although in its extreme form it manifests as in *The Secret Policeman*, it is also part of the everyday practice of many people, and as such only visible through careful and considered research.

BEST PRACTICE AND KNOWLEDGE TRANSFER

The examples discussed so far in this chapter are drawn from teaching within a specific area of social science and their applicability for other areas of teaching may not be readily obvious. However, this last section reiterates the reason why I use these methods to show that the needs of students are universal no matter what subject they study.

The first section of the chapter looked at the use of moving images to help illustrate difficult ideas for students who have not yet managed to engage with the literature in a subject. There is no doubt that students come to universities variably prepared for study at this level. At the most basic level of teaching, moving images provide an engaging method to present information that helps all students understand the instructor's point without relying on an assumption of the level of understanding of the students. Such a method as outlined above with *Batman Begins*, allows for the heterogeneity of the audience whilst still making a serious point about complex ideas. Those who have already studied sociology will apply that knowledge in a new context; those without such a background are introduced to the subject easily and engagingly without the need for that knowledge. Such an approach works with the cultural capital of the audience, rather than fighting against it. Every subject area will have its own ideas that need to be explained without relying on assumed knowledge that might not be there. For example, different styles of management might be explained by showing clips from various sources. One can imagine a lecture that draws on clips from the Ricky Gervais comedy *The Office* (Gervais & Merchant, 2001–2003), or *Yes Minister* (Lynn & Jay, 1980–1984) to demonstrate different forms of management and leadership. The use of engaging images to make serious points is perhaps the most important aspect of using moving images in teaching.

In the second example, I took this point further and showed how moving images can provide the content of knowledge where students may lack that information. Students who have grown up in an expanding economy may not have the knowledge of previous recessions. Similarly, many students were either too young to remember the television reporting of the terrorist attacks by the IRA or have not been taught about it at school due to the increasingly narrow, test-oriented curriculum. Consequently, it is useful to show students film-clips of such events. Television news reports of home repossessions and queues at job centres during the recession of the early 1990s adds content to student's historical imagination. For example, showing film of Kamikaze pilots flying planes into ships during WWII puts into context the terrorist attacks on September 11th 2001.

There is, of course, some overlap between the adding of content to students' knowledge of events and the last section of the chapter on providing support for difficult ideas that students may be reluctant to accept. Those who only know terrorism in a post-9/11 world or the relative prosperity of the Bill Clinton and Tony Blair years need to see the historical continuity of terrorist struggles or economic cycles. Moving images from various sources are able to provide this material and can be used as a metaphor for a more complex aspect of a topic or can provide the material knowledge that allows students to understand complex theoretical ideas without switching off because they have not heard of mods and rockers, punks, or even Margaret Thatcher.

REFERENCES

Cohen, P. (1972). Sub-cultural conflict and working class community. In *Working papers in cultural studies* (No. 2, Spring). CCCS: University of Birmingham.

Cohen, S. (1973/2002). *Folk devils and moral panics. The creation of mods and rockers* (3rd ed.). London: MacGibbon and Kee, with revised Introduction. London: Routledge.

Hall, S., & Jefferson, T. (Eds.). (1976). *Resistance through rituals: Youth subcultures in post-war Britain.* London: Unwin Hyman.

Films, Television Series, and Music

Cook, P., Jones, S., Lydon, J., & Matlock, G. (1977). *God save the Queen* [record]. London, United Kingdom: A&M.

Donner, R. (Director). (1987). *Lethal weapon* [Motion picture]. United States: Warner Bros.

Donner, R. (Director). (1989). *Lethal weapon 2* [Motion picture]. United States: Warner Bros.

Donner, R. (Director). (1992). *Lethal weapon 3* [Motion picture]. United States: Warner Bros.

Donner, R. (Director). (1998). *Lethal weapon 4* [Motion picture]. United States: Warner Bros.

Ford, M. (Producer). (2003). *The secret policeman* [Television series]. BBC, United Kingdom: BBC1.

Gervais, R., & Merchant, S. (Writers). (2001–2003). *The office* [Television series]. BBC, United Kingdom: BBC1 & BBC2.

Harlin, R. (Director). (1990). *Die hard 2* [Motion picture]. United States: Twentieth Century Fox.

Lynn, J., & Jay, A. (Writers). (1980–1984). *Yes Minister* [Television series]. BBC, United Kingdom: BBC2.

McTiernan, J. (Director). (1988). *Die hard* [Motion picture]. United States: Twentieth Century Fox.

McTiernan, J. (Director). (1995). *Die hard: With a vengeance* [Motion picture]. United States: Twentieth Century Fox.

Nolan, C. (Director) (2005). *Batman begins* [Motion picture]. United States/United Kingdom: Warner Bros. Pictures, Syncopy, & DC Comics.

Norman, L. (Series Producer). (1999). *Coppers* [Television series]. Historic Films, United Kingdom: Channel4.

Roddam, F. (Director). (1979). *Quadrophenia* [Motion picture]. United Kingdom: The Who Films & Polytel.

Temple, J. (Director). (2000). *The filth and the fury* [Motion picture]. United Kingdom: FilmFour.

Wiseman, L. (Director). (2007). *Die hard 4.0* [Motion picture]. United States: Twentieth Century Fox.

CHAPTER 7

GETTING TO "SO WHAT?"

Stephen D. Sloane

SEARCHING FOR ENLIGHTENMENT IN A FILM STORY

This chapter will analyze a film story, *Twelve O'Clock High* (King, 1949) as a case study that reveals significant truths concerning the human condition as people participate in the activity of complex organizations. First, let me explain how I came to realize the truth telling power of this film, as well as others.

When I became a member of the faculty at a liberal arts college, my formal training in the liberal arts was nil. I had earned degrees in engineering, public administration, and political science. All of these were based on thoroughly modern paradigms, on the idea that nature, the way the world works, is best explained by using methods of observation and objective analysis.

My life experience, however, encouraged me to question the usefulness of teaching and learning that eschewed imagination. The more I was jostled by the ebb and flow of my own experience, the more convinced I became that students needed to experience a search for meaning that goes beyond positive answers to empirical questions. I was convinced that students needed to be encouraged to cure the itch for knowledge with a

Moving Images: Effective Teaching with Film and Television in Higher Education,
pages 87–100

scratch of enlightenment. After all, the *Wizard of Oz* (Fleming, 1939) sat-isfied the Scarecrow's desire for a brain by awarding him a Ph.D. Yet the Scarecrow still lacked a brain!

It was the Scarecrow's advanced degree that gave him a positivist view of the world. So, a free falling body in a vacuum accelerates at a rate of thirty two feet per second every second. So, as he murmurs while skipping back along the yellow brick road, "The square of the hypotenuse equals the sum of the squares of the sides of the triangle." So what?

What does all this have to do with the unrecognized aspirations of students to fulfill their potential for living a well-lived life? The words and numbers that are the building blocks of logic can lead to objective answers to empirical questions. Most often, however, they cannot capture the complexity of hu-man experience. How could my teaching empower students to capture such complexity? How could I encourage my students to deal with the "so what?" question by searching for the meaning of the knowledge they acquire?

STARTING WITH THE GREAT BOOKS: THE PATH FROM INFORMATION TO WISDOM

My assignment to teach one course each semester in my school's Great Books Seminar program demonstrated that a path to enlightenment can be discerned by way of an examination of the images created by literature and art. The great books, I discovered, represented man's most noble attempts to find answers to the "so what" questions.

I had studied war as a social scientist. I had experienced war. Homer's sto-ries told me more about the *consequences* of war than even the best analysis provided by books and mentors, or by my own reflections on personal ex-perience. I had studied capitalism and experienced life as economic man. The images exhibited in Dickens' stories revealed the *meaning* of economics and the consequences of capitalism. I had examined and experienced the political environment of the civil rights movement. Toni Morrison provided my students with images that were considerably more informative concern-ing the *experience* of black people in America. I had reflected on the values of feminism and on the causes and consequences of the push of women toward gender equity. Such reflection produced limited *understanding* com-pared to the images evoked by Sappho and by Virginia Wolfe.

The great books that form the nucleus of liberal education, I discovered, provided the mortar that held together the bricks of objective reasoning. This was the mortar of *meaning*. Once my students gathered facts, once cause and effect relationships were established, the question, "So what?" still had to be dealt with. It was consideration of this question that would start them on a path from knowledge to wisdom.

The next step involved a transition from my teaching Great Books, to the courses that dealt with my formal training and expertise. I was assigned to expose my students to the study of modern organizations and the behavior of the leaders and followers who participate in the activity of organized systems.

My head and my book shelves were packed with the literature of organization theory and management practice. Yet none of these dealt with the "so what" questions that I found, by way of the Great Books, to be so important. The ubiquitous focus on the subject of motivation by those who study organization theory illustrates the problem.

The ideas of Aristotle crept into my thinking about the "so what" of motivation theory. Aristotle encouraged me to think about the concept of motivation in terms of organizational purpose and individual happiness.

Leaders use social science to engineer the behavior of subordinates. So . . . what is the purpose of a manager's attempt to control the behavior of subordinates? For the leader, the answer to this "so what?" question is . . . so organizational goals will be accomplished. When, however a subordinate whose behavior is being controlled asks, "so what?" this can lead to an attempt to relate the purpose of the organization with the happiness of the individual. Is the activity of organizational participants, a means to a valued end, or an end in and of itself?

Aristotle (1962, p. 15) suggested that happiness is:

> What is always chosen as an end in itself and never as a means to something else [but rather] is called final in an unqualified sense. This description seems to apply to happiness above all else: for we always choose happiness as an end in itself and never for the sake of something else.

Aristotle's idea of human happiness has to do with the chain of means and ends that leads to purpose, conceived of that which is ."..an end in itself and never as a means to something else..." Aristotle's notion of human purpose conflicts with the intended use of the literature of organization theory and behavior. Social science is not studied by emerging managers in order to understand the process of achieving human happiness. The literature of organization theory and behavior is useful to those who are involved in developing and implementing effective motivational strategies that enables managers to control employee behavior. It is the purpose of the organized system that is the goal of managers and not the purpose of the human being that at times can come into conflict with organizational purpose.

So what?

CONFLICT BETWEEN LIFE AND WORK: LOOKING TO THE SILVER SCREEN

Those who participate in the work of modern organizations are vulnerable to experiencing conflict between their lives as a whole and their working lives. This potential for disharmony results from the fact that organizational purpose (the need to accomplish a mission and to maintain the health and survivability of the organized system) and the psychological, emotional, and economic well being (i.e. the happiness) of the individual do not necessarily coincide. Whatever the "ends" are for the organization, these are not *necessarily* the same as the "ends" sought by the individual, or the ends that will satisfy the needs of the individual. At times, when people confront the conflict between life and work, they find themselves being encouraged by their leaders, in one way or another, to perceive that their life force is making a valuable contribution to the accomplishment of an organizational mission. Often, this finds an individual asking, "So what?" Often, the mandate to meld life and work can find a person wondering whether or not their life force is worth expending on the mission of an organization.

The use of film in the teaching of organization theory and behavior helps me to guide students to search for the answer to the "so what" question.

Why should we look to the silver screen for help in explaining and understanding the conflict between organizations and their members? How can the stories told by films suggest ways of dealing with this problem, ways to develop survival skills and coping mechanisms? Are there recurring themes that illuminate the way people can fall into the trap of failing to distinguish *being* from *doing*, between their humanity and their job?

What sort of picture do the stories told in films paint concerning the ecstasy and the agony of organizational life? Movies about organizations and the people who participate in the activities of organizations show us a picture that is not pretty. In *Twelve O'Clock High*, the 918th Bomber Group fails to put its bombs on target, is plagued by high losses of flying crews, and is threatened to be put out of existence by German fighters and flak. In *Network* (Lumet, 1976) the United Broadcasting System is in danger of being swallowed up by a giant conglomerate. The organization is losing the battle of the ratings as well as the commitment of the members of its News Department. *The Firm* (Pollack, 1993) shows us an organization that captures its members by taking advantage of their lust for material gain, luxury, and conspicuous consumption. *The Devil's Advocate* (Hackford, 1997) paints the same picture, in perhaps a more dramatic way. The police department of *Serpico* (Lumet, 1973) is corrupt. The main characters in *Lost in America* (Brooks, 1985) *Jerry McGuire* (Crowe, 1996), and *The Electric Horseman* (Pollack, 1979) flee from their corporations to search for happiness.

A CASE STUDY

Stories about military organizations are useful tools to deal with the problem of conflict between the parts of organized systems (people) and the whole system. The military unit is a useful metaphor for any organization because organizations are potential fields of "combat" and because the military situation, at least during a war, is often unambiguous with respect to what the organization is trying to accomplish. Gordon Gecko, in the movie *Wall Street* (Stone, 1987), is the quintessential modern executive. The bible that guides his organizational strategy has nothing to do with concepts of capitalism or management. Gecko's bible is *The Art of War* authored by the ancient Chinese military strategist, Sun Tzu.

Given Aristotle's connection between happiness and purpose, my use of film to explore the "so what?" of conflict between organizations and human beings is based on the complexity of purpose as revealed by the film *Twelve O'Clock High*. This is one example of the way that film can lead students to explore a deeper meaning of the organization science they find in their text books.

The film *Twelve O'Clock High* is a docudrama of historical events. The story takes place in the early years of U.S. involvement in World War II. U.S. leaders have decided to dedicate the Army's emerging aviation assets, organized into the form of the Army Air Corps, to daylight precision bombing of enemy targets in Europe. In daylight, accuracy of bombing will be greater than at night. The decision to fly bombing missions in daylight, however, presents some significant problems.

Bombing enemy targets in daylight is a very risky business because the bombers are vulnerable to enemy ground fire and fighter attack. For this reason the British strategic doctrine calls for the blanket bombing of cities and enemy installations at night. A second problem is that the U.S. is unprepared for its entry into the war. The American war machine has not yet come up to speed. There is a critical shortage of planes, in particular the B-17 Flying Fortresses that is used for the daylight bombing mission. Also, there is a shortage of trained crews. In a characteristic display of self-confidence, American leaders decide to muddle through until sufficient planes can be built and sufficient crews trained.

The organization that is the focus of the story is the 918th Bomber Group. In many respects this group, and others like it, are the guinea pigs that will test the concept of daylight precision bombing and hold the fort until the U.S. can mobilize its manpower and industrial strength. Based in England, the 918th consists of a number of squadrons that put up 20 or more aircraft each time Headquarters calls for a bombing mission, first against German targets in France and later against targets in the German homeland itself.

The Commanding Officer of the group, Colonel Keith Davenport, has great empathy for the crews of his planes. The 918th seems to be a "hard luck" group, losing men and machines to enemy action at an alarming rate. The situation is particularly grim because there are no relief crews on the horizon. The crews on scene will probably just keep flying until they fall victim to enemy action. "These boys can count," states Davenport. "They know they don't have a chance!" To make matter worse, the group is ordered to fly at lower altitudes to make their bombing more accurate.

Davenport objects strenuously. He points out to his bosses at headquarters that the lower altitude will make his crews even more vulnerable to enemy anti-aircraft fire. When one of his navigators is chided by higher command for making costly errors, Davenport refuses to relieve the young officer of his navigation duties.

General Pritchard, the leader of all the groups in England, is certain that Davenport has fallen victim to over-identification with his men and is no longer an effective group commander. Pritchard removes Davenport from his command position and taps General Frank Savage to shape up the 918th. Savage is a dedicated professional who sees his leadership task as taking a hard-nosed attitude. He gives the men a reality check by telling them that they "...have to fight

because they are in a war, a shooting war, and some are going to have to die." He advises them that "It is O.K. to be afraid," but they should "ignore that fear" and "consider themselves to be already dead." He challenges "anyone who is not man enough" to follow his suggestion to request a transfer from the group. The men unanimously opt for a transfer.

Aided by a loyal ground officer, Major Harvey Stoval, Savage manages to delay the written transfer requests of his aircrews. He uses the time to improve the technical skills of the crews and to encourage pride in his subordinates. Savage successfully solicits the cooperation of one of the youngest and most admired pilots, Lieutenant Jessie Bishop. When Bishop withdraws his request for transfer, so do the rest of the men.

Now the 918th really gets to work and starts making a useful contribution to the war effort. The odds against individual survival, however, remain high, and as Savage leads the group he loses many of his men. Although Savage does not consciously admit it, these men have become his comrades in arms. He empathizes with them. But he controls his feelings because he believes the group needs a harsh task master. Savage never lets his guard down. Acting the hard-nosed leader has worked for him in the past and he continues to maintain that posture. As a result, he ends his tour as commander of the 918th with a nervous breakdown. His attempt to bottle up his feelings for his men has taken a toll on his own mental stability. Savage has become a victim of the war and has learned the limits of his own humanity.

How can this story help us understand the idea of purpose and enable us to discern the basis of conflict between organizational purpose and individual human purpose? So, many men die in combat. So, General Savage has a nervous breakdown. So what?

As students view the story, they are presented with a description of a situation, with the facts of the story. Organizations indeed are entities that can be described by facts. The job descriptions of members, the assets and liabilities, the rules and regulations, the policy and procedures, and the ladder of authority are all factual constructs. Certainly, General Savage is a stickler for the formal (fact of life) rules. When an enlisted clerk is observed to be out of uniform, he reduces him in rank from sergeant to private. When a senior pilot, Lieutenant Colonel Ben Gaitley, leaves the base and gets drunk during the crisis of Davenport's dismissal, Savage removes him from his position in the hierarchy and assigns him as pilot of a crew filled with misfits to fly a plane that Savage names "The Leper Colony."

The structure of the organization, its anatomy, is described in factual terms. The decisions that formulate the day-to-day activity of the organization, its processes, its physiology, are based, at least in part, on factual premises. If the planes fly at 9000 feet of altitude they will destroy more targets than if they fly at 19,000 feet. The decision to lower the standard bombing altitude is based on this factual premise.

But organizations are not just machine-like producers of action based on a factual rationality. They are also institutions, i.e. complex social systems with deeply infused values. The complex mélange of values that define the soul of the organization represents a chain of means and ends that winds up identifying the highest or end game value of the organized system. This end game value expresses the formal purpose of the organization.

Technology and tactics are designed to help the pilots stay alive and do their jobs. Yet the aircrews and their skills are not an end in and of themselves. They are a means to achieving the objective of destroyed enemy targets, a valued goal. And the destroyed targets are a means to achieving the valued end of winning the war. So we might say that the purpose of the 918th is winning the war. And that is true. But that notion leaves out as much as it puts in. It only explains part of what is going on. One reason that organizations often seem, at least potentially, to be so imperfect or dysfunctional, is that in reality there is more than one governing purpose for which organizations exist, not just the one explicitly expressed by the formal purpose (i.e. mission). It is this complexity of purpose described in the film story that enables students to discover that there is more to what is going on here than is revealed by the objective facts.

Three Purposes

If a person from Mars were asked to observe organizational life and speculate on the purpose for the existence of modern organizations, the predominant social structure with which earthlings get things done, the Martian would conclude that there are three purposes. Only one of the three purposes is written into policy or into the organization manual: the formally stated mission. The other two can be inferred by the Martian (or my students) as they observe the behavior of the organized system and its parts.

The first, and most obvious, purpose (as has been mentioned) is the formal mission, the delivery of some goods or services to a client, customer, or constituency. For the 918th Bomber Group, this is helping to win the war for the American people. Yet there are times, as we observe the way the organizational process proceeds, as we examine the criteria that leaders and followers use for making decisions, that the purpose (end game value in the chain of means and ends) appears to be satisfaction of the needs of individual participants. Of course, everybody wants to win the war. But as these men try to do so, all the aircrews are going to lose their lives. Because of this, the leader, Colonel Keith Davenport, designs the organization and runs it so that the crews survive (purpose), rather than that the war is won. His decision to object to flying at a lower altitude reveals the value premise behind that decision. Similarly, Colonel Davenport's decision to refuse to fire the weak navigator is based on the young man's very strong need to prove himself to be a loyal American even though his parents are German immigrants. The value premise of decisions made by Colonel Davenport consists of the value of preserving the lives and dignity of the aircrews. This is in conflict with the factual premise of headquarters that flying lower will result in the destruction of more targets as well as the factual premise that there are plenty of trained proficient navigators. So we have the purpose of the organization, as expressed in the logic of the mission, in conflict with the purpose of the individual participant, to stay alive or to have his patriotism validated. If the organization is functional with respect to destroying enemy targets, it is dysfunctional with respect to preserving the lives of its members, and *vice versa*.

For the aircrew members who will almost certainly die in the performance of their duties, the leadership of General Savage is irrational. For General Savage, the refusal of the men to participate willingly in the activity of the organization is irrational. Savage is frustrated by the men's refusal to accept his suggestion that they "consider themselves already dead." On the other hand, at the level of analysis of the system, the social scientist conceives of organizations are entities of cooperation for rational action. How can two differing concepts of rationality exist in the same organized space? What is the meaning of this seeming inconsistency?

The idea of *rational* does not prescribe objective criteria for evaluating or predicting behavior. "Rational" means the optimization of some value. I drive a large pickup truck because I want to optimize the value of the capacity to tow my horses around the countryside. My wife drives a small 4 cylinder import because she wants to optimize the value of fuel economy. Both behaviors are rational because they result in an outcome that the decision maker finds useful.

General Savage wants to optimize the value of targets destroyed. For Colonel Davenport and for the young men who fly the aircraft of the 918th, the value to be optimized is the survival of aircrews.

It is important for my students to understand that organizations do not generally come into existence to serve the needs of participants. It is assumed that the members of the organization will serve a purpose derived from the original design of the organization. That assumption is generally true, albeit an oversimplification of complex reality. The assumption is rarely true in the absolute. Whether or not the purpose of serving the needs of members, when those needs come into conflict with the formal purpose of the organization, is legitimate or is pathological is a matter of philosophy and politics. In a socialistic political-economic system, the responsibility of institutions, both private and public, includes the nurturing of participants, perhaps to an extent above and beyond the straight forward exchange of labor for benefit. Here the dominance of the purpose of the individual might not be considered so irrational or pathological. Indeed, in the early days of the birth of a welfare state in the U.S., the federal government formed organizations, such as the Work Projects Administration (WPA), designed almost exclusively to serve the individual necessity of employees. In a free market capitalistic system, however, the benefits provided to the participants are believed to be in exchange for services that accomplish a mission. Nurturing the individual just for his or her own sake would not be considered rational.

Rationality and pathology notwithstanding, even in capitalistic nations people do *behave* as though the organization exists, at least in part, to serve their particular interests. In explaining this notion to my students I tell them that the college I work for exists, at least in part, to give me something to do when I wake up in the morning. Of course my students react to this rather glib statement by concluding that my tongue is firmly placed inside my cheek. This is not the case. If I believe that the relationship between me and my organization is based solely on the way I serve the more narrow rationality of the organization, I am vulnerable to perceiving myself as a tool in the hands of another. Because the hand that holds the tool also controls the tool, this might be the first step on the road giving up responsibility for my own happiness. Philosophically, at least for me, the sanctity of the individual person, the well being of mind, body, and soul, mitigates toward giving one the benefit of the doubt when, from time to time, the human being seems to be using the organization to a greater extent than the organization is using the human being. So, the second purpose of an organization is serving the needs of individual participants.

A third purpose is the survival and health of the organization itself. One of the problems faced by the 918th Bomber Group is that the tactic of daylight precision bombing is experimental and believed by many, the British and the ground forces of the U.S. Army in particular, to be too risky and nonproductive. The Army Air Corps is a relatively new organization. The willingness of American political and military leaders to devote scarce material and manpower to this organization, indeed to allow its continued existence, depends on the Corps' capacity to demonstrate that it can help win the war with daylight precision bombing. So, at times we see that the value premise of decisions optimizes the continued existence, indeed the survival as an institution, and the continued resource support, the health of the Army Air Corps.

The personification of this phenomenon is the general who leads the 8th Airforce, of which the 918th is part, General Pritchard. He tells the new leader of the group, General Savage, that his men must fly at lower altitudes and destroy more targets even though this means they may all be killed before they get relieved by other crews now in training. A sensible strategy might be to hold off and wait until they have enough crews and planes to let each crew fly a specified number of missions and then go home. This would motivate the men because they would expect the satisfaction of accomplishing a meaningful goal, the preservation of their lives. This is coming soon and this is what eventually happens. Pritchard, however, expresses his fears that if the Army Air Corps does not press on despite horrendous losses, daylight precision bombing will be discredited. That might mean the end of organizations like the 918th and perhaps of the Army Air Corps whose essence is strategic bombing. Of course, General Pritchard wants to win the war. Of course, he would prefer that the aircrews survive. But for a time he acts as though his highest value, his conception of organization purpose, is the survival and health of the 918th and the Army Air Corps.

The Role of a Leader

In the ideal, the three purposes: mission, self, institutional health and survival, are not in conflict. In this film story, one of the most important functions of the leader is to integrate the divergent purposes. The new leader of the 918th, General Savage, the hero of the story, figures out a way to do this, albeit at great cost to himself and at great loss of the life of the aircrews. Savage convinces the aircrews that placing bombs on target and the contribution of this to the war effort is more important to them, as individuals, than is their own lives.

When his advice to the men to ."..consider themselves already dead," results in massive resignations from a voluntary flying status, Savage focuses on a young pilot who, by virtue of his heroism and stoicism, is respected by all air crewmen.

The General tells Lieutenant Bishop that ."..a man has to decide for himself."

Bishop needs, more than anything else, to confirm his status as a man. To do so he must realign his values in an extreme way. He has to accept the proposition that the value of placing bombs on German targets is greater than the value of his own life. And this he does. General Savage gets Lieutenant Bishop and the others to replace their instinctive purpose, staying alive, with a societal purpose, winning the war.

General Savage convinces Lieutenant Bishop to give up his life for an organizational cause by taking advantage of Bishop's vanity, the satisfaction he can derive from dedicating himself to a worthy crusade. The cause that drives the formal mission of an organization is, however, not always universally and unambiguously admirable. In the film *Devil's Advocate*, the Devil in the form of the senior partner (Milton) in a law firm, takes advantage of a young lawyer's (Lomax) vanity to gain control of his soul. Both Bishop in *Twelve O'Clock High* and Lomax in *The Devil's Advocate* have free will, but their freedom is limited by the willingness, indeed the necessity, of the leader to push the goals of the organization against the interest of the lower level participant. "Vanity is my favorite sin," proclaims Milton (as the Devil). The vanity of his pilots, their need to act like *real men*, is also General Savage's favorite sin. The viewing student may conclude that Savage is good and Milton is evil. The form of the two stories is different. But the message is the same: The human being is potentially a victim of the organizational machine.

THE ANSWER TO THE "SO WHAT?" QUESTION

The fountainhead of human happiness is human purpose, those ends that are pursued for their own sake. Individual rationality depends on those values that embrace individual purpose. One person's feast in another's famine. Despite the efforts of philosophers, theologians, and artists, through the ages, human purpose remains a mystery. This is because the ends that people pursue for their own sake vary greatly among individuals and vary over time within the experience of a particular individual. Because organizational purpose includes goals, formal mission and institutional health/ survival, that can be in conflict with individual purpose, the expectation that an organization will be a *sufficient* supply of what is necessary to fulfill human desire is problematical.

The use of the film *Twelve O'Clock High* to explore the meaning of organizational purpose is but one example of the way I use film to teach those concepts that can help students to deal with the "so what?" question concerning conflict between organizations and their participants. My goal is to encourage students to respond to the analysis of film cases with, "So I can expect to experience the sort of problems people confront in these films. So I need to understand that my happiness depends on my own capacity to acquire wisdom concerning my own purpose. So I need to cope with the possibility of a day that I will experience a wakeup call that destroys the expectation that my human aspirations will be fulfilled by my organization"

In the following appendix I suggest films that can be used as case studies to explore specific causes of the problem I have suggested as well as coping mechanisms that can help people develop strategies for dealing with the problem.

APPENDIX

Here are some of the films that I have used to look at relevant concepts and coping mechanisms (Sloane, 2002):

Concepts

- Role Conflict: *The Electric Horseman* (Pollack, 1979), *Lost in America* (Brooks, 1985), *In Pursuit of Honor* (Olin, 1995)
- Socialization: *Twelve O'Clock High* (King, 1949)
- Isolation: *Groundhog Day* (Ramis, 1993)
- Hierarchy: *The Caine Mutiny* (Dmytryk, 1954), *Catch 22* (Nichols, 1970)
- Specialization: *Executive Suite* (Wise, 1954)
- Professionalism: *The Right Stuff* (Kaufman, 1983), *A Few Good Men* (Reiner, 1992)
- Fear of the future: *2001: A Space Odyssey* (Kubrick, 1968), *Rollerball* (Jewison, 1975)

Coping Strategies

Strategies ranging from conformity to alienation that protagonists use to deal with the epiphany - the inevitable wake up call - experienced when the potential for conflict between organizational and human needs becomes a reality can be explored as students discuss these films:

Conformity

- Personal transformation: *Lost in America* , *Twelve O'Clock High*
- A rite of passage: *The Caine Mutiny*
- The helping of leaders: *Twelve O'Clock High*

Alienation

- Creative rebellion: *Local Hero* (Forsyth, 1983)
- Uncooperative rebellion: *The Right Stuff, Silkwood* (Nichols, 1983)
- Exit: *The Electric Horseman*

REFERENCES

Aristotle (1962). *Nicomachean Ethics,* New York, NY: Macmillan.

Sloane, S. (2002). *Organizations in the Movies: The Legend of the Dysfunctional.* Lanham, MD: University Press of America.

Films

Brooks, A. (Director). (1985). *Lost in America* [Motion picture]. United States: The Geffen Company & Marty Katz Productions.

Crowe, C. (Director). (1996). *Jerry McGuire* [Motion picture]. United States: TriStar Pictures.

Dmytryk, E. (Director). (1954). *The Caine mutiny* [Motion picture]. United States: Columbia Pictures.

Fleming, V. (Director). (1939). *Wizard of Oz* [Motion picture]. United States: Metro-Goldwyn-Mayer.

Forsyth, B. (Director). (1983). *Local Hero* [Motion picture]. United Kingdom: Enigma Productions & Goldcrest.

Hackford, T. (Director). (1997). *The devil's advocate* [Motion picture]. United States: Warner Bros.

Jewison, N. (Director). (1975). *Rollerball* [Motion picture]. United Kingdom: Algonquin.

Kaufman, P. (Director). (1983). *The right stuff* [Motion picture]. United States: The Ladd Company.

King, H. (Director). (1949). *Twelve o'clock high* [Motion Picture]. United States: Twentieth Century Fox.

Kubrick, S. (Director). (1968). *2001: A space odyssey* [Motion picture]. United Kingdom/United States: Metro-Goldwyn-Mayer (MGM) & Stanley Kubrick Productions.

Lumet, S. (Director). (1973). *Serpico* [Motion picture]. United States/Italy: Artists Entertainment Complex & Produzioni De Laurentiis International Manufacturing Company.

Lumet, S. (Director). (1976). *Network* [Motion picture]. United States: Metro-Goldwyn-Mayer & United Artists.

Nichols, M. (Director). (1970). *Catch-22* [Motion picture]. United States: Paramount Pictures.

Nichols, M. (Director). (1983). *Silkwood* [Motion picture]. United States: ABC Motion Pictures.

Olin, K. (Director). (1995). *In pursuit of honor* [Motion picture]. United States: Home Box Office.

Pollack, S. (Director). (1979). *The electric horseman* [Motion picture]. United States: Columbia Pictures.

Pollack, S. (Director). (1993). *The firm* [Motion picture]. United States: Paramount Pictures.

Ramis, H. (Director). (1993). *Groundhog day* [Motion picture]. United States: Columbia Pictures.

Reiner, R. (Director). (1992). *A few good men* [Motion picture]. United States: Castle Rock Entertainment & Columbia Pictures.

Stone, O. (Director). (1987). *Wall Street* [Motion picture]. United States: Twentieth Century Fox.

Wise, R. (Director). (1954). *Executive suite* [Motion picture]. United States: Loew's.

SECTION II

CRITICAL ISSUES

CHAPTER 8

USING FEATURE FILMS AS CRITICAL DOCUMENTARY IN MANAGEMENT EDUCATION

Over the last thirty years, a number of Hollywood 'blockbuster' films have successfully engaged the public's interest in the activities of the world's more powerful corporations, and the potential which exists for 'organizational misbehavior': corruption, oppression and/or exploitation (Vardi & Wiener, 1996). For example, films such as *Wall Street* (Stone, 1987), *Syriana* (Gaghan, 2005), *Erin Brockovich* (Soderbergh, 2000), *Silkwood* (Nichols, 1983), *The Insider* (Mann, 1999) and *Blood Diamond* (Zwick, 2006) explore a range of controversial organizational practices, varying from corporate raids and aggressive takeovers, cavalier policies on environmental pollution, radiation and public health to the effect of Western consumerism on indigenous communities (Bell, 2008; Hassard & Buchanan, 2009). At the same time, these films often reveal the stark differences between the lives of employees at different levels of organizational structures; particularly in the

Moving Images: Effective Teaching with Film and Television in Higher Education,
pages 103–117

103

ways that blue collar workers may be the butt of corporate practice whilst senior management benefit.

As well as being hugely entertaining, these films can provide a useful resource in management education to enable students to explore and debate issues of business ethics and corporate social responsibility. The moral and ethical implications of management practices can be considered on a range of scales: how they may impact on society, how they may play out at different levels of organizational hierarchies, as well as how they might be dealt with on a personal level, by individuals in their role as managers. Feature films can thus usefully work alongside other film media such as critical documentaries (for example, *The Corporation* [Achbar & Abbot, 2003] or *Super Size Me* [Spurlock, 2004]) as well as viral videos (for example, *The Meatrix* [Fox, 2003] or *The Story of Stuff* [Fox, 2007]) to illustrate and highlight issues of social justice and environmental responsibility.

On the face of it however, it might appear somewhat contradictory to use feature films to engage students in the critical analysis of corporate activities. After all, critics from the Frankfurt School of the 1940s to the present day have argued that feature films are themselves, in the main, produced by powerful media conglomerates which together form one of the largest and most lucrative industrial sectors in the global economy (Adorno & Horkheimer 1944, Harrington & Bielby 2005). From this perspective, the main function of feature films is to sustain the status quo of capitalism; i.e., to continue and increase the potential to make a profit. As such it would seem unlikely that they would represent narratives which might challenge or undermine the basis on which this ability has been constructed (Harrington & Bielby, 2005; Jancovich, 1995; Rhodes & Westwood, 2008; Storey, 1993). However, I would argue that the complexities of popular culture mean that it cannot be simply 'read off', or reducible to, the economic context of its production. The meanings of cultural products cannot be simply contained within a particular ideological regime, but can be appropriated and renegotiated at all stages of the production and reception process (Rhodes & Westwood, 2008).

A further counter-argument exists in the conventional assumption that feature films are usually fictional, produced for mass 'entertainment' rather than for information, education or critical/political analysis (Dyer 1992). This means they are made 'easy' for the audience: rather than aiming to challenge worldviews or destabilize 'common sense', they draw on stereotypical characterizations and generic narrative forms which have been well established through the 'Hollywood' film system and proved to be popular at the box office (Gramsci et al, 2001; Lacey, 2000; Phillips, 1996). Such films are dominated by the 'star' system, using actors with mass appeal rather than people who may be more representative of the actual political and social issues featured in the film (Dyer, 1979; McDonald, 1995). In addition, analysts such as Arijon (1991) and Tan and Fasting (1996) argue that feature films frequently make use of specific cinematic techniques or 'grammar', which are designed to manipulate the emotions and sometimes the intellect of audiences, rather than encourage the ability to evaluate critically (Arijon, 1991; Tan & Fasting, 1996). However, this argument also over-prioritizes the power of the producer in the construction of meaning. As has been well-documented, audiences negotiate a broad range of meanings from their interactions with cultural texts, some of which may be interrogative and/or resistant (Hall 1980). As such, feature films cannot be understood in monosemic terms, but instead as offering a multiplicity of functions and interpretations, including the ability to 'document' organizational life—and be critical of it.

This chapter argues therefore that feature films are in fact a rich resource for teaching and learning. The cinematic techniques mentioned above are valuable to teaching and may be productive in bringing the complexities of many management and organizational practices 'to life'. Film not only enables the 'visual exaggeration' of behavior, which helps to illustrate and reinforce organizational issues and debates (Champoux, 2001), but also employs the 'textual exaggeration' of storylines and dialogue to the same effect. Whilst this sort of embellishment quite clearly plays with notions of 'accuracy' and 'reality', this technique of amplification can be useful in helping to sediment and reinforce the key aspects of certain management and organizational issues and debates. Feature films also present topics in ways which are 'more graphic, engaging and memorable than conventional classroom methods' (Hassard & Buchanan, 2009, p. 621), and as such can be a valuable means of motivating students. Whilst it is true to say that films are affective, engaging us at the level of our emotions, they can also offer cognitive pleasures which can be exploited after the film in the classroom by involving students in sharing their views and critical analysis in discussion. Finally, and importantly, they enable students to encounter situations, events and contexts which they may have had no previous experience of, or access to, in their own lives.

However, quite clearly, if feature films are going to be used effectively in the management classroom, they need to be more than merely entertaining and transporting. The purpose of this chapter is to explore how feature films can be used as critical documentary, offering an effective and productive resource for questioning corporate ethics and responsibilities. Students are, of course, already likely to be skilled in consuming films as general members of film audiences. Far from being 'cultural dopes' (Garfinkel, 1967), passively absorbing the ideologies of powerful media moguls, contemporary audiences are now highly skilled in decoding and interpreting films and other media. As our responses to media varies according to our own socio-cultural situations, a range of multiple and diverse responses exist amongst audiences which it is interesting to explore (Hall, 1980; Ross & Nightingale, 2003). This is perhaps especially the case when the topic under discussion may produce principled reactions, as is the case with moral or ethical decisions. However this is certainly not to say that, as educators, we cannot develop and hone these skills. Specific pedagogical techniques can be employed to enable students to use feature films as a productive means of exploring the ethical and social responsibilities involved in their work as managers.

FEATURE FILMS AS CRITICAL DOCUMENTARY

Although movies do not offer an unmediated window on 'reality', the representations and interpretations of organizational behavior within feature films can be a useful resource to trigger critical questions and lively debate within the classroom. There is a growing body of film that explores a range of important and sometimes controversial issues which it is important to address in the analysis of corporate behavior and practice in our increasingly globalized world. These include issues of power, gender, inequality, oppression, exploitation, conflict and resistance (Bell, 2008; Rhodes & Westwood, 2008; Hassard & Buchanan, 2009). As the films featured in the other chapters of this book illustrate, these issues are often contextualized in international political landscapes, thus enabling the critical reading of management and organizational decision-making in global contexts. Through the use of diverse characters, each representing a particular position or point of view, films can also be an important tool for encouraging students to 'see diversity'. They can enable events to be seen through *multiple* voices and *diverse* standpoints: not just through a managerialist or perhaps a white, middle class, male, lens that may be over-represented in management textbooks. Thus although films often feature (overly) dramatic and large scale events, they can be used to provide a metaphor for the everyday: to open up discussion on the small scale, routines and practices that occur in our daily working lives and yet which may still have ethical implications. In this way, the issues covered can be made to resonate with students' own lives and experiences.

Below I suggest a selection of feature films which provide critical documentary of management and organizational activities. These cover a wide range of topics, but all can be used to explore and question the behavior or 'misbehavior' of organizations (Vardi & Wiener, 1996).

Health and Safety; Environmental Pollution

Silkwood explores the true story of Karen Silkwood, a union activist for the Oil, Chemical, and Atomic Workers in a processing plant in Utah. Her particular concern was health and safety, and she was regarded by the corporation as a 'trouble maker'. Because of the nature of the work in the plant, questionable safety laws, and even the possibility of deliberate company sabotage, Silkwood becomes contaminated with plutonium. The film raises interesting questions about the extent of corporate responsibility in ensuring the personal safety of workers, as well as the negotiation of competing interests and worker resistance.

The way in which inadequate corporate safety legislation can affect the wider community is explored in several films about environmental pollution. One example is *The China Syndrome* (Bridges, 1979). Interestingly, this film was released just twelve days before the real life Three Mile Island accident and reveals the potential dangers of nuclear energy plants. 'The China Syndrome' refers to the idea that, if an American nuclear plant melts down, the core will melt down into the earth until it hits China. In the process, of course, the surrounding area would be contaminated with radioactive steam. The film explores issues of inadequate safety policies and cover ups.

Erin Brokovich tells the 'true' story of the case against brought against the Pacific Gas and Electric Company by Erin Brokovich, an American legal clerk and environmental activist. The case alleged contamination of the water supply, including local drinking water, with hexavalent chromium. Settled in 1996 for US$333 million, this was the largest settlement ever paid in a direct action lawsuit in US history. The film is useful for examining the separation of business and community as well as the supposed immunity that large corporations assume they have from effective local level contestation. The energizing of the community by Brokovich shows that it *is* possible to confront and beat large corporations however. The film can also be used therefore to demonstrate the sort of leadership that people can aspire to in their everyday lives.

The Insider explores one of the greatest corporate frauds of recent times: the testimony of the CEOs of the giant tobacco companies (the seven dwarves) that their in-house research had proven that nicotine is non-addictive. The drama centers on a tobacco research scientist turned whistle blower, and his struggles to tell the truth and to have his story heard. Not only does his own employing organization attempt to silence him through 'confidentiality' clauses; but so does CNN, the news media giant, which is shown to be implicated in a relationship with the tobacco company. As Zaniello argues 'the business of a global company has rarely seemed so scary, in real life or on the screen' (Zaniello, 2007, p. 100).

Takeovers, Mergers and Liquidations

Wall Street explores the world of corporate raiders through the contrasting lives of three people at very different levels of the employment structure. Gordon Gekko (Michael Douglas) is a highly successful insider trader, Fox (Charlie Sheen), his apprentice, is a young stockbroker, whilst Fox's father (Martin Sheen) is a blue collar factory worker. Whilst Gekko, as one character explains, received 'an ethical bypass at birth' (Zaniello, 2007, p. 176), moral dilemmas are more obviously evident in the character of Fox, who is asked to use his own father as a source of important inside information. Not only does the film raise questions about the ethics of takeovers and how they are handled, it also explores how such activities are experienced by workers at different levels of organizational hierarchies. A similar theme is explored in *Other People's Money* (Jewison, 1991) in which 'Larry the Liquidator', a Wall Street investor and asset stripper shows little concern for the workers of the companies he destroys. A more complex film is *Syriana* which explores the collusion of the American government with oil corporations. The highly questionable involvement of the United States in trying to affect who becomes the next heir of a 'friendly' Middle Eastern nation is gradually revealed through the tangled relationships of a CIA agent, an oil advisor, and the son of an ageing emir.

The Effect of Consumerism

Another theme explored in the multi-stranded *Syriana* is the effect of consumerism on societies, politics, organizational behavior, as well as individual employees. The acquisition of oil for a fuel hungry west is seen to come at a high price involving murder, torture and betrayal. *Blood Diamond* also explores dirty practices between business and governments and how these can wreak havoc on indigenous communities. The title refers to diamonds mined in African war zones and sold to finance conflicts, thereby profiting warlords and diamond companies across the world.

Employment Hierarchies and Relations

As I have already indicated above, *Wall Street* is a rich resource to explore the differences in lives and outlooks of men located at different points within organizational and class structures. In addition, as Rhodes and Westwood (2008, p. 53) argue, *Glengarry Glen Ross* (Foley, 1992) also offers 'a complex and trenchant critique of the ethos of contemporary capitalism and its effects on those who labor within it'. The film focuses on four salesmen in a real estate agency and their manager, and through these relationships the damaging and dehumanizing effects of hierarchy and competition can be explored. In addition, as Rhodes and Westwood (2008) reveal, the film is useful as an exploration of masculinity and the potentially damaging implications for men through their work in contemporary organizations. The film depicts how office work can constrain acceptable performances of masculinity to the predictable and the mundane, albeit with occasional explosions of violence. Similar themes of hierarchy, masculinity and the effects of work on the self are raised in *Office Space* (Judge, 1999).

Sexual/Racial Harassment and Discrimination

A League of Their Own (Marshall, 1992) explores how the world of women's baseball is shaped by corporate and patriarchal constraints. The film shows how a women's baseball team, the Rockford Peaches, is forced to operate within the constraining gender stereotypes of their sponsors. In order to make the sport more palatable to spectators, the women are made to wear impractical, scanty uniforms 'which clearly signpost the unmistakable femininity of their bodies' (Taylor, 1995, p. 167). However while the team agree to comply with some of the terms laid down for them by the manager, such as the wearing of short skirts, the film also shows how they succeed in turning management terms around to suit their own objectives.

Disclosure (Levinson, 1994) explores the issue of sexual harassment within an office environment. What is particularly interesting is that it can reverse the expectations of some viewers, as the perpetrator is a woman. The film is thus useful in inviting viewers to examine critically topics such as the ease with which allegations of sexual harassment can destroy careers; and whether a double standard exists when such allegations are levied by men or women.

North Country (Caro, 2005) is a film which was inspired by the book *Class Action: The Story of Lois Jenson and the Landmark Case That Changed Sexual Harassment Law* (Bingham & Gansler, 2002) which chronicled the case of *Jenson v. Eveleth Taconite Company*. It explores the story of a woman working in the male-dominated world of iron mining who attempts to join the ranks of the highly paid ore-blasters. Although she is prepared to work hard in back-breaking and often dangerous conditions, the bigger challenge proves to be the *harassment* that she and the other female miners encounter from their male coworkers. This includes verbal, physical and sexual abuse. The company's response is complete disinterest, but when she attempts to take the case further, the wider community is also unsupportive, fearing the mine will be closed down. The film explores corporate responsibility and policy in matters of sexual harassment, as well as the ways in which a single dominant employer can shape communities.

The Impact of Unemployment (Personal and Community)

Many good films exist which explore the impact of unemployment, particularly in relation to the decline of traditional working class masculine identities and community as a result of deindustrialization. There are some particularly touching British films in this genre. For example, *Brassed Off* (Herman, 1996) explores the impact on community life and gender when the major employer, in this case the coal mine, closes down. *The Full Monty* (Cattaneo, 1997), whilst exploring similar issues, focuses more particularly on the impact on masculinity following the closure of the steel mines in Sheffield, England. In both films, the loss of certain 'heroic' aspects of working class masculine identities is central, emphasized through the representation of declining, industrialized urban space. The men's attempts to find alternative employment are parodied through the tropes of clowns and strippers, and the intertextual connections of these with children, women and families underline the challenge to traditional masculinity as well as suggesting the rise in the (economic) power of femininity.

Exploitation (National and International)

The exploitation of labor makes for a powerful feature film, often by giving a voice to the oppressed. Issues such as gross underpayment or denial of union membership or representation have been featured in both domestic and international contexts. A good example is *Bread and Roses* (Loach, 2000), named after the 1912 textile strike in Lawrence, Massachusetts. The plot deals with the struggle of poorly paid janitorial workers in Los Angeles and their fight for better working conditions and the right to unionize. It is based on the 'Justice for Janitors' campaign of the Service Employees International Union (Stern, 2007). The film criticizes inequalities within the United States, particularly looking at the issue of *health insurance.* A more complex film is *The Constant Gardener* (Meirelles, 2005) which is set in Kenya. The plot centers on a low rung British diplomat, Quayle, whose highly political and activist wife is murdered. As he tries to uncover the mystery surrounding his wife's death, Quayle discovers that a large drug corporation is using the local population for the fraudulent testing of a *tuberculosis* drug, 'dypraxa.' Whilst dypraxa has known harmful side effects, the health of the test subjects, poor and uneducated as they are, is seen to be of little consequence.

Use and Abuse of Knowledge, Power and Technology

A good example here is *Rogue Trader* (Dearden, 1999), a film portraying the 'true' story of former derivatives broker Nick Leeson, whose activities were seen to bring about the collapse of Barings Bank in 1995. Leeson was the General Manager of the Trading Floor in Singapore, and the film follows his rise to become one of Barings' key traders. However, encouraged by the greed of his managers, his ability to use technology to cover up what he was doing, and his manager's inability to monitor his activities, Leeson starts to gamble the bank's money. In the end, as is now well known, the bank's losses were so great that the bank collapsed. As well as raising issues of the use and abuse of technology, the film is also useful to explore inadequate management techniques to control such activity.

TOWARDS A CRITICAL APPROACH

As discussed above, these films need to be approached with a critical eye. They *represent*, rather than *reflect*, reality, and tend to 'exaggerate, sensationalize and glamorize characters and events' (Buchanan & Huczynski, 2004, p. 314) often through the use of genre and (oppressive) stereotypes (Hall, 1997). Although the films listed above offer a useful selection of topics through which to explore and critique organizational practices, it can be argued that they favor a somewhat narrow range of identities, contexts and subjects (Bell, 2008). Identification and evaluation of these demands the acquisition of 'film literacy' by students; that is, the ability to 'read' films with a critical and analytical approach. Students need to be equipped to 'deconstruct' filmic representations, and to 'read' the 'language' and 'grammar' of films in order to recognize how meanings are constructed, packaged and delivered (Aryon, 1991; Hassard & Buchanan, 2009). In addition, there are always multiple ideological discourses and meanings in play. There is never one, singular 'correct' reading of a film. Instead, the diversity of audiences and their individual biographies and socio-cultural situations cause the construction and negotiation of multiple responses and meanings. In student discussion, particularly of moral dilemmas, this multiplicity needs to be acknowledged and taken into account, (Hassard & Holliday, 1998; Morley, 1992).

It is useful here to draw on concepts developed within cultural studies on the different responses to media messages; the notion of 'preferred', 'oppositional', and 'negotiated' responses is particularly valuable (Phillips 1996). A '*preferred*' reading of a media text is where the viewer takes the intended meaning and aligns themselves with the messages and ideologies of those who produced the film. Within the typology his response is understood as the most pleasurable, albeit a comfortable pleasure of reassurance and familiarity. An '*oppositional*' reading is one in which the viewer rejects the ideologies and views promoted by the film, and as such the viewing experience may be unpleasurable. A '*negotiated*' reading, possibly the most common, involves a negotiation between the viewer and the messages of the film to produce new meanings and understandings (Phillips 1996).

In this understanding of the viewer as active in the meaning-making process of films, it is clear that stereotypical representations in film can be mediated. Rather than seeing viewers as immobilized by the discourses of, for example, the capitalism, or patriarchy that arguably tends to dominate Hollywood feature films, the activity of viewing can function as a form of critique and/or resistance to specific power relations (Radway, 1987; Taylor, 1989; Taylor, 1995). For example, Helen Taylor's (1989) research on women's responses to *Gone with the Wind* (Fleming, 1939) revealed a wide diversity of reactions according to race, class, age and sexuality. Thus, whilst many of the black women rejected the 'one-sided and patronizing' representations of race in the film as 'childlike, dependent and rather stupid' (Taylor, 1989, p. 193), some of the white women accepted these unquestioningly (Taylor, 1995). Taylor (1989) also demonstrates how meaning emerges from the relationship between the audience and the film text, rather than existing as a single, unified object which resides in the text, waiting to be revealed by the skilful viewer (Taylor, 1995). This enables potentially resistant readings. For example, some of the respondents saw Scarlett O'Hara the central character as a strong, feminist figure.

Informing management students of some key cultural studies concepts and research findings such as these may be useful therefore in encouraging them to recognize the active agency involved in viewing and the multiplicity of responses which may be negotiated.

PEDAGOGIC TECHNIQUES

The acquisition of this sort of film literacy is a skill that we can teach in the management classroom. The following techniques can be used. First, the facilitator needs to identify an appropriate film by which to explore a particular issue of business ethics or corporate responsibility. As well as the suggestions given within this book, many of the references featured at the end of this chapter provide additional sources of help with this task. The facilitator must obviously watch the film carefully themselves; hard work but someone has to do it! Key scenes should be identified as a useful basis for discussion. Clearly there is usually not time to watch a whole film together in the classroom, so students should be encouraged (and usually want to) view this in their own time prior to the session. These activities can be used to develop the following viewing or 'reading' techniques and strategies.

1. Segmentation

The first technique to undertake is a detailed analysis of the structure and action of the film. This task is ideally done in advance, whilst students are watching the film, as it involves constructing a full record of it. The key parts of the film are broken down into segments, running times recorded and the main action described. In order that this does not become too onerous and time consuming, this task can be broken down into group work so that each student takes responsibility for, say, 30 minutes of film and brings this with them to the classroom. The notes can then be pieced together to form a coherent record. This can then be used as a basis for the more detailed analytical techniques which now follow.

2. Connotation

The second technique helps students develop their ability to 'read' films and/or their constituent parts. The task is to watch a segment carefully and add to the above notes on time, place and action with a descriptive record of key spoken dialogue, nonverbal communication (eye movement, facial expression, bodily comportment and movement), signs and symbols such as costumes, props, objects and artifacts, and music, soundtrack, lighting, and other cinematic techniques such as camera use and position, special effects, and so on. For the first time, this should be done together so that the facilitator can show the group how this can be done. Thereafter, once the technique has been acquired, students can again undertake this phase in their own time to save valuable classroom time.

3. Analysis

The third technique is to develop the ability to explore the meanings of the film. The task here is to encourage students to interpret or 'decode' the meanings of the contexts, events, dialogue, non-verbal communication, symbols, and so on that have been noted and recorded. What do they think is the importance of a particular event, speech act, incident of non verbal communication such as a look or a gesture, or key object such as a diamond (*Blood Diamond*) or a brass instrument (*Brassed Off*)? Key questions should be identified by the facilitator for exploration and contemplation, either at the level of the whole film if they have watched this in advance and or in terms of the key segments which have been played in the classroom. The following are examples of the sorts of questions which can then be explored, perhaps as group work before returning to whole class discussion:

- What are the central questions raised by the film (or segment, scene or clip)?
- Is there an ethical/moral dilemma for the organization and what is this?
- Is there an ethical/moral dilemma for the manager and what is this?
- What ethical/moral dilemmas are faced by the other characters?
- How are each of these represented and what are the similarities and differences between them?
- What ethical guidelines are used to decide a course of action, and how do these vary by character (standpoint)?
- Who behaves ethically or unethically?
- What is the impact on others and is this justified?
- What questions are raised about Rights? Justice? Social responsibility? Utilitarianism? Leadership? Integrity? Equality/diversity? Representation of race and gender?
- How does the film answer these questions?
- Do you agree with this answer?
- What are the multiple ideologies of the film? (i.e., messages of film vs. American production context?)

4. Personal Response

The fourth technique is to invite students to explore and discuss their responses to the film. If they have watched the whole film at home and undertaken the technique of segmentation, they can also be invited to make a record of their initial responses as they watch. They can then bring these notes to the classroom for group discussion of such questions as:

- How did you respond to the film?
- Do you think your response was preferred/oppositional/negotiated?
- What emotions were created?
- Did you identify with any of the characters?
- What are your positions on the central ethical dilemmas?
- What would you do in these situations?
- What is the impact of the film?
- Do films such as these enable or achieve changes in behavior or resistance to organizational misbehavior (Vardi & Wiener, 1996)?

CONCLUSIONS: FILM LITERACY AS A KEY MANAGEMENT SKILL

This chapter has argued that feature films can be used as a key teaching resource in management classrooms to engage students in the critical debate of the ethics of organizational activity and managers' roles and responsibilities within this. Deployed skillfully, feature films facilitate the discussion of complex issues in the classroom which it can be difficult for the educator to explain with sufficient intricacy. It may also enable the introduction and thorough exploration of particular issues of oppression and exploitation, such as sexism and racism, which it can sometimes be problematic for teachers to introduce. It can also push debate on the extent of personal responsibility and the development of codes of action.

However, I would also argue that the ability to read and deconstruct films critically is an important and valuable management skill with more general applicability. Developing this ability can help to extend students' critical faculties, and can thus be usefully applied to other theories and concepts in organization and management that students will meet elsewhere in their studies. Just as film relies heavily on conventions such as genre, narrative and character, so organization theory *also* makes use of conventional rhetorical devices (Leonard, 2002, 2004). I have argued elsewhere how, when we read organization theory, we may make intertextual links with other media such as feature films, and draw on our knowledge of aspects such as narrative and genre in our interpretations and responses (Leonard, 2002, 2004). By developing the critical abilities of our students, we can encourage them to deconstruct and analyze theoretical texts in order to reveal the ways in which they *too* may construct 'truths' according to familiar stereotypes (Leonard 2004). Developing our students' film literacy may therefore encourage the creativity and confidence to develop new knowledge, as well as sensitivity to their moral and ethical responsibilities as managers.

REFERENCES

Adorno, T., & Horkheimer, M. (1944). *Dialectic of enlightenment.* London, UK: Verso.

Arijon, D. (1991). *Grammar of the film language.* Los Angeles, CA: Silman-James Press.

Bell, E. (2008). *Reading management and organization in film.* Basingstoke, UK: Palgrave Macmillan.

Bingham, C., & Gansler, L. (2002). *Class action: The story of Lois Jenson and the landmark case that changed sexual harassment law.* New York, NY: Doubleday.

Buchanan, D., & Huczynski, A. (2004). Images of influence. *Twelve Angry Men* and *Thirteen Days. Journal of Management Inquiry, 13*(4), 312–323.

Champoux, J. (2001). *Using film to visualize principles and practices.* Cincinnati, OH: South Western College Publishing.

Dyer, R. (1979). *Stars.* London, UK: BFI.

Dyer, R. (1992). *Only entertainment.* London, UK: Routledge.

Garfinkel, H. (1967). *Studies in ethnomethodology.* Englewood Cliffs, NJ: Prentice Hall.

Gramsci, A., Forgacs, D., & Nowell-Smith, G. (Eds.), & Boelhower, W. (Trans.) (2001). *Selections from cultural writings.* London, UK: Electric Book Company.

Hall, S. (1980). Coding/encoding/decoding. In S. Hall, D. Hobson, A. Lowe, & P. Willis (Eds.) *Culture, media, language* (pp. 107–166). London, UK: Hutchinson.

Hall, S. (1997). The spectacle of the 'other.' In S. Hall (Ed.) *Representation: Cultural representations and signifying practices.* London, UK: Sage.

Harrington, C., & Bielby, D. (2005). Constructing the popular: Cultural production and consumption. In C. Herrington & D. Bielby (Eds.) *Popular culture: Production and consumption.* London, UK: Blackwell.

Hassard, J., & Buchanan, D. (2009). From *Modern Times* to *Syriana:* Feature Films as Research Data. In D. Buchanan & A. Bryman (Eds.) *The Sage handbook of organizational research methods.* London, UK: Sage.

Hassard, J., & Holliday, R. (1998). *Organization representation: Work and organizations in popular culture.* London, UK: Sage.

Jancovich, M. (1995). Screen theory. In J. Hollows and M. Jancovich (Eds.) *Approaches to popular film.* Manchester, UK: Manchester University Press.

Lacey, N. (2000). *Narrative and genre: Key concepts in media studies.* Basingstoke, UK: Macmillan.

Leonard, P. (2002). Organizing gender? Looking at metaphors as frames of meaning in gender/organizational texts. *Gender, Work and Organization, 9*(1), 60–80.

Leonard, P. (2004). Westerns, weddings and web-weavers: Gender as genre in organizational theory. *Gender, Work and Organization, 11*(1), 74–94.

McDonald, P. (1995). Star studies. In J. Hollows & M. Jancovich (Eds.) *Approaches to popular film.* Manchester, UK: Manchester University Press.

Morley, D. (1992). *Television, Audiences and cultural studies.* London, UK: Routledge.

Phillips, P. (1996). Genre, star and auteur-critical approaches to Hollywood cinema. In J. Neimes (Ed.) *An introduction to film studies*. London, UK: Routledge.

Radway, J. (1987). *Reading the romance: Women, patriarchy and popular literature*. London, UK: Verso.

Rhodes, C., & Westwood, R. (2008). *Critical representations of work and organization in popular culture*. London, UK: Routledge.

Ross, K., & Nightingale, V. (2003). *Media and audiences: New perspectives*. Maidenhead, UK: Open University Press.

Stern, A. (2007). Bread and roses forward. *Service Employees International Union*. *http://en.wikipedia.org/wiki/Bread_and_Roses_(film)*

Storey, J. (1993). *An introduction to cultural theory and popular culture*. Hemel Hempstead, UK: Harvester Wheatsheaf

Tan, E., & Fasting, B. (1996). *Emotion and the structure of narrative film: Film as an emotion machine*. Mahwah, NJ: Lawrence Erlbaum.

Taylor, H. (1989). *Scarlett's women: Gone with the Wind and its female fans*. London, UK: Virago.

Taylor, L. (1995). From psychoanalytic feminism to popular feminism. In J. Hollows & M. Jancovich (Eds.) *Approaches to popular film*. Manchester, UK: Manchester University Press.

Vardi, Y., & Wiener, Y. (1996). Misbehavior in organizations: A motivational framework. *Organization Science, 7*(2), 151–165

Zaniello, T. (2007). *The cinema of globalization: A guide to films about the new economic Order*. New York, NY: Cornell University Press.

Films

Achbar, M., & Abbott, J. (Directors). (2003), *The Corporation* [Motion picture]. Canada: Big Picture Media Corporation.

Bridges, J. (Director). (1979). *The China syndrome* [Motion picture]. United States: IPC Films.

Caro, N. (Director). (2005). *North country* [Motion picture]. United States:: Warner Bros.

Cattaneo, P. (Director). (1997). *The full Monty* [Motion picture]. United Kingdom: Redwave Films.

Dearden, J. (Director). (1999). *Rogue trader* [Motion picture]. United Kingdom: Granada Film Productions.

Fleming, V. (Director). (1939). *Gone with the wind* [Motion picture]. United States: Selznick International Pictures.

Foley, J. (Director). (1992). *Glengarry Glen Ross* [Motion picture]. United States: GGR.

Fox, L. (Director). (2003). *The meatrix* [Motion picture]. United States: Free Range Studios.

Fox, L. (Director). (2007). *The story of stuff* [Motion picture]. United States: Free Range Studios.

Gaghan, S. (Director). (2005). *Syriana* [Motion picture]. United States: Warner Bros.

Herman, M. (Director). (1996). *Brassed off* [Motion picture]. United Kingdom & United States: Channel Four Films.

Jewison, N. (Director). (1991). *Other people's money* [Motion picture]. United States: Warner Bros.

Judge, M. (Director). (1999). *Office space* [Motion picture]. United States: Twentieth Century Fox.

Levinson, B. (Director). (1994). *Disclosure* [Motion picture]. United States: Warner Bros.

Loach, K. (Director). (2000). *Bread and roses* [Motion picture]. United Kingdom, France, Germany, Switzerland, Spain, & Italy: Parrallax Pictures.

Marshall, P. (Director). (1992). *A league of their own* [Motion picture]. United States: Columbia Pictures.

Mann, M. (Director). (1999). *The insider* [Motion picture]. United States: Blue Lion Entertainment.

Meirelles, F. (Director). (2005). *The constant gardener* [Motion picture]. United Kingdom & Germany: Potboiler Productions.

Nichols, M. (Director). (1983). *Silkwood* [Motion picture]. United States: ABC Motion Pictures.

Spurlock, M. (Director). (2004). *Supersize me* [Motion picture]. United States: Kathbur Pictures.

Soderbergh, S (Director). (2000). *Erin Brockovich* [Motion picture]. United States: Jersey Films.

Stone, O. (Director). (1987). *Wall Street* [Motion picture]. United States: Twentieth Century Fox.

Zwick, E. (Director). (2006). *Blood diamond* [Motion picture]. United States & Germany: Warner Bros.

CHAPTER 9

UNDERSTANDING AUDIENCES

Emma Bell

Many management educators see film as a valuable pedagogic device that can be used to gain insight into organizational behavior. However, rarely is much attention devoted to the role of film audiences in interpreting these messages. Do audiences passively and uncritically absorb the images of management and organization contained within film? Or do their interpretations vary according to gender, age, ethnicity, personality, social position, values and beliefs and life experiences? When management educators use film in the classroom do they assume audiences will understand its message in the same way as themselves? Or do they seek to explore differences in interpretation between groups and individuals?

The approach taken here assumes that films are a series of interrelated texts which can be read for meaning in a similar way to written texts (Bell, 2008). Embedded within these texts are the creative interpretations of their creators or authors. The meaning of these texts is not fixed but dynamic and open to reinterpretation as part of an ongoing circuit of communication involving the author, the reader, and the text (Hall, 1980). Hence despite shared recognition, there are always possibilities for alternative readings (Hassard & Holliday, 1998).

Moving Images: Effective Teaching with Film and Television in Higher Education,
pages 119–131
119

In this chapter I review the way that management scholars have understood the role of the film audience. I argue that audiences are generally understood as relatively passive and unknowledgeable, or principally as recipients of meaning. I suggest that management educators need to develop a more sophisticated understanding of the relationship between the film reader and text that recognizes its ambivalence as well as its significance. The chapter calls for greater awareness of audiences and emphasizes the need for management educators to resist the imposition of a single, authoritative interpretation. Finally, I propose some methods for researching audiences and show how these can provide a valuable analytical resource for management educators in the classroom.

LOCATING THE AUDIENCE

Many management educators suggest that film gives students, especially those with limited direct managerial experience, insight into a wide range of organizational behaviors and the opportunity to apply complex organizational theories to 'real' situations (Buchanan & Huczynski, 2004; Marx & Frost, 1998). It is quite common for organizational behavior textbooks to provide recommendations of films (Clegg, Kornberger & Pitsis, 2008; Huczynski & Buchanan, 2008) as a means of keeping students interested in subjects that can appear relatively abstract (Champoux, 1999; Comer, 2001; Holmes, 2005). Several writers have recommended particular films to teach certain subjects such as leadership, conflict, gender or business ethics (c.f. Berger & Pratt, 1998; Comer & Cooper, 1998; Harrington & Griffin, 1990; van Gelderen & Verduyn, 2003).

These analyses are predominantly reflectional in that they suggest film represents the social world to which it refers in a mirror-like fashion (Bell 2008). They thereby assume a high degree of correspondence between the film text and a pre-existing and objectively-knowable reality. The role of the management educator is therefore to raise students' awareness of the message contained within the film and to demonstrate how it relates to organization theory. This assumes that audiences will understand and respond to film in a similar way.

In addition to the use of film as a teaching resource, a newly emerging strand within organizational analysis suggests that film, alongside other forms of narrative fiction such as novels (Czarniawska-Joerges & de Monthoux, 1994), provides a source of data from which to generate theory (Foreman & Thatchenkery, 1996, 2003; Hassard & Buchanan, 2009). Influenced by the impact of the linguistic turn (Rorty, 1979), these writers reject the idea that knowledge is produced through scientific exploration. Instead they emphasize narrative knowledge, the value of which is measured by the convincingness of the interpretation rather than whether or not it is based on scientific data (Czarniawska, 1999; Linstead, 2003; Phillips, 1995).

The role of the management researcher is therefore to provide a convincing interpretation of the film using organization theory that makes sense of the narrative. Almost no attention is paid to audiences within these analyses since the only significant reader of the text is the organizational theorist. This is reinforced by the use of language such as 'the message of [the film] tells us' and 'the filmic representation also shows' (Foreman & Thatchenkery, 1996, p. 59) to indicate the singular authority of the interpretation that is offered.

Another way in which film has been understood in organization studies relates to its role as a device for communicating managerial ideologies and conversely, as a means of resisting and challenging these ideologies. Several authors working under the umbrella of Critical Management Studies have argued that film is of particular value in understanding organizational power relations through its depiction of issues of control, conflict and resistance (Bell, 2008; Hassard & Holliday, 1998; Parker, 2002; Rhodes & Westwood, 2008). These analyses focus on the role of film as a device of mass communication. They build upon insights from critical theory and specifically on the work of Marxist theorists Horkheimer and Adorno who, having fled from Germany to New York in the 1930s, were struck by the extent of mass consumerism in US society which they saw as related to the controlling effects of the culture industry. In *The Dialectic of Enlightenment*, Horkheimer and Adorno (1944) argue that film serves to construct illusions that perpetuate false consciousness in the general population, shaping individual subjectivities in ways that serve the interests of the capitalist system. They regard the Hollywood film industry as a device of moral correction, its purpose to ensure ongoing conformity and passivity by creating artificial and unrealizable desires for consumer goods and lifestyles that audiences see on the screen. Film is viewed as a narcotic distraction that distorts and impedes individuality by manipulating people's tastes and preferences and audiences are able to be 'injected' with a message, a perspective that is referred to as the 'hypodermic needle' model (Brooker & Jermyn, 2003). For Horkheimer and Adorno (1944), film audiences are child-like in their vulnerability, absorbing the messages communicated by the text and acting in accordance with them.

At an organizational level, this implies that film is a predominantly stabilizing influence which serves to reinforce existing organizational power relations and inequalities. Film, alongside other aspects of popular culture, functions as a safety valve for audiences, helping them to cope with their everyday organizational lives by expressing their frustrations, and thereby diffusing the possibility of more meaningful organizational protest. For example, in a scene from the comedy film *Office Space* (Judge, 1998), the young, male office workers take out their frustrations on the malfunctioning fax machine by 'kidnapping' it and taking it to a deserted field where they smash it to pieces with a baseball bat and their bare hands, backed by a Gangsta Rap soundtrack. Despite limited box office success, the film attained cult status on DVD (Sailer, 2006). Its success may be related to the way the film expresses common organizational frustrations (malfunctioning technology, irritating colleagues) and fears of audiences (downsizing, redundancy, management consultants). From a critical perspective, films like *Office Space* provide a hidden mechanism for maintaining stability in 'real' organizations. By providing a fictitious outlet for the expression of negative feelings, audiences are seen as less likely to resist them in their everyday lives. Films like *Office Space* and television shows like *The Simpsons* have been suggested to be of limited effectiveness in resisting managerial ideology since by 'encouraging viewers to laugh at their own employment situations', they act as a 'safety valve that actually buttresses organizations from a more thoroughgoing critique' (Rhodes, 2001, p. 382). This perspective leads to a negative view of film as an ideological instrument used to oppress subordinate groupings by manipulating them into inactivity.

However, some critical writers challenge this view of film audiences as victims of ideological indoctrination that serve organizational interests. Rhodes and Westwood (2008) argue that film and other aspects of popular culture are resistant to incorporation by the dominant culture. Moreover, they suggest film can overtly challenge many aspects of contemporary organization in a way that is often more effective than academic analyses. They emphasize the potential of film texts as a source of resistance that has the potential to transform organizations through the articulation of discourses that are critical of global capitalism and contemporary managerial practices. Parker (2002) too suggests the emergence of negative representations of organization in popular culture coincides with the emergence and growth of a broad societal critique of management since 1975. A further example of the transforming potential of film is provided by Ritzer (2007), who uses the example of *Fight Club* (Fincher, 1999) to illustrate how the 'globalization of nothing' may be confronted and resisted. He suggests that a 'dramatic change takes place when the movie's "hero" is introduced to the Fight Club, a place where he is able to find at least part of what has been lost in a modern consumerist society' (Ritzer 2007, p. 203). These writers see film as a catalyst for organizational resistance through communicating critiques to audiences that resonate with their everyday experience.

To summarize, critical authors have drawn attention to the role of film in communicating and resisting managerial ideologies. Within this category there are two strands of analysis. One emphasizes the role of film as a device that reinforces existing organizational power relations and inequalities. This assigns a passive role to audiences and tends to be deterministic, overestimating the extent of ideological domination, and denying the possibility of struggle. The second strand suggests film can be understood as challenging many aspects of contemporary organization. It assigns a highly active role to the audience, suggesting they are able to resist dominant organizational cultures through their engagement with film. It may therefore be criticized for overemphasizing the creativity of audiences and their potential for radicalism (Hall, 1986). Like other management educators, critical analysts portray audiences as a relatively homogenous grouping that can be commented on from a distance. Hence they refer to 'the viewer' as an anonymous entity whose responses are the same as their own (Spicer, 2001) or construct themselves as a 'model reader' (Eco, 1976) who reads the text from the perspective of its creator (see for example Rhodes & Westwood's [2008] analysis of the film, *Glengarry Glen Ross* [Foley, 1992]). They thereby claim an authority for their reading that detracts attention from the possibility of alternatives.

DIVERSE READINGS

The argument put forward in this chapter is that management scholars have underestimated audiences in their analyses of film. When audiences are mentioned they are usually assumed to be relatively passive and homogenous. This reinforces a stimulus-response model that portrays audiences as able to be injected with a message. However, the overwhelming trend in audience analysis suggests this is not the case (Brooker & Jermyn, 2003). Instead, studies have consistently demonstrated that audiences are active in their interpretations of film texts, to such an extent that the intended meaning of a film can sometimes be turned around by audience members who read it in a way that reverses the intended meaning. This is referred to as a 'boomerang effect' (Lazarsfeld et al., 1968).

One example of a boomerang effect concerns the film *Wall Street* (Stone, 1987) and the character, Gordon Gekko, a financial investor who represents the ruthless, short-term, asset-stripping culture associated with the late 1980s. Probably the most infamous line in the film is uttered by Gekko in his speech at a shareholders' meeting where he declares that 'greed is good'. The film's director, Oliver Stone intended the film as a social commentary on a society driven by material wealth and status (Denzin, 1990). The story ends with Gekko being imprisoned for his illegal insider-dealing activities. However, this was not how some members of its audience interpreted it, as represented in the film *Boiler Room* (Younger, 2000). In one scene from *Boiler Room* a group of young stock brokers sit at home watching *Wall Street* on TV and drinking beer. Far from finding Gekko's character problematic they appear to idolize him and can recite the words of his speech line by line, modeling their own organizational behaviors on the character. As this example powerfully illustrates, the way that audiences interpret the text depends on the cultural and organizational experiences that they bring to bear upon it and how they choose to read it. This can include using the text to develop and reinforce attitudes that are the opposite of those intended by the author.

Another example that illustrates the potential for diverse readings concerns the different interpretations of management educators presented with the same text. The film *Disclosure* (Levinson, 1994) represents the issue of sexual harassment in the workplace. According to producer-director Levinson, through a reversal of roles that makes the man rather than the woman the subject of harassment by a woman, the film sensitizes the audience to issues that they might not otherwise be aware of (cited in Brewis, 1998, p. 87). Comer and Cooper (1998) claim that their classroom audiences are convinced by the message of the film and conclude that its use as a teaching resource helps to reduce the prevalence of sexual harassment in the workplace. However, Brewis (1998) rejects this reading of the film in favor of a more critical interpretation. She argues that the film constitutes and consolidates understandings of working women as threatening and having no legitimate claim to organizational success. Brewis further suggests that by representing sexual harassment as highly erotic, the film invites a reading which fails to see it as unwanted and abusive. These authors are thus diametrically opposed in their reading of the same text and the conclusions they derive from it.

If management educators disagree in their interpretation of a film we should not be surprised if the gender, ethnicity, socio-economic class position, cultural values, lived experiences, and individual psychology of classroom audiences affects how they read film and the messages they take from it. What appeals to one audience member may horrify or bore another. A film that signifies subtleties of taste and cultural knowledge for certain audiences may seem outdated and irrelevant to others. In addition, management educators must acknowledge the possibility that their own tastes may be incomprehensible to others who do not interpret the text in the same way (Willis, 1995). Moreover, the choice of certain films and the preference for particularly masculine genres, such as science fiction (Corbett, 1995; Smith et al., 2001) or gangster films (Parker, 2008), may reveal more about the identity of the management educator than it does about the utility of certain films in illustrating management theory.

Instead of seeing these differences of interpretation as problematic because they disrupt the traditional model of using film to capture the attention of students as a precursor to the delivery of more traditionally packaged managerial knowledge from books and articles (Marx, Jick & Frost, 1991), they can provide a rich educational and analytical resource. However, for this to be realized, management educators must take a different approach to understanding the relationship between film and management theory. Rather than assuming that illustrations of a theory are contained in a particular film and all audiences have to do is watch and discuss it for this to become evident, a more inductive approach is needed. The role of the management educator in this context is to facilitate a process whereby audiences play a more active role in creating meaning through the text, helping them to draw out generalizable inferences from their engagement with the film rather than seeking to impose a particular interpretation upon them. The educator must assume that each reader negotiates their relationship with the film differently and explore what it means to each member of the audience. This approach carries greater uncertainty of learning outcome. It may be that audiences do not take away a message about leadership or strategy from a film because that is the topic that is being covered in the classroom that week. However, what they do learn is likely to better enable them to build relate abstract theory to lived experience.

This has the potential to stimulate greater reflection among students concerning the practice of management and their own identity as managers. It involves acknowledging the often profound investments that some audience members make in certain texts (Hollows & Jancovich, 1995) and exploring the role of these texts in conferring and confirming their identities. It also involves greater awareness of notions of relevance and comprehension and recognition that audience responses are dependent on their ability to make sense of a text (Morley, 1992). In addition, it requires an understanding of the motivations and pleasures of specific audiences in consuming these texts, including their social uses and the ways in which they enter into their lived organizational experience. Meaning is thus the result of a complex dialectical interplay between text and reader influenced by the historical and cultural context in which the reading takes place. Text and audience cannot therefore be seen as independent, nor can they be studied separately (Livingstone, 1993).

This may be more useful in the long run to students in a profession that lacks a secure body of knowledge to guide practice (Schon, 1983) and who may find themselves in situations where they are uncertain as to what management or being a manager really is (Watson, 1994). It involves recognition of the fact that it is through the activity of reading these texts that social activities like management are constructed and some of the identity work of being a manager is carried out. The section that follows outlines how this more audience-focused approach to the use of film as a teaching resource in management might be developed.

INTERPRETING AUDIENCES

One of the great advantages of using film as a management educator is that it provides the opportunity to understand film from the point of view of the audience. This entails exploration of the relationship that management students have with film texts. Writers like Ang (1991) suggest that one of the challenges in audience research arises from the dispersed nature of audiences and the private nature of their engagement with texts, viewing often taking place at home. This has led to a focus on methods of investigation that are primarily quantitative (e.g. box office figures and television viewing patterns), thereby overlooking the film's meaning, salience or impact on audiences. Management educators have access to students from a wide range of backgrounds. The challenge therefore is to identify methods for the qualitative investigation of this empirical resource that have mutual benefits to educators and students. In the section that follows, three qualitative methods that could be used by management educators to research film audiences are proposed: interviewing, ethnography and focus groups.

Interviewing Audiences

One way of investigating audiences is by conducting interviews with individuals who have seen a film that represents characters and issues that are closely related to their own identity. For example, in the film *Human Resources* (Cantet, 1999), Franck, an undergraduate student of business at a prestigious University in Paris returns to his home town to take up an industrial placement at his father's place of work. Unlike his father who works on the factory floor, Frank is given a position in the Human Resources department where he will be assessing the impact of recent legislation that limits the length of the working week. In another film, *Fear and Trembling* (Corneau, 2003), a young Japanese-born Belgian woman named Amélie gets a job in a large Japanese corporation where she is given all kinds of menial tasks including photocopying and making the coffee to test her loyalty and punish individualistic behaviors that her bosses associate with Westerners. In both films the central characters appear relatively powerless despite their education, more powerful organization members controlling their activities to a high degree.

I was interested in how undergraduate students who took my classes responded to these two films about being a junior employee in a large organization. Many of them study modern languages alongside their business school courses and are involved in university exchanges and workplace placements in other European countries. Did they empathize with the central characters and accept the *preferred* reading of the text as a commentary on the powerlessness of junior employees in large organizations? Or did they construct a *negotiated* reading in which they accepted parts of the text and rejected others? The final possibility was that they would reject the message of the text through an *oppositional* reading (Hall, 1980). I therefore devised the following set of questions:

- What is the film about?
- What did you think of it?
- What did you like about it?

- What didn't you like about it?
- Which character did you admire the most?
- What kind of person is the hero?
- What was the best scene? Why?
- Have you thought about the film since seeing it?

The questions were designed to allow the students to decide for themselves on the meaning of the films. From their answers it was possible to explore their interpretations as a process which involved them resisting, engaging with and creating meaning through their reading of the text in a way which was shaped and limited by their affiliations to management and management education and by their different cultural experiences.

Audience Ethnography

One way in which greater understanding may be gained of how audiences respond to and use film texts is through audience ethnography. Ethnographic methods offer the possibility for developing understanding of how people construct meaning around film through lived experience and cultural practices. For example, a number of recently released documentary feature films have been highly critical of management and business, including *The Corporation* (Abbot & Achbar, 2003), *Super Size Me* (Spurlock, 2004), *Fast Food Nation* (Linklater, 2006), *Black Gold* (Francis & Francis, 2006), and *Walmart: The High Cost of Low Price* (Greenwald, 2005). Greenwald has developed a system that involves 'Brave New Friends', people who volunteer to host film screenings in venues such as universities, churches, schools and local theatres. Details of the events are posted on the Brave New Theaters website: http://bravenewtheaters.com/home and many screenings include discussions after the film. Management educators could become involved in attending film screenings or in organizing them at their universities as a means of creating the opportunity for ethnographic study of audiences. This type of activity could provide a rich resource for understanding how certain groups use film texts as a resource for resisting management and organizations. It might involve analysis of why individuals identify with particular films and exploration of the influence that their spectatorship has on their everyday lives.

Focus Groups

Studies of audiences have shown that if a group identifies strongly with the issues represented in a film they are likely to develop a stronger attachment to it, often watching it several times and discussing it at length (Winick, 1963). Focus group interviewing can be used to gain access to such interpretive communities and their consumption of film texts. For example, a group of part-time, post-experience MBA students might be asked to nominate their own top ten favorite films about management. These lists are relatively common on the internet (e.g. Amazon.com 'Top 10 Business Movies'; the American.com '10 Best Business Movies' and 'Management Goes to the Movies' http://www.moviesforbusiness.com). Students could be encouraged to visit these sites as prior research for the task. The lists could then be collated and the three most popular films overall watched by the whole group. Focus group discussion following each screening would explore why the students were fans of the film. To increase the informality of the viewing environment a social atmosphere could be cultivated by serving drinks and snacks. This could thereby reduce the likelihood of students responding to the academic norms of a formal university context by expressing views that they think the management educator would want to hear (Ruddock, 2001). Discussion could explore audience members' evaluations and judgments of the fictional characters they see on the screen as a way of accessing definitions of what makes a good manager or an effective leader. It might also facilitate audience discussion of why the film is important to them and how their engagement with the text contributes to their own identity construction. The discussion could be video-recorded and used to produce a verbatim transcript. Analysis would involve looking for recurring themes that indicate commonalities of perception and interpretation. It might also enable comparison of the way that different groups, such as male and female students or students working in different sectors, interpret the same film. Internet and online university student discussion forums could also be used to study interpretive communities of management film audiences using similar methods.

CONCLUSION

This chapter has introduced the idea that audiences consume film actively and creatively, potentially deriving quite different meanings and messages from the same text. However, within management education audiences have usually been portrayed as passive recipients of meaning. Consequently, the role of the educator has focused on helping them to decipher the singular meaning of the text. Through outlining qualitative research methods which management educators could use to explore differences of interpretation among management students, the chapter has sought to develop a more sophisticated understanding of audiences. With the advent of YouTube and film distribution via the internet, the importance of film as a communicative resource among management students is only likely to increase. It is therefore important that we find new ways to explore how audiences interpret these texts and to understand how this informs their behavior and identity.

REFERENCES

Ang, I. (1991). *Desperately seeking the audience.* London, UK: Routledge.

Bell, E. (2008). *Reading management and organization in film.* Basingstoke, UK: Palgrave Macmillan.

Berger, J., & Pratt, C.B. (1998). Teaching business-communication ethics with controversial films. *Journal of Business Ethics, 17*(16), 1817–1823.

Brewis, J. (1998). What is wrong with this picture? Sex and gender relations in *Disclosure.* In J. Hassard & R. Holliday (Eds.) *Organization representation: Work and organizations in popular culture* (pp. 83–99). London, UK: Sage.

Brooker, W., & Jermyn, D. (2003). *The audience studies reader.* London, UK: Routledge.

Buchanan, D., & Huczynski, A. (2004). Images of influence: *12 Angry Men* and *Thirteen Days. Journal of Management Inquiry, 13*(4), 312–323.

Champoux, J. E. (1999). Film as a teaching resource. *Journal of Management Inquiry, 8*(2), 206–217.

Clegg, S., Kornberger, M., & Pitsis, T. (2008). *Managing and organizations.* London, UK: Sage.

Comer, D. R. (2001). Not just a Mickey Mouse exercise: Using Disney's *The Lion King* to teach leadership. *Journal of Management Education, 25*(4), 430–436.

Comer, D. R., & Cooper, E. A. (1998). Gender relations and sexual harassment in the workplace: Michael Crichton's *Disclosure* as a teaching tool. *Journal of Management Education, 22*(2), 227–241.

Corbett, M. (1995). Celluloid projections: Images of technology and organizational futures in contemporary science fiction film. *Organization, 2*(3/4), 467–488.

Czarniawska, B. (1999). *Writing management: Organization theory as a literary genre.* Oxford, UK: Oxford University Press.

Czarniawska-Joerges, B., & Guillet de Monthoux, P. (Eds.) (1994). *Good novels better management: Reading organizational realities in fiction.* Chur, Switzerland: Harwood Academic Publishers.

Denzin, N. K. (1990). Reading *Wall Street:* Postmodern contradictions in the American social structure. In B. S. Turner (Ed.) *Theories of modernity and postmodernity* (pp. 34–44). London, UK: Sage.

Eco, U. (1976). *The role of the reader: Explorations in the semiotics of texts.* London, UK: Indiana University Press.

Foreman, J., & Thatchenkery, T. J. (1996). Filmic representations for organizational analysis: The characterization of a transplant organization in the film *Rising Sun. Journal of Organizational Change Management, 9*(3), 44–61.

Foreman, J., & Thatchenkery, T. J. (2003). Representation of organizational change in Ron Howard's *Gung Ho.* In S. Linstead, (Ed.) *Text/Work: Representing organization and organizing representation.* London, UK: Routledge.

Hall, S. (1980). Encoding/Decoding. In S. Hall, D. Hobson, A. Lowe, & P. Willis (Eds.) *Culture, media, language* (pp. 128–138). London, UK: Hutchinson.

Hall, S. (1986). Cultural studies: Two paradigms. In R. Collins et al. (Eds.) *Media, culture and society: A reader* (pp. 33–48). London, UK: Sage.

Harrington, K. V., & Griffin, R. W. (1990). Ripley, Burke, Gorman and friends: Using the film "*Aliens*" to teach leadership and power. *Journal of Management Education, 14*(3), 79–86.

Hassard, J., & Holliday, R. (1998). (eds.) *Organization representation: Work and organizations in popular culture.* London, UK: Sage.

Hassard, J. S., & Buchanan, D. A. (2009). From *Modern Times* to *Syriana*: feature films as research data. In D. A. Buchanan & A. Bryman (Eds.) *Handbook of organizational research methods.* London, UK: Sage.

Hollows, J., & Jancovich, M. (1995). Popular film and cultural distinctions. In J. Hollows & M. Jancovich (Eds.) *Approaches to popular film* (pp. 1–14). Manchester, UK: Manchester University Press.

Holmes, R. A. (2005). Finding OB in Disney's *Finding Nemo. Organization Management Journal, 2*(2), 70–79.

Horkheimer M., & Adorno, T. (1944). *Dialectic of enlightenment: Philosophical fragments.* Stanford, CA: Stanford University Press.

Huczynski, A., & Buchanan, D. (2008). *Organizational behavior.* Harlow, UK: Pearson.

Lazarsfeld, P., Berelson, B., & Gaudet, H. (1968) *The people's choice: How the voter makes up his mind in a presidential campaign.* New York, NY: Columbia University Press.

Linstead, S. (2003). *Text/Work: Representing organization and organizing representation.* London, UK: Routledge.

Livingstone, S. M. (1993). The rise and fall of audience research: An old story with a new ending. *Journal of Communication, 43*(4), 5–12.

Marx, R. D., & Frost, P. J. (1998). Towards optimal use of video in management education: Examining the evidence. *Journal of Management Development, 17*(4), 243–50.

Marx, R. D., Jick, T. J., & Frost, P. J. (1991). *Management live! The video book.* Englewood Cliffs, NJ: Prentice Hall.

Morley, D. (1992). *Television, audiences and cultural studies.* London, UK: Routledge.

Parker, M. (2002). *Against management.* Cambridge, UK: Polity.

Parker, M. (2008). Eating with the Mafia: Belonging and violence. *Human Relations, 61*(7), 989–1006.

Phillips, N. (1995). Telling organizational tales: On the role of narrative fiction in the study of organizations. *Organization Studies, 16*(4), 625–649.

Rhodes, C. (2001). D'Oh: *The Simpsons*, popular culture, and the organizational carnival. *Journal of Management Inquiry, 10*(4), 374–383.

Rhodes, C., & Westwood, R. (2008). *Critical representations of work and organization in popular culture.* London, UK: Routledge.

Ritzer, G. (2007). *The globalization of nothing 2.* Thousand Oaks, CA: Pine Forge Press.

Rorty, R. (1979). *Philosophy and the mirror of nature.* Princeton, NJ: Princeton University Press.

Ruddock, A. (2001). *Understanding audiences.* London, UK: Sage.

Sailer, S. (2006). Mike Judge: *King of the Hill, VDare.Com* [http://www.vdare.com/sailer/060326_judge.htm—consulted 14.09.08]

Schon, D. (1983). *The reflective practitioner.* London, UK: Temple Smith.

Smith, W., Higgins, M., Parker, M., & Lightfoot, G. (Eds.). (2001). *Science fiction and organization.* London, UK: Routledge.

Spicer, A. (2001). Out of the cynical bind? A reflection on resistance in *Fight Club*. *Ephemera*, *1*(1), 92–102.

van Gelderen, M., & Verduyn, K. (2003). Entrepreneurship in the cinema: Feature films as case material in entrepreneurship education. *International Journal of Entrepreneurship Education*, *1*(4), 539–566.

Watson, T. (1994). *In search of management: Culture, chaos and control in managerial work*. London, UK: Routledge.

Willis, A. (1995). Cultural studies and popular film. In J. Hollows & M. Jancovich (Eds.) *Approaches to popular film* (pp. 173–191). Manchester, UK: Manchester University Press.

Winick, C. (1963). Tendency systems and the effects of a movie dealing with a social problem. *Journal of General Psychology*.*68*(April), 289–305.

Films

Achbar, M. & Abbott, J. (Directors). (2003). *The corporation* [Motion picture]. Canada: Big Picture Media Corporation.

Cantet, L. (Director). (1999). *Ressources humaines (Human resources)* [Motion picture]. France: La Sept-Arte & Haut et Court.

Corneau, A. (Director). (2003). *Stupeur et tremblements (Fear and trembling)*. [Motion picture]. France & Japan: Canal+, Divali Films, France 3 Cinéma, & Les Films Alain Sarde.

Fincher, D. (Director). (1999). *Fight club* [Motion picture]. United States & Germany: Fox 2000 Pictures & Regency Enterprises.

Foley, J. (Director). (1992). *Glengarry Glen Ross* [Motion picture]. United States: GGR.

Francis, M., & Francis, N. (Director). (2006). *Black gold* [Motion picture]. United Kingdom & United States: Fulcrum Productions & Speak-it Productions.

Greenwald, R. (Director). (2005). *Walmart: The High Cost of Low Price* [Motion picture]. United States: Brave New Films.

Judge, M. (Director). (1999). *Office space* [Motion picture]. United States: Twentieth Century Fox.

Levinson, B. (Director). (1994). *Disclosure* [Motion picture]. United States: Warner Bros.

Linklater, R. (Director). (2006). *Fast food nation* [Motion picture]. United Kingdom & United States: Recorded Picture Company, Participant Productions, Fuzzy Bunny Films, & BBC Films.

Spurlock, M. (Director). (2004). *Super size me* [Motion picture]. United States: Kathbur Pictures.

Stone, O. (Director). (1987). *Wall Street* [Motion picture]. United States: Twentieth Century Fox.

Younger, B. (Director). (2000). *Boiler room* [Motion picture]. United States: New Line Cinema & Team Todd.

CHAPTER 10

THE DRAMA OF FILMS

Andres Fortino

THE USE OF FILM TO TEACH MANAGEMENT

It is important to discover the basic principles under which successful drama is crafted and how it may be used appropriately as a basis for management education. Once understood and mastered, the use of film to teach management concepts and practices may be used appropriately in one's own classroom. When orchestrated carefully, the use of drama can provide a powerful transformative experience for the student. This practice should extend to all aspects of management beyond the usual application to the fields of organizational behavior and leadership so often seen, to include other areas, even those such as innovation management.

The award-winning, full-length motion picture *Shadow Magic* (Hu, 2000) is based on historical facts and fictionalizes the introduction of film technology to China at the start of the twentieth century. Used together with Everett Roger's work on the diffusion of innovation (Rogers, 1995), it assists in teaching aspects of the diffusion of innovation and various principles of technology adoption. Viewing the film becomes a common shared experience by the students in a class which, as I explain in the next section, may stimulate a 'cycle of learning' (Kolb & Fry, 1975). This may then be built

Moving Images: Effective Teaching with Film and Television in Higher Education,
pages 133–147

133

on by the instructor for further in-class case study work. Another major value of the work is self-reflection on the part of the students to discover their technology adoption roles (attitudes and preferences as adopters of technology). This chapter presents the use of the film in a technology and innovation management class, with appropriate assignments, to teach innovation management, technology adoption patterns, how to overcome barriers to adoption, and develop self-knowledge as a technology adopter.

STORY TELLING

According to the playwright David Mamet, "It is in our nature to dramatize" (Mamet, 2000, p. 2). The use of storytelling—dramatic storytelling—has its roots deep in human history. The Greeks used it to transmit cultural traditions and to teach character development to their youth through such works as Homer's Odyssey (Pagels, 1996). The same is true in all cultures. The need to dramatize goes beyond cultural purpose and permeates all aspects of our lives. Some argue that drama fulfills a basic human need.

> The dramatic urge [is] our impulse to structure cause and effect in order to increase our store of practical knowledge about the universe... It is enjoyable, like music, like politics, and like theater, because it exercises, it flatters, and it informs our capacity for rational synthesis—our ability to learn a lesson, which is our survival mechanism. (Mamet, 2000, p. 7)

As management educators we can take advantage of this deep need and overarching human drive to create order by harnessing drama to teach management principles. Rather than become dramatists ourselves (although we may occasionally lapse into this role to make a point), we could make use of good drama to educate, to exemplify principle, and to illumine a point of practice.

> We dramatize an incident by taking events and reordering them, elongating them, compressing them so that we understand their personal meaning to us—to us as the protagonist of the individual drama we understand our life to be. (Mamet, 2000, p. 5)

Key to this process is to (a) select good drama, as embodied in a film in our current case; (b) envision the application of the story and its characters to the management point being illustrated; and finally, (c) orchestrate the educational experience for best effect.

The Kolb Cycle and Use of Transformational Experiences

David Kolb (together with Fry) created the now famous model of learning consisting of four elements: the concrete experience, followed by periods of observation and reflection, followed by the formation of abstract concepts, and then the testing of new-found knowledge and wisdom in new situations (Kolb & Fry, 1975). He claimed these steps are foundational to learning by adult learners.

Figure 1 diagrams the cycle and the four elements as applied to the use of film as experiential learning. Although Kolb argues that the cycle is a spiral and that the learner may start the learning cycle at any one of the four points, the learner most often begins by carrying out a particular action (step 1) and then observing the effect of the action in a given situation (step 2). The period of reflection would follow and starts the internalization process, from which general principles are derived (step 3) and used as a foundational model of reality to be used as a basis for future action (step 4.).

In translating Kolb's model to the use of drama and film, activity of viewing the film becomes the initial action by the learner which starts the learning cycle. The learner must come to the experience with some foreknowledge of the topic to be studied. To this store of knowledge we add the film, plus the orchestrated set of questions on which students must focus their attention. The film becomes the concrete case where the principles are showcased and played out. The assignment must be reflective, both to allow the student to extract meaning from the experience and to derive new knowledge, and to be self-reflective to allow for the generation of self-knowledge. The application of this new knowledge comes from additional assignments in the course. The educator then has a common shared experi-

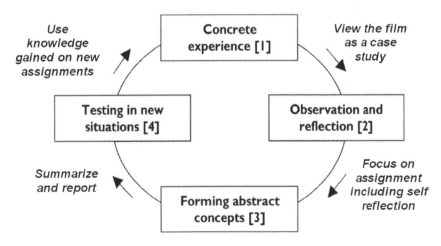

FIGURE 1. The Kolb Learning Cycle applied to the use of film viewing for learning.

ence (the film) with students which can be used for further case discussion and to build upon for future assignments.

Use of Film Embodies Good Educational Practice

Chickering and Ehrmann (1996) advocates the use of technology as good educational practice in teaching students with diverse learning styles. In his paper on educational practice, the last, and seventh, "good practice" he advocates is respect for students' diverse talents and ways of learning. All students need opportunities to show their talents and learn in ways that work for them. Technology (film in this case) can be harnessed as a:

> different method [...] of learning through powerful visuals and well-organized print; through direct, vicarious, and virtual experiences; and through tasks requiring analysis, synthesis, and evaluation, with applications to real-life situations. They can encourage self-reflection and self-evaluation. They can drive collaboration and group problem solving. Technologies can help students learn in ways they find most effective and broaden their repertoires for learning. (Chickering & Ehrmann, 1996, p. 4)

Film viewing as a group activity, together with case questions based on the film to be answered by the group as a whole, both capitalizes on the diversity of talent and viewpoints, and allows for the effect Chickering and Ehrmann (1996) advocates. Not only will students find the mastery of principles easier but they will assimilate knowledge more quickly. Chickering and Ehrmann(1996) argues that the whole experience of viewing a film with subsequent assignments and application to further learning produces a deeper transformation. Films are one embodiment of the more encompassing genre we term drama. We use films because of the accessibility and convenience as containers of drama. It is drama in general I use in the discussion of educational practice advocated here.

THE NATURE AND APPLICATION OF DRAMA

Basic Components of Drama

Mamet is acclaimed as one of the modern era's greatest playwrights and dramatists. His classic book *The Three Uses of the Knife* (Mamet, 2000) is used regularly and widely to teach young dramatists their craft. It provides an excellent source of guidance for how good drama is constructed, and more importantly, why it is created.

> Artists don't set out to bring anything to the audience or to anyone else. They set out to ... cure a raging imbalance. Artists don't wonder, 'What is it good for?' They aren't driven to 'create art,' or to 'help people,' or to 'make money.' They are driven to lessen the burden of the unbearable disparity between

their conscious and unconscious mind, and so to achieve peace. (Mamet, 2000, p. 67)

These comments give us the insight that, in selecting good drama for teaching, it is not that important to find out 'what the artist intended', or 'what point' the artist was trying to make. The drama itself depicts a slice of life, a commentary on historical or current events. It is a compressed look (over several hours) at the human condition. It can be effectively used to teach management principles, no matter what the artist intended, because

> It is in the nature of our reasoning faculty to order perceived elements of threat, to identify and structure them so that we can consider alternative methods of overcoming them, and implement the best plan....The drama excites us as it recapitulates and calls into play the most essential element of our being, our prized adaptive mechanism. (Mamet, 2000, p. 67)

Most drama is created in three acts: hero is given a quest, hero struggles with the quest, hero triumphs in the quest (heroines too). 'Hero quests' are part of the mythology of all cultures (Campbell, 1972). These three acts are fundamental to drama.

> Dramatic structure is... an exercise of a naturally occurring need or disposition to structure the world as thesis/antithesis/synthesis. Dramatic structure is not an arbitrary—or even conscious—invention. It is an organic codification of the human mechanism for ordering information. Event, elaboration, denouement: thesis, antithesis, synthesis: boy meets girl, boy loses girl, boy gets girl: act one, two three. (Mamet, 2000, p. 67)

This sort of 'Good' drama keeps our attention through all of its three acts and smoothly carries us through from start to end. Recognizing well-crafted drama is important in selecting the appropriate film to orchestrate the learning experience. For maximum transformation it must have an emotional impact and it must grip the student. This seldom includes a great deal of violence (and often none at all). And it always illumines some aspect of the human condition.

Since dramatists strive for emotional engagement, rather than crafting a message, we should rely upon the work of fiction to do two things: (1) to help us make *our* point, assist the student in realizing the point we are trying to make and draw their own conclusions; and (2) to be good drama in order to maximize its transformative power. The good dramatist understands that:

> the purpose of the theater is not to fix the social fabric, not to incite the less perceptive to wake up and smell the coffee, not to preach to the converted about delights (or the burdens) of a middle class life. The purpose of the

theater, like magic, like religion—those three harness mates—is to inspire cleansing awe. (Mamet, 2000, p. 69)

Capturing the powerful force of drama to teach is a great asset to us as management educators.

Selecting Dramas and Films to Teach

The use of film to teach management concepts and practice has been gaining greater acceptance among management educators. Compilations of films and guides to using them are increasingly common (Champoux, 2000). Presentations on the use of film as teaching platforms by Academy of Management members at its annual conferences is routine (Johnson, 2003). Some films, such as documentaries, are both factual and educational in nature to start with. They represent good history or good reporting and have their place as teaching vehicles. However an additional and different approach is advocated here: the use of dramatic fiction, properly orchestrated, can effect an emotional transformation that drives home important educational lessons in the viewing student.

When using fiction, and drama in particular, one may show short clips or use the entire film. Some educators use short film clips in class to make a point and as a basis for class discussion. This can be a powerful tool if effectively used. It is similar to the foundational scenes in the settings of case studies (Barnes, Christensen, & Hansen, 1987). Clips help all students understand the setting for the case to be studied and discussed or the principle to be taught in the lectures that follow.

Use of Full-Length Films

Some films, as well as some assignments, lend themselves to the use of the entire film. In such cases it takes the majority, if not the entire film, to see the principles played out and demonstrated. Such is the case for example with using *Jurassic Park* (Spielberg, 1993) to teach principles of software system design. The film shows the disastrous consequences of developing a software system by a single developer of dubious loyalty; one who is the sole owner of passwords, source code and system details; and who, when he dies, takes with him the necessary information that can restore order to *Jurassic Park* after disaster strikes. Throughout the film, many best practice system design rules are broken. The drama that unfolds is punctuated with these "should have" lessons in system design. Some two dozen such lessons are sprinkled through the film, and these would lose their dramatic and transformative impact if shown as short clips. For full effect, one must see the cumulative impact and consequence of these poor practices as the story unfolds.

Assigning the students to view the entire *Jurassic Park* film in teams allows for sufficient discussion and discovery of all best practices. The assignment could be to create the most exhaustive list of best practices (or poor practices) as possible, with elements of team competition thrown in to enhance the transformation that takes place. This film makes a good assignment in Management Information Systems courses.

The same is true with the film *Executive Suite* (Wise, 1954) where a major drama unfolds in corporate governance. Once again, this can only exemplify basic principles if viewed in its entirety. Although the film was created in the fifties, the drama played out in film, the issues presented, and the character types depicted, are all timeless. The film affords the educator the opportunity to teach organizational leadership at top corporate levels, including a healthy dose of corporate ethics which are so important in to-day's curriculum. Again, this is an example where re-viewing the entire film maximizes the educational impact.

Shadow Magic, the subject of the in-depth case study below, is another example of a drama best used in its full length.

CASE STUDY: USING THE FILM *SHADOW MAGIC*

The film *Shadow Magic* depicts in fictional form the introduction of film technology to China at the start of the twentieth century. It shows both the diffusion of the producer side of the technology, the birth of the nascent film industry, as well as the trials and tribulations of the adoption of films as entertainment by the Chinese people. It is a good case study on the stages of innovation introduction and development and the subsequent diffusion of the innovation through the adoption cycle. All major actors in the innovation process are well illustrated (Rogers, 1995). The hero of the story, for example, illustrates the trials and tribulations of an early adopter. In addition, some elements of the innovator after the process of re-invention is shown as well. The time frame of the one-and-a-half-hour film takes place over twelve months, with follow-up documentary material at the end of the film to demonstrate the full diffusion of the technology over subsequent years.

The film is based on apparent documented historical fact of a well-known Chinese opera actor being recorded for a documentary (shown at the end of the film) as well as scenes of early twentieth century Chinese village life. The film fictionalizes established traditional businesses defending their investment in the incumbent technologies of still photography, as well the live entertainment arts (Chinese opera performances) attacking the technology of film making and the innovative business of entertainment. The innovation of film eventually gains acceptance by the majority of consumers (the Chinese people), but not before having to gain the very necessary approval of influential opinion makers, such as the Chinese Empress herself. As the technology gains acceptance and develops a consumer base, the business managers of opposing businesses begin to see the opportunities and, as late adopters, begin to join rather than fight the protagonist, taking advantage of the success of the new technology.

Using Film to Teach Innovation Management

The film may be used to teach technology managers some basic principles of innovation and technology management. It is important for the technology manager (TM) to understand the process by which innovations appear and the creative destruction process that develops in its wake. Some TMs may be creators of technology, but all of them are adopters of technology. Using a film such as *Shadow Magic* allows the student of technology to observe within only an hour and a half, and in a very dramatic manner, the entire cycle of creation, disruption, diffusion, defense by incumbent technologies, the eventual triumph of the innovator, and the accommodation of the new technology by the incumbents.

Why is this important to the technology manager? Technology churn brings with it many challenges, and the TM must be prepared to cope and profit from these. By observing the cycle of innovation introduction and diffusion, the TM may be able to analyze current technologies and their status and in the process be able to evaluate the readiness of a technology for adoption. Adopt too early and the manager incurs the bleeding edge risk of failing, due to too high an expense, or betting on a technology that may not cross the chasm (Moore, 1999). Adopt too late and the TM incurs the trailing edge risk of not taking advantage of technology being used by competitors and of being left behind in the competitive business struggle. The TM wants to know when to get on the leading edge of a technology and adopt organizational-wide for greatest benefit.

Through the film-viewing experience and subsequent reflective assignments, the TM can learn to be an astute industry watcher waiting and adopting as technologies cross in and out of the leading-edge domain. And the TM can only do this successfully if aware of what the process is, what the signs are, and how to interpret them properly. All the principles of creative destruction of Schumpeterian economics (Schumpeter, 1942), and diffusion of innovation (Rogers, 1995), may be seen, understood and assimilated by properly guiding the viewing experience and by giving critical follow-up assignments and discussion. (Appendix A shows a typical assignment).

Orchestration of the Transformation

Drama may be used effectively to teach these principles. It can be done with short clips or the full-length motion picture. In this case we expect to take advantage of the entire film since all aspects of the diffusion process are shown, including excellent depictions of all major adoptive categories through very impressive dramatic performances.

Viewing the film, as well as crafting answers to a lengthy set of questions based on the definitions of the diffusion of innovation (Rogers, 1995), may be assigned as a required group activity. Assigned reading of Roger's book and a short lecture on diffusion of innovation sets the stage for the transformative experience of viewing the film and answering the questions. A follow up discussion after the assignment is completed wraps up the experience and drives the major points home.

In-Class Viewing Versus Assigned Viewing

I would recommend that the actual viewing of the film should not take place in class. Class time is becoming more and more rare as we move toward a blended model of education (using distance technologies) and away from the Carnegie Unit model of graduate education (Lagemann, 1983). It is useful to make this a group rather than an individual experience to allow for maximum exercise of students' learning modalities (Chickering & Ehrmann, 1996; Gardner, 1993).

Interpersonal learners get an opportunity to discuss the meaning of the film with fellow classmates in the context of the questions. The visual learners, of course, get a high-content visual and aural experience; and the musical learners have a high-value musical score of the film to accompany the learning experience. The intrapersonal learners will have a reflective experience to go with this assignment (see below). Compiling answers and writing the report on behalf of the group satisfies those who learn best via the written word; and due to the informal nature of the experience, the kinesthetic learner is free to move about during the viewing (something not possible in the three hours of class time). In this way, the principles of active learning are satisfied and a major transformational experience is accomplished, without using a minute of class time watching a film.

As the students return to class the following session, the tutor may debrief and encourage them to explore the experience more deeply, anchoring the lessons of the assignment.

Self-Reflective Assignment

The subject matter (diffusion of innovation with actors), purpose of the assignment (discover how innovations diffuse and who the actors are), and the nature of the experience (dramatic) lends the assignment to fulfill additional purposes. In the true tradition of the self-reflective manager (Argyris, 1999), we can assign the TM student to reflect on their role in the technology adoption process. They can ponder what role they are comfortable with by identifying with any one person or group of characters in the drama. In the case of adoption of innovation, they can carry this identification to their role as adopters of technology. It is important to make it clear that there is no right answer to this part of the assignment, but one of true self-discovery. The educator points out that it is important to know the level of risk and personal comfort level one TM is willing to accept as a TM with respect to the creative destruction process. Thus if in their current job they are asked to go against type (they are a late adopter by temperament but are tasked to take high risks as innovators), they can successfully carry out their task, albeit uncomfortably.

In the assignment the students are asked to identify further how they personally adopt technology to discover their true adopting nature, what role they are asked to take on the job, and become aware of any underlying dichotomies. Calibration of their self-knowledge discoveries may be done by requiring the student to query work colleagues and/or student team members to give them feedback on the accuracy of their findings.

Each group assignment is complemented by individual reports on each student's self-reflections. The group answers are graded for accuracy and perceptiveness in understanding the diffusion process as depicted in the film. The individual answers are graded for effort, honesty and level of self-discovery (epiphanies) demonstrated in the self-reflective process.

Self Identification With the 'Hero' of the Story—A Caveat

To achieve maximum effect the dramatist strives to make the viewer identify with 'the hero' (Mamet, 2000). This is the nature of traditional drama, to follow the hero through trials and tribulations, and eventually triumph in the assigned quest. The film maker, due to the nature of the craft, is able through the use of camera techniques, dialogue and action sequences to focus our attention even further on the hero. Identification and empathy with the hero is one of the cornerstones of good film making.

In the use of film to teach management, the educator must be aware of the consequences of students identifying too closely with the hero, which may yield a false positive in the self-reflective assignment. The hero of *Shadow Magic* happens to be an early adopter of technology and even a re-inventor in his own right. Some of the characters have been made distasteful for the purpose of the drama. Identification with these characters may be difficult because of emotional expectations and barriers. Care must be exercised to warn to the students to this effect and to be critical and impartial in their analysis to obtain an honest and authentic self-assessment.

Several groups of students that have completed an assignment based on *Shadow Magic* appeared to have an unusual high number of self-reported early adopters. The question is: Do these students identify too closely with the early adopter hero, and thus miss identification of their true adopter style? Several independent tests were devised to assure the students that they were not under the influence of the dramatic constructs of the film and to reinforce that self-reflection is a useful process. It was found that technology managers who had not seen the film classified themselves in the same proportions of adopter categories (with a high percentage of self-reported early adopters) as the students who had seen the film when give the opportunity to reflect on their own roles. Further, the students were asked to fill out an online survey that ranked their propensity to adopt leading edge technologies (Newsweek, 2003). The score on the Digital IQ test conducted online by *Newsweek* correlated very well with Roger's innovation adopter categories as well as student's self-reported adopter status (see Figure 2).

It should be noted that even actions by the anti-hero or unsavory characters may be used to illustrate a point. The educator may point out in the discussion that follows viewing that even if the CFO in the film performed unethical acts, as in *Executive Suite*, the vast majority of CFOs are ethical business people and conduct themselves in a professional manner. In *Shadow Magic* the apparent villain in the character of the owner of the incumbent still photography business demonstrated the role of the laggard

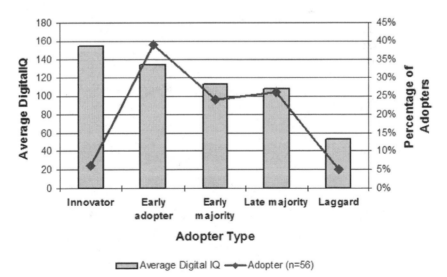

Digital IQ Identification of Adopter Type

FIGURE 2.   Relationship between self-reported Newsweek's Digital IQ test score and adopter category, including self-reported adopter modality.

adopter. Students, who upon self reflection discovered they were laggard adopters themselves, nevertheless were articulate defenders of this point of view after viewing the film.

Additional Teaching Opportunities—Teaching the Cultural Dimension

The educator should be alert for additional teaching opportunities when a using film or drama. Sometimes it happens that the story line is based on another culture. If the cultural dimension is depicted accurately and with sensitivity, additional lessons may be possible. Management students should not miss opportunities to develop and deepen their cultural mind-sets (Jeannet, 2000). In our use of *Shadow Magic* we found North American students became better acquainted with Chinese culture and appreciated that the process of introduction of innovation is universal but with important local cultural variations. When presented with such opportunities, it is useful to add assignment questions to explore the cultural dimension, whether to compare and contrast with each student's personal culture or to show the universality of certain principles that cut across cultures.

CONCLUSION

Orchestrating learning experiences in management topics using drama, specifically using full-length motion pictures, can be a powerful transformative experience. Orchestration of the experience must be carefully carried out. Knowledge of how drama is created by modern storytellers assists the faculty to properly select the film and match it to the subject to be taught and the type of experience being designed. It would very useful to continue to extend the work of creating a database of films (Champoux, 2000) and their appropriateness to teaching certain subject matter.

APPENDIX A: INTRODUCTION OF MOVING PICTURE TECHNOLOGY IN CHINA AT THE TURN OF THE TWENTIETH CENTURY

Diffusion of Innovation Team and Individual Assignment based on Everett Rogers' Diffusion of Innovation and the film "Shadow Magic"

Instructions

- Read the instructions for the assignment before starting.
- Read the questions at the end this assignment.
- Read the definitions used by Rogers in his book "Diffusion of Innovation" as summarized in the handout.

Team assignment

- Watch the film "Shadow Magic" with your team. Keep in mind the questions below as you watch.
- Go through the questions and answer each one as a team. Use the summary of Rogers' definitions as a guide as the meanings of the questions.
- Submit a team written report as paragraphs under each question as if you were writing an FAQ.
- Clearly identify your team and teammates names at the header of the report. A written report team is expected.

Individual Assignment

- Each team member should consider their own attitude towards innovation (are they an innovator, early adopter, late adopter or laggard). There is no right answer here, just an honest self examination.
- Identify your perceived role in the diffusion process and your comfort level with being a change agent or not. Write a paragraph on your analysis on which adopter category you consider yourself in with examples showing how you take this approach towards innovation, and a paragraph or two on your comfortableness, or not, with the role of change agent. Which character in the film do you identify with?
- Your one page report should be handed in attached to the team report. It should have your name at the top left, and the date and be labeled: "Personal Self-Assessment of Adopter and Change Agent Role."

Questions

1. What was the **innovation** being diffused in the film? Describe it.
2. Over what period of **time** was the innovation introduced as shown in the film? Short term over the length of the film, long term over the whole innovation diffusion cycle.
3. Describe the **social system** as the environment for the diffusion of the technology.
4. What was the **technology** being introduced (refer to definitions)? Describe it.
5. What technology was being replaced or threatened?
6. What industry was being replaced or threatened?
7. In the **innovation-decision process** shown in the film was the innovation adopted or rejected? Give examples to illustrate your answer.

8. Categorize each of the main characters and groups of the film into the various adopter categories: **innovators, early adopters, early majority, late majority, and laggards**. For each person give one or two attributes that exemplifies why they are being characterized as such and one or two sentences describing a situation where they exhibit this adoption characteristic.
9. Briefly describe the **social system** that is the setting for the diffusion of the innovation.
10. Describe some of the **norms** of the social system.
11. Who held the **opinion leadership** position in the social system?
12. Who acted as the **change agent**?
13. Who made the **collective innovation-decisions** to adopt?
14. Name all those who made the **authority innovation-decisions** in the end and the result of their decision.
15. What did people believe that the innovation was going to replace and what did the early adopters believe was the **relative advantage** of the innovation.
16. Did the innovation replace or extend the early activity/process?
17. Was the innovation shown in the film perceived as **compatible** with the existing values, past experiences, and needs of potential adopters?
18. At what point in the film did the innovation achieve **critical mass** for adoption?
19. At what point in the film was a threshold for adoption reached? Describe.
20. Give at least two **consequences** as a result of the adoption of the innovation. Classify each as (1) desirable versus undesirable, (2) direct versus indirect, and (3) anticipated versus unanticipated.

REFERENCES

Argyris, C. (1999). *On organizational learning*. Cambridge, MA: Blackwells.

Barnes, L. B., Christensen, C. R., & Hansen, A. J. (1987). *Teaching and the case method*. Boston, MA: Harvard Business School Press.

Campbell, J. (1972). *The hero with a thousand faces (Mythos Books)*. Princeton, NJ: Princeton University Press.

Champoux, J. E. (2000). *Management: Using film to visualize principles and practices*. Cincinnati, OH: South-Western College Publishing.

Chickering, A., & Ehrmann, S. C. (1996). *Implementing the seven principles: Technology as lever*. AAHE Bulletin, October, 3–6.

Jeannet, J. P. (2000). *Managing with a global mindset*. Englewood Cliffs, NJ: Financial Times Prentice Hall.

Johnson, C. D. (2003). *Turning the silver screen into classroom gold! Using full length films for competency development*. Paper presented at the Academy of Management Annual Meeting, Seattle, WA.

Kolb. D. A., & Fry, R. (1975). Toward an applied theory of experiential learning. In C. Cooper (Ed.) *Theories of group process.* London, UK: John Wiley.

Lagemann, E. C. (1983). *Private power for the public good: A history of the Carnegie Foundation for the Advancement of Teaching.* Middletown, CT: Wesleyan University Press.

Mamet, D. (2000). *Three uses of the knife.* New York, NY: Vintage Books.

Moore, G. (1999). *Crossing the chasm* (revised ed.). New York, NY: Harper Business.

Newsweek (2003). *Test your digital IQ.* Retrieved January 4, 2004 from http://msnbc. msn.com/id/3338562/

Pagels, R. (Trans.). (1996). Homer. *The Odyssey.* New York, NY: Viking Press.

Rogers, E. M. (1995). *Diffusion of innovation* (4th ed.) New York, NY: The Free Press.

Schumpeter, J. A. (1942). *Capitalism, socialism and democracy.* New York, NY: Harper Perennial.

Films

Hu, A. (Director). (2000). *Shadow magic* [Motion picture]. China, Germany, Taiwan, & United States: Beijing Film Studio, C & A Productions, Central Motion Pictures Corporation, China Film, Filmstiftung Nordrhein-Westfalen, Post Production Playground, Road Movies Vierte Produktionen, Schulberg Productions, & Taiwan Central Motion Picture Corporation.

Spielberg, S. (Director). (1993). *Jurassic Park* [Motion picture]. United States: Universal Pictures.

Wise, R. (Director). (1954). *Executive suite* [Motion picture]. United States: Loew's.

CHAPTER 11

USING MOVING IMAGES IN MANAGEMENT EDUCATION

Technology, Formats, Delivery, and Copyright

Joseph E. Champoux and Jon Billsberry

Although it may be true to say that "technology is moving faster today than ever before," it should not be forgotten that technology is always changing. This is particularly true of the technology used to show moving images in the classroom. Over the past fifty years, educators have gone from using reels of film on projectors through to online and digital sources today. Changes to both the hardware and software is removing the walls from the management classroom and allowing students to view moving images wherever and whenever they wish. At times there seems a dizzying array of technological choices to be made. Our intention in this chapter is to consider the main technological choices that educators have to make when considering the use of moving images in their classrooms. We hope this is a practical chapter giving advice and suggestions based on our mistakes, disasters and occasional triumphs.

Moving Images: Effective Teaching with Film and Television in Higher Education,
pages 149–158
Copyright © 2012 by Information Age Publishing

IN THE 'CLASSROOM'

Live Broadcasts

Many people's first memory of encountering moving images in the class-room will be sitting around a television with classmates whilst at school. In the UK, weekday morning television used to consist of broadcasts made by the BBC for schools. Children would gather in front of a television in their classroom at the appointed hour and be part of a national viewing audi-ence. Jon, the second author, remembers the weekly viewing of the 25-min-ute program *Music Time* (BBC, 1970–1991) and playing along to Prokofiev's Lieutenant Kijé as a eight or nine year old primary school pupil in the early 1970s. The local council would hold recitals based on the broadcast material that enabled classes from schools in the town to perform together. Thinking back to his primary school, this is one of the most vivid educa-tional memories; in fact he cannot recall any other aspect of the teaching in those years, not even the name of his teachers.

These days, having students watch a live broadcast in the management classroom is an unlikely occurrence. The stricture of timetabling makes it a lucky chance coincidence if a desirable live broadcast fits with a teaching slot. Additionally, live broadcasts can usually be 'taped' to give the instruc-tor more flexibility in the use and analysis of the clip. Where live broadcasts may be useful is when an instructor wants to explore the implications of one event on predictable outcomes. Imagine, for instance, in a finance class where the announcement of corporate results (often done on live podcasts rather than live television) or of major Governmental initiatives, or the tes-timony of an important official to an important oversight committee, might be predicted to have an impact on stock prices or exchange rates. Analyz-ing these events live may add a frisson as well as show the immediacy of response.

It is perhaps too obvious to mention, but the key bit of advice with using live broadcasts, regardless of the media used, is to tune in early. Establish the link and resolve any technical problems long before the broadcast starts. We have heard of televisions that are delivered to rooms without the right cabling, televisions not tuned in, and live podcasts requiring passwords. Do not expect to be able to switch on the equipment at the appointed hour and have a trouble-free viewing.

Reels of Film

Arguably, none of the modern ways to watch films capture the excite-ment of watching films shown from a real reel-to-reel projector in the class-room. The sound of the machine, the flickering images, and the shaft of light aimed at the screen all provide intimacy and fix attention. There is something wonderfully atmospheric watching films in this way. This is likely to be something that people who attended school in the 1970s and before have experienced. Jon vividly recalls the use of reel-to-reel projectors in his geography lessons in the late-1970s. The memories of rubber production in Malaysia, women walking around with large water butts in their heads in East Africa, and town planning in Milton Keynes are as vivid to him today as the first time he saw the films.

Although it might be a challenge to find a reel-to-reel projector these days, this technology still has a place in the management classroom. At the Academy of Management in Philadelphia in 2007, we spent a pleasant afternoon at the top of the Loew's Hotel in the company of Chuck Wrege viewing a selection of films from his extraordinary archive. These included early corporate promotional films, 'fly-on-the-wall' type documentary films about work, advertisements, and more general films about work and working life in the first half of the 20th Century. These are valuable as historical documents and help to put research from the period into perspective. The images of the Hawthorne Works, for example, illustrate its vastness, the nature of work there, and act as vital background to films like *Metropolis* (Lang, 1927), *À Nous la Liberté* (Clair, 1931), and *Modern Times* (Chaplin, 1936).

Getting access to such films is problematic, but film libraries still exist and they will loan out films. Other libraries are digitizing these films making access much easier, even though this does lose a little of the 'magic.' The Library of Congress, available through iTunesU or directly (http://www.loc.gov/library/libarch-digital.html), is a particularly good starting point. Using them in the classroom works well with teaching approaches where students are encouraged to seek out, analyze and critique primary data.

VHS Videotapes

Video Home System (VHS) videotapes changed the usage of film in education. Both pre-recorded and user-recorded tapes made showing films considerably easier than previously. With the arrival of VHS tapes (and Betamax, but we will concentrate on the victor in this format battle in this chapter) came a much greater availability of films. It allowed movies and TV programs to feature in the armory of the educator for the first time, practically speaking. Assuming the hardware to play VHS tapes was available in the classroom, all the instructor had to do was purchase the tape, cue it up to the appropriate point, and press 'PLAY' on the machine for the material to spring into life. With VHS, analysis of film was practical for the first time. Films could be rewound, played in slow motion, or even frozen allowing the study of micro-behavior as well as the bigger issues from the source. Having the ability to record from broadcast sources further expanded the usefulness of this source and, in many countries, it was, and still is, legally permissible for instructors to show their own recordings from broadcast sources in the classroom in many countries; please note that this differs by country and is not allowed in the USA (see later).

VHS tapes offer the considerable advantages of ease of use, simple cueing, the ability to record content from other sources, and a relatively straightforward process for duplicating material. However, they are not perfect. Trying to show more than one clip from a film, unless they are sequential clips, is clumsy; fast forwarding to the appropriate place is difficult to achieve smoothly. Also the quality of the image and sound could easily be compromised. 'Tracking' would often be off, meaning that the image might wobble or be distorted. The sound has some 'tape hiss.' And it is uncommon to have more than one player in the room making group work with VHS films rarely possible.

DVDs

Using Digital Versatile Disks (aka Digital Video Disks; DVDs) resolved many of these problems. In particular, the image and sound quality was much better with its digital source and navigation to different parts of the film or program could be quick and slick (after a little practice).

DVDs are not the perfect solution. The most annoying feature of most DVDs is that when you put one in a drive they insist on playing copyright notices and film trailers before the film menu is available. On some disks, it can take ten minutes before the film can be accessed. This presents a considerable problem if the film cannot be cued-up beforehand. It makes using more than one DVD in a session particularly awkward. Fortunately, there is a trick that can be used to get around this problem. Most DVD players and playing software has a 'play from last position' function, which overrides the disk's desire to be played from the start of the notices and advertisements. All you need do is to insert the disk and go to the position on the disk where you want to start. Press pause or stop and eject the disk. Do this for each disk. Then, when you put each one in, it should start playing from where you left off.

One important benefit of DVDs is the ubiquity of hardware needed to play them. Most students' personal computers will have a DVD drive and appropriate software enabling them to play DVDs on their own machines. This feature changes the possibilities for using film in the management classroom. No longer is film just a supplement to a lecture. Instead, activities can be created that allow students to read, explore, analyze, and critique films individually or in small groups.

Digital Files

Technically, the DVD is really just a delivery format. It is a collection of digital files on a 'handy-to-use' disk. At the time of writing (2011), the

DVD may itself be rapidly becoming obsolete. A much improved form of disk called 'Blu-Ray' has won a high definition format battle (akin to the VHS vs. Betamax battle of the early 1980s) and is rapidly gaining a presence in the market. A Blu-ray disk looks just like a DVD, but it can contain approximately ten times the amount of information (depending on which formats of DVD and Blu-ray disks are being compared) and this results in much sharper pictures and better sound. Lecture theatres are now being equipped with these players, but it is still unusual for personal computers to have Blu-ray drives.

Digital files do not need to come on a disk, DVD or Blu-ray. A digital file is simply a computer file and as such can use all the media associated with transferring computer files such as USB sticks, hard drives, and online delivery. Interestingly, some Blu-ray releases of films are coming out with three formats in the box; a DVD disk, a Blu-ray disk, and a digital file. *Toy Story 3* (Unkrich, 2010), *Despicable Me* (Coffin & Renaud, 2010), *Harry Potter and The Deathly Hallows Part One* (Yates, 2010), *Inception* (Nolan, 2010), and *Paranormal Activity 2* (Williams, 2010) are early examples of films released in a package with this 'triple play' option. Given the easy transportability of digital files, they might seem the answer for distributing films and television programs to students. Unfortunately, it is not that straightforward as these digital files come with sophisticated encryption protection and are covered by copyright law. This actually makes the sharing of films in this format more difficult than sharing disks.

The online delivery of films and television programs is likely to be increasingly useful for management educators. There are many online rental suppliers, which students can be referred to (and we consider some of these later in the chapter), but in some countries, notably the UK, changing copyright law is allowing the streaming of films through closed computer intranets. This is permitted as an extension and new interpretation of copyright legislation regarding broadcast material. University lecturers in the UK have always been allowed to tape broadcasts from the television and play them in their classes to their students. The Educational Rights Agency (ERA; www.era.org.uk) has formalized the process and now clarified that any program (including films) that has been broadcast may be recorded and played for non-commercial educational purposes in universities and colleges. This allows universities to stream films and television programs over a closed intranet allowing an exciting range of possibilities with students having access to material whenever they connect to their universities' or colleges' network.

Please note that it is not permissible to use material recorded from broadcasts in this way in the USA, which is unfortunate given the benefits of using digital files. Such files let students watch and study films and television programs in their own space and time. They can slow-down, speed-up, and freeze the action to analyze events and behavior. Lecturers in Britain seem to be particularly fortunate with the ERA initiative; instructors in other countries may not be so fortunate.

One solution that enables similar access, although at a cost to either the students or the university, is to rent material from online sources. Sites vary in their charges for films and film scenes. They also vary in the degree of control that one has over playing the film or film scenes. Some sites have video players that replicate the playability of standalone DVD players; other sites have cruder players that allow little more flexibility than stopping and starting the action. Useful suppliers for streamed rental material are Amazon (www.amazon.com), Hulu (www.hulu.com), iTunes (www.itunes.com), Jaman (www.jaman.com), LoveFilm.com (www.lovefilm.com), Netflix (www.netflix.com), and Blockbuster (www.blockbuster.com). There are many other less well-known suppliers who are worth searching out as well. The Jaman site is particularly interesting and different from the others. Its library includes documentary and feature films. The site describes itself as a secure way for filmmakers and studios to market and distribute their films worldwide and, as a result, has a lot of innovative and independent material not available elsewhere.

Fasting streaming rates have changed the game with online delivery of video material. Rather than the slow downloads, jerky pictures, pixilation noise, and buffering, streamed video is now quick(ish) and smooth. Many major television companies now offer a method to download and play their programs free of charge, usually for 30 days after the broadcast. These 'iPlayers' vary in functionality, but most allow pause and navigation allowing for scenes to be found easily and analyzed.

There is also a rapidly increasing volume of free material on the internet that can be assessed even more easily. Websites such as YouTube (www.youtube.com), contain a vast library of video material that students can be directed to easily (it is easy to email a link to students or to embed a link on a webpage) and this material is played within the site meaning that no software has to be downloaded. However, a word of warning is needed. Just because a film or program is available on a site like YouTube, you are not exempt from the copyright legislation. Many of these sites contain pirated or illegal copies and such material should not be used in the classroom. However, many independent filmmakers will release their films free of charge on such internet platforms when they cannot gain distribution elsewhere in the hope that the publicity will help them gain future deals.

YouTube expands the possibilities for teaching with moving images. Students can upload their own films and video projects for easy sharing with classmates, or the rest of the world, depending on how you set up your part of YouTube. Whereas instructors used to need a lot of computer support to do this sort of thing, nowadays everything (e.g., technical support, help, advice) is taken care of by the website.

Cinema

For all our discussion of the various ways of bringing moving images, especially films, into the management classroom, there is no denying that the best place to view a film is in a cinema. That is where they are designed to be shown; that is where they have most impact. The massive screen, the surround sound, the dimming of the lights, the comfy chairs, and the smell of the popcorn all add to the magic that make movies so compelling. Why not consider using cinemas for showing films to your students? They are, after all, the places designed to show films for maximum impact.

The most obvious way to do this is simply to ask your students to attend a screening at their local 'World of Cine' before discussion of the film in class. This has some drawbacks. There is a cost involved, screenings may be full, and there may not be suitable films to coincide with the course timetable. You might be able to work with a university film club to request particular films and to allow free entrance for your students. It is also possible to do a similar thing with cinemas. Cinemas are always keen to use their facilities in the quieter periods, especially in the mornings and afternoons. You could request private screenings, but this will bring a (not insubstantial) charge. An alternative is to arrange for open screenings of the films you want to show. You might be able to enhance the screening with an introductory lecture and you can negotiate lower rates for your 'guaranteed' audience of students. In such a situation, everyone is a winner and it helps outreach and community involvement initiatives as well. And you have not seen PowerPoint until you have seen it projected 30 feet high!

COPYRIGHT ISSUES

Copyright is the one issue above all others that concerns instructors keen to use moving images in their classes. Is it legal to use films and television programs? Sadly, it is not possible to answer this question definitively here for two reasons. First, the relevant laws are different in almost every country. Second, laws are open to interpretation and different people have different interpretations even within the same territory (and institution). We can offer some general guidelines. We will focus on the USA and UK. These two territories have quite different laws and will guide readers in other territories to the relevant issues. We recommend that you speak to the copyright experts in your own college or university for advice. Larger universities are likely to employ a specialist in this area. If your institution runs media studies or other such courses, all of these matters are likely to have been worked out long ago.

USA

You have different restrictions depending on whether you are showing the film privately or publicly. A private showing is defined tightly as one made to family or a small group of friends. It would also allow showing the film to a *small group of people* in a hall of residence. A performance is public if it goes beyond the reasonable interpretation of 'small group' or is open to members of the public. So, if you showed the film in any circumstances where people other than your known small group might watch it, the screening would be designated 'public.' If someone has copyright on the material you wish to show, most films and television programs certainly will, then you need to get written permission from the owner of the copyright to show the film, which is a major hassle and can be expensive. But don't panic; there are two important avenues you should explore.

First, there is some excellent copyright-free material available. In addition to some of the sources already mentioned in this chapter, Joe, the first author of this chapter, has licensed film scenes related to some management issues for his *Our Feature Presentation* series from South-Western Cengage Learning (Champoux, 2004, 2005, 2006, 2007). These scenes can be used in any educational environment, profit or non-profit, face-to-face, online, or blended. McGraw-Hill also has their *Management in the Movies* collection.

Second, US Copyright Law includes an important exclusion. Section 110 (1) of the law allows the use of copyrighted video material for public performance if, and only if, all of the conditions set forth by the law are met. It reads thus,

> Notwithstanding the provisions of section 106, the following is not an infringement of copyright: (1) performance or display of a work by instructors or pupils in the course of face-to-face teaching activities of a nonprofit educational institution, in a classroom or similar place devoted to instruction, unless, in the case of a motion picture or other audiovisual work, the performance, or the display of individual images, is given by means of a copy that was not lawfully made under this title, and that the person responsible for the performance knew or had reason to believe was not lawfully made... (Title 17, U.S.C., Copyrights, Section 110 (1), Limitations on exclusive rights: Exemption of certain performances and displays)

Different universities and colleges interpret this exemption differently. At the University of New Mexico, for example, university counsel has said that 10 percent of a film's running time is fair-use. But there are different readings of this exemption including those who would allow the screening of whole films. It is important to check with your own institution and act on their advice. On face value, if you are screening a film for instructional purposes, you are present during the screening, and the material is legally purchased, you can show films. Sadly, there are much more stringent constraints on distance modes of teaching. Also, you may not record a film or television program and show that through any mode of teaching.

UK

In the UK, the law surrounding the playing of DVDs and related material is even murkier. Any viewing on university or college premises is likely to be viewed as a public screening, even if this is one student loaning out a university library owned DVD and playing it on a university computer in the university library. Others might see the screen and therefore it could be deemed a public performance. However, all is not lost; far from it. The relevant legislation is S.34 of the Copyright, Designs and Patents Act 1988 which deals with the screening of copyrighted works to an educational audience. It says that

> The playing or showing of a sound recording, film or broadcast before [an audience consisting of teachers and pupils at an educational establishment and other persons directly connected with the activities of the establishment] at an educational establishment for the purposes of instruction is not a playing or showing of the work in public for the purposes of infringement of copyright. (The section in square brackets is from S.34(1); JISC, 2011)

This means that if the DVD is being shown for educational purposes you do not need to obtain a license to do so.

There is one wrinkle. Many DVDs contain a provision that says something like 'Domestic Use Only.' Although this has the potential to defeat the educational provision, many institutions have decided that the intention of this notice is not to deny the educational exemption and therefore ignore it (JISClegal, 2011). Unfortunately the law has not been tested in this regard and therefore it is vital that you check your institution's own position if you want to show a DVD marked 'Domestic Use Only.'

However, the good news in the UK is the law surrounding recorded material discussed earlier. If your institution has an ERA license, you can show pre-recorded material to your students and may even stream it through your intranet.

SUMMARY

In this chapter, we have focused on some of the practical issues you might face using moving images in your classroom. It was less about teaching practice and more about the technology and the law. In doing so, we hope we have addressed many of your concerns and perhaps given you a few new ideas to think about. When we first sketched out ideas for this chapter a couple of years ago, we found ourselves writing about the new opportunity of downloading rented films. Already this is looking 'old hat' with downloading replaced with streaming. As we look at the new technology that is arriving, we see a new world of palettes, apps, and clouds, all of which may move us forward again. One of the ironies of the quicker, faster, higher definition technology is that much of it is also more secure and less transportable making it less useful to the instructor. Nevertheless, instructors have many more options than ever before and these open up the opportunities for teaching with moving images.

REFERENCES

Champoux, J. E. (2004). *Our feature presentation: Management.* Mason, OH: South-Western, a division of Thomson Learning.

Champoux, J. E. (2005). *Our feature presentation: Organizational behavior.* Mason, OH: South-Western, a division of Thomson Learning.

Champoux, J. E. (2006). *Our feature presentation: Strategy.* Mason, OH: Thomson South-Western.

Champoux, J. E. (2007). *Our feature presentation: Human resource management.* Mason, OH: Thomson South-Western.

Copyright Law of the United States: And related laws contained in Title 17 of the United States code. (Circular 92). Washington, DC: U.S. Government Printing Office.

JISClegal (2011). *Legal Guidance for ICT Use in Education, Research and External Engagement.* Available from www.jisclegal.ac.uk/Default.aspx%3Ftabid%3D463+Copyright+for+Showing+Movies+in+university+UK. [Accessed 24 February 2011].

Films and Television Series

BBC (Multiple producers). (1970–1991). *Music time* [Television series]. British Broadcasting Corporation, United Kingdom: BBC1.

Chaplin, C. (Director). (1936). *Modern times* [Motion picture]. United States: Charles Chaplin Productions.

Clair, R. (Director). (1931). *À nous la liberté* [Motion picture]. France: Films Sonores Tobis.

Coffin, P. & Renaud, C. (Directors). (2010). *Despicable me* [Motion picture]. United States: Universal Pictures.

Lang, F. (Director). (1927). *Metropolis* [Motion picture]. Germany: Universum Film.

Nolan, C. (Director). (2010). *Inception* [Motion picture]. United States: Warner Bros.

Unkrich, L. (Director). (2010). *Toy story 3* [Motion picture]. United States: Pixar Animation Studios & Walt Disney Pictures.

Williams, T. (Director). (2010). *Paranormal activity 2* [Motion picture]. United States: Paramount Pictures.

Yates, D. (Director). (2010). *Harry Potter and the Deathly Hallows: Part one* [Motion picture]. United Kingdom & United States: Warner Bros.

SECTION THREE

IMAGINING INCLUSION

CHAPTER 12

USING FILM TO CONTEXTUALIZE THE TEACHING OF PUBLIC INVOLVEMENT

Julie Charlesworth

THEMES IN PUBLIC INVOLVEMENT

Public involvement, civic engagement, public participation, active citizenship, consultation, partnership working, communitarianism, deliberative democracy, to name but a few, are all terms used to describe or theorize how governments (whether at international, national, regional or local level) try to engage with citizens but also how citizens themselves seek greater involvement in governance and politics. It is certainly not a top-down process. Indeed, films tend to portray the grass-roots level, local activism and communities helping themselves considerably more than they focus on the state perspective in leading or facilitating involvement. Clearly (and as this chapter will show) this makes for more interesting story-lines but it is also the case that in reality, policy is often made through an iterative process involving complex negotiations between politicians, civil servants, managers,

Moving Images: Effective Teaching with Film and Television in Higher Education,
pages 161–169

front-line workers, and citizens. There is always scope, however, for considerably more consultation, engagement, and participation.

In addition to illustrating key aspects of public involvement, the use of feature film ensures the *historical* perspective is emphasized. Some students may perceive active citizenship to be a recent phenomenon but in fact, many older films depict communities banding together to help each other fight authority or other external threat. The study of public services management is impossible without understanding its history and therefore, for students who have not lived through turbulent periods of public sector reform (for example, under Thatcherism in the UK) or have little understanding of the past (for example, the desire to foster a shared sense of community during and after the Second World War), then film can bring these elements to life.

The themes chosen for discussion here examine the means of achieving community empowerment and enrichment. This chapter focuses on both older and more recent films, thereby illustrating continuity in themes even if the 'coziness' of older films has been replaced with more gritty and realist settings in recent times. The films explored are: *Passport to Pimlico* (Cornelius, 1949), *Blazing Saddles* (Brooks, 1974), *King of New York* (Ferrara, 1990), and *Vote for Huggett* (Annakin, 1949). There are of course many other examples from which to choose.

TEACHING 'COMMUNITY'

The subject of 'what is community?' is extensive and a crucial element in understanding public involvement. Community is often perceived as a locus for mobilizing public participation. The concept can provide a starting point for discussion as most students will have some idea of what community means. Community is not a new concept and sociologists such as Townsend (1954) and Wilmott and Young (1957) conducted extensive studies of particular communities in the 1950s and 1960s. Its return to favor in recent years has a nostalgic feeling to it, perhaps as it provides a haven from ever encroaching globalization and mass society. Bauman's (2001) critique suggests that the appeal of the notion derives from the coziness and feelings of security it denotes: if you are in your own community, you feel safe, people know you and can help you.

Community denotes more than just a place, although it is often used in a geographical sense (i.e., residents in a particular neighborhood or street). It can also be used to describe people sharing ethnic origin, religion, occupation, interests, or a vision of collective action. In the latter sense, it is a more dynamic concept, a process or agent (cf. Crow & Allan, 1994; Taylor, 2003). Yet it is hard to identify a community without some degree of tension, conflict or divergent views. The coziness of community also disappears when one considers how the people within a particular community may become hostile to outsiders. Furthermore, there is no easy leap from a group of people apparently having shared interests to one that is prepared to act collectively and agree on a shared vision.

Not surprisingly, many films include some concept of community. Historically, films from the Second World War in the UK and Europe inevitably focused on communities fighting together to defend themselves, their homes and families; there was a common purpose and shared vision for the future. As Butler (2004) highlights, the films of the time were not just concerned with geographical community but also with communities in factories for example, *Millions Like Us* (Gilliat & Launder, 1943) and on ships, for example, *In Which We Serve* (Coward & Lean, 1942), and with an emphasis on the 'ordinary' working classes. The theme of community continued into the postwar period as film-makers depicted people trying to rebuild their lives and communities after the devastation of war. Plots involving one person or a small group fighting to save their community from outside threats or internal divisions continues as a powerful motif in films.

RESISTING EXTERNAL THREATS

In the UK, the Ealing Studios produced a number of films during the 1940s and 1950s with community as their main theme, the classic one is the comedy *Passport to Pimlico.* This film was extremely well-known although students under the age of 25 may not have encountered it now that UK television does not show older films so frequently and international students of all ages may never have come across it. It is worth showing the whole of this film as much is relevant and the twists and turns in the fortunes of the community (mostly) pulling together against outside threats and the bureaucracy of the state at the time illustrates key learning points about community as well as having entertainment value. In this film, a working-class geographical community (in Pimlico, London) finds an ancient document in the crater left by a bomb, which states that the community is in fact part of Burgundy, France. Initially there are tensions within the community: several people try to claim responsibility for the discovery of the treasure in the belief that there will be a reward; street traders move in to avoid postwar restrictions elsewhere in London, and residents become upset about the prospect of lawlessness. But gradually, the delight at the prospect of being freed from the austerity of postwar Britain (rationing, shortages, etc) unites the community, and it declares itself 'Burgundian' and therefore not subject to the laws of the UK.

The government is not prepared to tolerate an independent state in the heart of London and puts pressure on the community to give up their claim and toe the line, and tries to force their submission through bureaucratic procedures, passing them from one government department to another. However, this reinvigorates the residents in their shared purpose of defending themselves against an external threat and they elect a small group to run their community. When their food supplies are destroyed in a flood, media sympathy and support ensures that members of the public turn up to help by throwing food over the barricades so that they do not have to submit defeat to government. Ultimately, however, they realize that life has become too difficult and decide to rejoin Britain and loan their treasure to Britain. They secure agreement from government that they can spend the interest from the loan on a scheme to redevelop the bomb site as a community resource (i.e., playground and lido).

In a similar vein, and some thirty years later, the comedy *Blazing Saddles* focuses on the town of Rock Ridge in mid-western USA in the nineteenth century. The community is an isolated town whose white residents are under attack from (unbeknown to them) a corrupt mayor who wants to make money from putting the railroad through the town. In an early scene, the community meets to discuss what action they should take to protect themselves from being attacked by outsiders. Some of the residents feel they should leave but one of the older residents—in a series of clichés—says they should stay, fight it out and appeals to the past (a common theme in community/place identity). They decide to ask for a new sheriff to help them deal with the threat, and the mayor surmises that he could destroy the community from inside by giving them a black sheriff, believing that they will not tolerate him and it will drive the residents out. Although thirty years on, this film feels at times very politically incorrect, it made some efforts to be tackling racism at a time when films still had few black leading characters or portrayed positive role models.

When the new sheriff, Bart, rides into town, all the local residents are out ready to greet and welcome him but are collectively stunned when they realize he is black. Their immediate reaction is to want to kill him as the idea of a black sheriff is one they cannot comprehend, as all their shared experience is of white authority figures within their community. A black sheriff is an outsider and a threat to their community. The exception in the community is the drunk Jim, aka 'Waco Kid', and who, although happy to be friends with Bart, says 'you can't win these people over, no matter what you do.' Bart tries to remain positive and responds 'once you establish yourself, they have to accept you.'

After rescuing the community from a thug sent in by the mayor, the residents start to accept the sheriff but still do not believe he is capable of saving them from the outsiders who wish to destroy their community, particularly when word reaches them that the mayor has put together an army of the 'worst' men. The residents pack up and prepare to leave. However, the sheriff has a plan and enlists the local railroad workers to help but the local residents are unsure when they realize that most of the workers are black or Irish. Bart says they have to accept *everybody*. The community is successfully defended when all the residents and railroad workers pull together, and in fact, the workers stay, thereby potentially creating a new, more open, less racist community, united through their defense of the town. In a stark contrast to how they welcomed the sheriff, the residents prepare a big speech saying they need him to stay but Bart, feeling his work is done, leaves the new community.

This is a difficult film in teaching terms: some students might find it offensive so thought is needed about whether to show the whole film or just relevant clips. Providing historical context about representations of minority ethnic characters in film and television might also help students' viewing and understanding. However, *Blazing Saddles* does provide a strong visual statement about the impact of perceived outsider threats to communities and the ability of residents to absorb new cultures and backgrounds into a more shared, heterogeneous space.

DIVIDED COMMUNITIES

King of New York offers a less straightforward and bleaker representation of community, where everything does not turn out alright in the end with divisions resolved. The story concerns the criminal underworld and the police of New York, dominated by the role of Frank White, recently released from prison who wants to help his community. His ideas on how this should be achieved (through violent means) are in conflict with others' perceptions. Frank moves easily between the criminal world and the respectable community, mixing with councilors and taking part in community fundraising events. In an early scene, he teases people that he has reformed and wants to be Mayor, suggesting that he might consider legal means of helping his community but at the same time, his supporters are already killing drug-dealers. He perceives stealing money from drug-dealers to be a legitimate means of funding a hospital, given that the city authorities cannot afford to fund one in his district and he says to the city councilor: 'privileged districts shouldn't be the only ones with hospitals.'

Essentially, the film focuses on a number of conflicts and divisions within the city:

- within the criminal world—between different gangs of drug-dealers;
- between Frank and the police—an obvious conflict but interesting in this context as they seemingly want the same outcome;
- within the police about how to deal with Frank and the other criminals.

We could add a gender division within these communities too: women in this film are relegated to the background as sexual objects and with no status. This is unsettling to watch as a viewer but may reflect some of the reality of drug-dealing gangs. The character of Jennifer is not well-developed—she is an attorney working closely for criminals (beyond representing them in the legal system) and in a relationship with Frank but seems to do what she is told.

These divisions are clearly highlighted in the film through visual contrasts between and within scenes, with violence and 'normal' life frequently juxtaposed: for example, a bloody shoot-out between Frank's men and a gang of drug-dealers is followed by Frank relaxing in a plush hotel, with classical music playing, and champagne and flowers in the room. In another scene, Frank discusses a major deal with a gang-leader whilst the two of them take a tour of the local hospital, which Frank has pledged to help financially; a small child in a hospital bed plays with her teddies and hands them to Frank as he negotiates the deal in front of her.

The different gangs of drug-dealers are inevitably divided along ethnic, territorial and leadership lines. Frank is white and his followers are from black, Asian, and white ethnic groups. None of the gangs want to cut a deal with Frank and it is actually unclear what Frank would have done if they had. Presumably he would have used the profits but it is more likely he just made the contact in order to access their communities to kill them and steal the money.

Frank's motivation for killing the drug-dealers (and whole gangs are eliminated in the film) is two-fold: first, he takes their money which he then plans to use to help his community; secondly, he regards them as more criminal than he is and that consequently they deserve to die. In a scene towards the end of the film, where he justifies his actions to the chief police officer, he describes how the other gang-leaders abused their own communities: using teenage girls as prostitutes, renting appalling properties at high rents to their own people, and so on. Frank says 'I don't want to make money that way' and is surprised that he is perceived as 'Public Enemy No. 1' by the police. He says he is not the problem and is 'just a businessman.' He is of course a murderer and a drug dealer and the police inevitably want him brought to justice. They do not distinguish between him and the other violent criminals in the same way as Frank does. He—as they do—wants the community free from drugs and exploitation so they share a desired outcome but the means to achieve this is different, which for Frank is through murder and violence. As he says to the chief police officer, whilst he was in jail, and therefore off the streets, the drugs problem continued and the authorities struggle to deal with it.

This conflict about the methods to create a better community also causes tension within the police force. The chief police officer, Bishop, wants Frank brought to justice through the legal system but when his team sees Frank on television at the fundraising event, they become angry. One of the police officers, Gilley, says 'I thought the law counted for something but this whole system favors the scumbag' and that they risk their lives everyday whilst Frank gets rich on killing people. Gilley then suggests they should kill Frank and make it look like a rival gang shooting, but the chief police officer says disagrees: 'you can't kill everyone you can't arrest.'

Gilley and some of his colleagues do in fact take this route—so like Frank, they are acting illegally to achieve their desired outcome—and attack Frank and his followers at a party. Frank escapes and Jimmy, one of his close followers, is involved in a battle with a police officer, Flanagan. The fight becomes personal: they are both black men on opposite sides of the law. The decision to act outside the law proves disastrous with several officers killed including Flanagan. Gilley is then shot dead by Frank at the police officers' funeral. At the end, Bishop is killed by Frank but not before he has fatally injured Frank, who dies in a cab surrounded by police. All those people who thought they were acting for the good of the community are dead.

Clips or the whole film could be used in teaching but it is a violent film that some students could find offensive or uncomfortable but it does provide an unusual and powerful perspective on divided communities, as well as the rights and wrongs of using criminal means to achieve good.

LOCAL DEMOCRACY

In contrast to *King of New York*, the British comedy film, *Vote for Huggett*, illustrates how using a local democratic route might achieve desirable outcomes for the local community. Again, in common with the other films discussed here, the seemingly cozy picture of the local community is inaccurate; it is strongly divided by class and the desire to achieve wealth through manipulating local politics. Even the Huggetts as a close-knit family become disrupted by conflict and actions of the head of the household.

Vote for Huggett is comparable with *Passport to Pimlico* because both main protagonists develop schemes for the community and are 'upholders of that progressive, egalitarian, co-operative spirit which had developed during the war and swept the Labour party to victory in 1945' (Murphy, 1989, p. 216). In *Vote for Huggett*, Joe and his family are fighting corruption on the local council. Joe proposes the idea of a lido for the local community but it conflicts with a scheme proposed by a powerful local councilor who wants a community centre. This appears to be a respectable idea for a local facility, but he is championing it because he wants his building company to win the contract.

Joe's ideas cause conflict within the family, whose attitudes are working-class and resistant to change. Grandma, in particular, does not agree with Joe 'putting himself forward' when she sees his letter about a lido printed in the local newspaper. Joe's wife, Ethel, is horrified by the idea of Joe being a councilor and exclaims 'but nothing like that ever happened before.' Ethel is still deferential to middle-class people and so is Joe to some extent, although once he gets used to the idea of being a councilor, he is very enthusiastic and confident. The councilor who would lose out by Joe's proposal describes him as an 'impudent, impertinent upstart' and the councilor's wife says 'he's only a workman' and 'can you imagine that funny little Mrs Huggett being a councilor's wife.'

Throughout the film, people try to manipulate the Huggetts to achieve their goals: the owners of a key site who would benefit from Joe's scheme persuade him to stand as a councilor, and the boss of the firm also makes advances on Joe's daughter, who works as his secretary. The councilor with a vested interest in his own scheme for the community centre sends his wife to the Huggett home in order to put Ethel off the idea of being a councilor's wife. When it is discovered that Ethel and her niece own a key piece of land, attempts are made by the councilor and the developers to persuade her to sell, as do Ethel's mother and niece but she stands her ground. In the end, Joe uses his charm to persuade three elderly sisters to provide their land for a park, thereby thwarting all the others. So, although all the characters attempt to manipulate others, only Joe is thinking of the local community and perhaps himself to some extent once the idea of being a councilor is implanted in his mind.

This film is very much of its time and some students without a background in post-war history may require some context. It still provides a good illustration of how somebody unaccustomed to fighting a local battle might take up the reins of local politics and fight corruption in order to achieve a good outcome for the community, despite the conflict caused to the family and within the community.

CONCLUSION

These films provide a starting point for thinking about how to illustrate themes in public involvement, particularly the conflict and division inherent in the complex notion of community, as well as what are legitimate means to achieve desirable outcomes. The films also demonstrate how both historical and more recent films can be used, as well as films from different genres. Most films, however, require some contextual background and scene-setting so that students fully understand their relevance. Discussing why a teacher might use film in a non-film studies course will also be important.

REFERENCES

Bauman, Z. (2001). *Community: Seeking safety in an insecure world.* Cambridge, UK: Polity.

Butler, M. (2004). *Film and community in Britain and France. From La Règle du Jeu to Room at the Top.* London, UK: I B Tauris.

Crow, G., & Allan, G. (1994). *Community life: An introduction to local social relations.* New York, NY: Harvester Wheatsheaf.

Murphy, R. (1989). *Realism and tinsel: Cinema and society in Britain 1939–48.* London, UK: Routledge.

Taylor, M. (2003). *Public policy in the community.* Basingstoke, UK: Palgrave Macmillan.

Townsend, P. (1954). *The family life of old people.* London, UK: Routledge & Kegan Paul.

Willmott, P., & Young, M. (1957). *Family and kinship in East London.* London, UK: Routledge & Kegan Paul.

Films

Annakin, K. (Director). (1949). *Vote for Huggett* [Motion picture]. United Kingdom: Gainsborough Pictures.

Brooks, M. (Director). (1974). *Blazing saddles* [Motion picture]. United States: Crossbow Productions & Warner Bros.

Cornelius, H. (Director). (1949). *Passport to Pimlico* [Motion picture]. United Kingdom: J. Arthur Rank Organisation & Ealing Studios.

Coward, N. & Lean, D. (Directors). (1942). *In which we serve* [Motion picture]. United Kingdom: Two Cities Films.

Ferrara, A. (Director). (1990). *King of New York* [Motion picture]. Italian, United States, & United Kingdom: Caminito, The Rank Organisation, Reteitalia, & Scena International.

Gilliat, S. & Launder, F. (Directors). (1943). *Millions like us* [Motion picture]. United Kingdom: Gainsborough Pictures.

CHAPTER 13

TO BOLDLY GO WHERE FEW HAVE GONE BEFORE

Teaching Strategy With Moving Images

Véronique Ambrosini, Jon Billsberry, and Nardine Collier

Many authors have discussed the role of films as a teaching resource (e.g., Bumpus, 2005; Champoux, 1999; Huczynski & Buchanan, 2004). The films advocated are as diverse as the concepts taught, with for instance *Dead Poets Society* (Weir, 1989), *The Magnificent Seven* (Sturges, 1960), *For Love or Country: The Arturo Sandoval Story* (Sargent, 2000) and *12 Angry Men* (Lumet, 1957) used to illustrate a range of concepts from risk-taking and leadership, influencing strategies, and effective communication (Billsberry & Gilbert, 2008; Bumpus, 2005; Champoux, 2001; Huczynski, 1994; McCambridge, 2003; Serey, 1992). Champoux (1999, p. 206) advocates the use of films because "films scenes can offer a visual portrayal of abstract theories and concepts taught in organizational behavior and management courses." This quality of films is of particular value when teaching inexperienced students or those students who have little experience of work. This is of particular relevance when teaching strategic management, not just because of the increasing trend for students to take MBA and related courses straight after

Moving Images: Effective Teaching with Film and Television in Higher Education,
pages 171–191
Copyright © 2012 by Information Age Publishing
All rights of reproduction in any form reserved.

their undergraduate studies, but also because strategic management ideas are most often relevant to senior management decisions, of which even fewer students have experience.

Strategic problems are largely complex, idiosyncratic, interrelated, and often have more than one correct answer. Moreover strategy making is, to a large extent, as much based on intuition and tacit knowledge as on rational decision making (White, 2004). This makes teaching strategic management difficult when students lack practical work knowledge. It is relatively straightforward to teach students most strategic analysis frameworks or rational theories, but it is less so for concepts and ideas which are procedural, complex, or context dependent. Showing films can help students understand and learn these concepts. They can help to illustrate concepts 'in action'; they create experience (Stadler, 1990). Moreover, these references to popular culture help students access, and relate to, the concepts being illustrated. As a whole, when watching films or reading the literature on using films as a teaching resource, one can find many examples relating to organizational behavior and general management (e.g., Champoux, 2000a, 2000b, 2003a, 2003b, 2004, 2005; Clemens & Wolff, 2000). There is, however, a paucity of guidance on films related to strategic management, especially in non-military and non-sporting contexts.

In similar vein to Ambrosini, Billsberry and Collier (2009), the purpose of this paper is to address this gap, and suggest a range of films that can be used in the strategic management classroom. The paper is structured as follows. First we explain why we believe that films may be a useful addition to the strategic management instructor's arsenal of teaching tools. We argue that films can be employed for experiential learning, which is invaluable when teaching a topic such as strategic management that is both about practice and analysis. We also reflect on some of the pitfalls of such a tool, notably the hazard of using military and sport films. In the second section we describe a typical strategic management curriculum and suggest a series of films or film clips that can facilitate the teaching, and students' learning, of strategy concepts, and specifically those principles that are difficult to grasp when one has little organizational experience. We conclude with a summary and by highlighting the motivational effects on students of using films in the classroom.

FILMS AS A STRATEGIC MANAGEMENT INSTRUCTIONAL TOOL

Lampel (2005, p. 21) wrote: "We need to rethink our approach to teaching strategy." This view is widely shared. Many (e.g., Greiner, Bhambri, & Cummings, 2003; Mintzberg & Gosling, 2002; Pfeffer & Fong, 2002) have voiced criticism about the current state of strategy teaching, which emphasizes economic principles and downplays the role of practice rather than connects analytical and behavioral skills or articulation and intuition.

There are two main reasons why it is not easy to teach strategic management. Firstly, as strategy is about both practice and analysis, it is difficult for students lacking managerial experience to relate to and comprehend strategic management principles (Short & Ketchen, 2005). Hence, to be effective strategy teaching methods need to somehow 'make real' organizational contexts that many students are not familiar with (Joshi, Davis, Kathuria, & Weidner, 2005). Secondly, in the last couple of decades, the field has become increasingly complex, and developed multiple perspectives and concepts. As a result, traditional methods such as texts and teaching case studies are no longer adequate, and cases alone are likely to be "insufficient in bridging the gap between these students' knowledge, experience, and their preparation for the real world" (Joshi et al., 2005, p. 676). With this is mind, we suggest that teachers should consider films as a strategic management of instructional tool. We believe that films can work in combination with all of the other tools to help teach and facilitate the learning of strategic management. In other words we want to add films to Forrest and Peterson's (2006) list of instructional strategies[1].

Pfeffer and Fong (2002) argue that management is best taught as a craft: it is about practice, actions, and learning from experience. Nadkarni (2003, p. 340) also comments that "management courses are qualitative, applied, and subjective, where student learning is comprised not only of the conceptual understanding of the domain, but also of the application of these concepts in a variety of 'real' situations." This suggests that instructors should be encouraged to use experiential learning methods to teach strategy topics which need to be related to concrete experience to be fully meaningful. The core principle of experiential learning is that experience is the basis for observation and reflection (Kolb, 1984). Learning is described as a process "whereby knowledge is created through the transformation of experience" (Kolb, 1984, p. 38). Experiential approaches to learning are a way by which strategy instructors can bridge the experience gap (Joshi et al., 2005).

As mentioned in the introduction, films can be used as a substitute for experience (Stadler, 1990), and thus they can be argued to be used as an experiential learning method. Films illustrate ideas in a pictorial and evocative manner. They stress the role of context. They also highlight how nonverbal cues from eye movement, facial expression, and body movement can load images with information a viewer interprets (Champoux, 2006). Some films can also help show uncertainty and the ambiguous and unknowable

---

[1] Forrest and Peterson's (2006) list of instructional strategies is comprised of: labs, role-playing, multiple choice, mentoring, team assignments, group discussion, small group, journals, portfolio, drama, examinations, lecture, scavenger hunts, team tests, service learning, problem-based learning, class presentations, research papers, just-in-time learning, readings, and essays.

nature of life and organizational life. Films are a means by which one can show that there is no single, or 'one right answer,' to some questions, and that dilemmas can be variously interpreted. Films can also help the transfer of tacit knowledge; show the role of intuition as pictures help express more than words can do, show phenomena that texts do not as they cannot be easily codified. They also show that people do not always make decisions as the result of rational analysis. In other words films may "be able to portray more effectively some aspects of organizational experience" (Buchanan & Huczynski, 2004, p. 314) than conventional methods and they may be considered as an educational approach that can be applied to workplace and informal learning (Reynolds & Vince, 2004), as well as the classroom.

In addition to being a substitute for concrete experience, films are also effective as a teaching and learning device in that they help students remember course ideas. Similar to storytelling, they serve as memory-trigger devices (Short & Ketchen, 2005). Films scenes combine images with sound, to create a 'whole' atmosphere that students may associate with a strategy concept, thereby rendering it 'alive' (hence creating an experience-like effect) and making the memory of it more vivid. Films also help students critically explore theories and concepts. They evoke emotion, encourage discussion, and prompt students to be more imaginative, creative, and critical than when using traditional materials.

As explained earlier, management education emphasizes theory (Kolb & Kolb, 2005) and strategy instructors tend to favor text and cases i.e. they put an accent on reading and listening teaching methods. One needs these methods, however they are insufficient. This is not only because they do not allow for the teaching of principles requiring experience to be learned, but also because these methods are essentially about comprehension (Baker, Jenson & Kolb, 2005), that is that they emphasize abstract learning and focus on the abstract thinking stage of Kolb's (1984) learning cycle model.

Based on our discussion so far, films can be seen to be about apprehension (Baker et al., 2005) i.e., concrete knowing and experiential learning:

> Some people grasp new information through experiencing the concrete, tangible, felt qualities of the world, relying on their senses and immersing themselves in concrete reality. Others tend to perceive, grasp, or take hold of new information through symbolic representation or abstract conceptualization—thinking about, analyzing, or systematically planning, rather than using sensation as a guide. (Baker et al., 2005, p. 412)

The presence of these two learning styles makes us believe that films should be used as a complement to, rather than a substitute for, traditional case studies or other methods. In order to cater for both main styles we need a variety of tools, this is important as "the better the fit between the learning style of students and the instructional style, the more favorable the learning outcomes resulting from the activity of learning" (Nadkarni, 2003, p. 337). To help students with a disposition towards abstract learning, teachers need to provide readings, lectures and allow them to explore analytical models (Kolb & Kolb, 2005), hence the need for cases, traditional lectures and texts. For those who favor experiential learning, films together with simulations, practical applications (Kolb & Kolb, 2005), role-play (Forrest & Peterson, 2006), or acting (Baruch, 2006) may be better suited. Another point that reinforces the need for this mix is that it is also important to recognize that learning is not about absolutely one style or another: it is about integrating the two (Baker et al., 2005). Teaching effectiveness and learning is facilitated when one uses a variety of instructional methods (Baruch, 2006).

Finally, before proposing a selection of films that we recommend for teaching strategic management principles, we must make a few comments about film selection and notably about some aspects that need to be considered when choosing films. Hassard and Holliday (1998) highlight that some films strive on stereotypes. For instance, they mention that films such as *Working Girl* (Nichols, 1988) or *Disclosure* (Levinson, 1994) "draw upon rather crass stereotypes of the 'career bitch' or the choice between a career or a man (a woman can't have both)" (Hassard & Holliday, 1998, p. 8), or that films such as *The Man in the White Suit* (Crichton, 1951) or *The Hudsucker Proxy* (Coen, 1994) suggest that organizations are boring, mechanical and rife with corruption. If the topic of teaching is such a subject, this is not a problem, but one needs to be clear of the message that one wants to convey to ensure that we do not engrain clichés.

Similarly, it is important to be aware of the problems associated with the use of war films or sport films. They usually display extremes and commonly depict caricatures. These films are usually a poor analogy of organizational life: the style of decision making showed is usually top-down. The organizations are often portrayed as very hierarchical with little discussion or search for consensus taking place. Essentially strategy is portrayed as being about planning. People seem also to have clear job specifications, organizations have only one measure of performance, one type of leadership dominates ('the great man'), and by and large, male characters dominate. Moreover, individual behavior is depicted at a time of high risk, crisis, or drama. Although these are occasional features of working life, they are not as pervasive as depicted in war and sports films. In short, war and sport films are often simplistic. They do not usually reflect the complexity of organizational life; they give a 'black and white' view of organizations, and hence such films should be used with caution.

A STRATEGIC MANAGEMENT CURRICULUM

In this section we identify and describe a series of scenes from films that can be used to illustrate strategy concepts. Our discussion is structured according to a 'typical' strategic management curriculum for a core strategy course.

To generate a 'standard strategic management curriculum', we reviewed the content of six seminal teaching texts in the field of strategic management (Barney & Hesterly, 2006; de Wit & Meyer, 2004; Dess, Lumpkin, & Taylor, 2005; Grant, 2005; Hitt, Ireland, & Hoskisson, 2005; Johnson, Scholes & Whittington, 2005). We synthesized the subject content of these texts to produce a coherent listing of the strategic management topics that are commonly dealt with in the teaching curriculum (see Table 1).

Our intention here is to identify material from feature films that strategic management educators can use both to illustrate and enliven their teaching and also to promote critical discussion in the classroom. The above summary of the typical strategic management curriculum demonstrates the breadth of the subject. Clearly, it is beyond the scope of this paper to cover all of these topics in any meaningful depth, hence we must make a selection of which subjects to cover. The review of these text books demonstrates that there are rational (generally economic-based) and interpretive/soft (generally organizational behavior-based) subjects within the curriculum, and that these approaches receive different emphasis in the textbooks (Burke & Moore, 2003). Echoing Burke and Moore (2003) our experience tells us that it is the teaching of the soft subjects that is most challenging. These ideas are less easy to exemplify and, given their innate complexity and subjectivity, lend themselves to illustration through media that relates matters in a complex, ambiguous and differently interpretable manner. Accordingly, we have chosen to focus on the soft subjects in the remainder of this paper. These are:

1. *An introduction to strategic management*: Strategy development process, planning process, synergies, and strategic intent.
2. *Resource-based view of the firm*: Fit vs. resource-based strategy, valuable, rare, imperfectly imitable, and imperfectly substitutable resources, tacit knowledge, causal ambiguity, and path dependency.
3. *Internal environment*: Organizational knowledge, organizational culture, and, taken for granted assumptions.
4. *Methods of development*: Mergers and acquisitions and strategic alliances.

In the following section, we examine each of the above themes. For each, we briefly define the topics before identifying and describing relevant film clips (or whole films) that may be useful to teachers of strategic management to aid the development of understanding and learning.

TABLE 1. Content from Seminal Textbooks (not in chapter order)

Exploring Corporate Strategy	Strategic Management	Strategy	Strategic Management and Competitive Advantage	Strategic Management	Contemporary Strategy Analysis
Johnson, Scholes, & Whittington (2005)	Hitt, Ireland, & Hoskisson (2005)	de Wit & Meyer (2004)	Barney & Hesterly (2006)	Dess, Lumpkin, & Taylor (2005)	Grant (2005)
Introduction to strategic management					
What is strategy?	Strategic intent and fit	The nature of strategy	What is strategy?	What is strategic management?	Strategic intent and fit
Strategy context	Strategy development processes	Strategy processes	Strategic management processes	Strategic management processes	
Strategic development	Purpose of organization	Organizational purpose		Organizational purpose	
Purpose of organization	Mission	Synergy			
External environment					
PESTEL framework	External analysis	Industry context	External environment	Environmental analysis	Environmental analysis
Porters diamond	Industry analysis	Porter's five forces	Industry structure	Industry life cycle	Industry analysis
Porter's five forces	Customer analysis		Porter's five forces	Porter's five forces	Porter's five forces
	Porter's five forces			Strategic groups	Competitive analysis
	Strategic groups				
	Competitor analysis				

(continued)

TABLE 1. Continued

	Exploring Corporate Strategy	Strategic Management	Strategy	Strategic Management and Competitive Advantage	Strategic Management	Contemporary Strategy Analysis
Internal environment	Resource-based view Value chain analysis Core competencies Organizational knowledge Cultural context Leadership	Resource-based view Value chain Core competencies Knowledge Organization culture Leadership	Resource-based approach Value chain Core competencies Learning organization Culture Leadership	Resource-based view Value chain Core competencies Internal capabilities evaluation Learning curve	Resource-based view Value chain Core competencies Evaluation of firm performance Identifying, evaluating, and managing intellectual capital and learning Leadership	Resource-based view Value chain Capabilities Knowledge and learning Organization culture Modes of leadership
Competitive strategy	Type of competitive strategy Game theory	Type of competitive strategy Strategic and tactical decisions Entrepreneurial strategies Innovation	SBU strategy Porter's generic strategies Value Innovation	Cost leadership strategies Product differentiation strategies Entrepreneurship	Porter's three generic strategies Entrepreneurship Managing innovation	Sources of competitive advantage Cost advantage Differentiation advantage Game theory Innovation

Corporate strategy

Merger and acquisition	Merger and acquisition	Corporate strategy	Merger and acquisition	Alliances and joint venture	Diversification
Alliances	Strategic alliances	Alliances	Strategic alliances	Vertical integration	Managing diversified multi-business organizations
Diversification	Diversification	International context	Vertical integration	Diversification	Strategy in global industry
International strategies	International strategies	Governance	Diversification	International strategies	
Corporate governance	Corporate governance			Corporate governance	
	Ethics			Ethics	

TEACHING STRATEGIC MANAGEMENT WITH FILMS

Introduction to Strategic Management

Many strategic management curricula begin with a description of *strategy development processes*. This subject matter is concerned with the way that strategy is formed and, in particular, whether it is planned or emergent. This is an area of the curriculum that abounds with material. Many crime and heist films, e.g. *The Italian Job* (Collinson, 1969), *Pulp Fiction* (Tarantino, 1994), *The Lavender Hill Mob* (Crichton, 1951), provide material illustrating precise and deliberate planning having to be altered or abandoned in light of changing circumstances. An alternative rich seam is the prison break-out movies involving an intended strategy. Examples include *The Shawshank Redemption* (Darabont, 1994), *Escape from Alcatraz* (Siegel, 1979), *The Last Castle* (Lurie, 2001), *The Great Escape* (Sturges, 1963), and *Chicken Run* (Lord & Park, 2000). *The Great Escape* demonstrates the intended versus emergent strategies very well. We see 'Big X' (Richard Attenborough), the officer responsible for the mass escape, informing others of his intended strategy (i.e. to dig three tunnels leaving the camp in different directions). As the digging progresses, we see both Big X and his colleagues developing strategies to solve the numerous difficulties as they arise. A particularly good example is the problem of how to get rid of the dirt from the tunnels, which is ingeniously solved with several strategies. This example illustrates the common assertion that most strategies involve a combination of both intended and emergent approaches before they are realized.

One related element that is often addressed extensively in the strategy texts is the topic of the *planning process*. It deals with the formal processes by which the firm develops its strategy, and formally organizes its resources and actions in relation to its external environment in order to achieve its objectives. The two film genres described earlier under strategy development processes are relevant here as well. It is interesting to compare two of these films, *The Last Castle* and *The Great Escape*, as the failure of the first to depict the planning process undermines the believability of the story and causes it to pale in comparison to the second. Instead, in *The Great Escape*, Sturges (the director) goes to considerable lengths to show how the inmates overcome the myriad of different problems thrown at them through effective planning.

Synergies are benefits that are gained from activities that complement each other such that 1+1=3. Many films involving formed partnerships demonstrate this effect. *Men in Black* (Sonnenfeld, 1997), for example, illustrates how the different skills of Agents K (Tommy Lee Jones) and J (Will Smith) combine to make an effective unit. This theme of law enforcement partnerships being synergistic can also be seen in *Lethal Weapon* (Donner, 1987) and *Se7en* (Fincher, 1995). Another example is *Rush Hour* (Ratner,

1998). In this film, a Chinese consul recruits a Hong Kong inspector (Jackie Chan) to help rescue his kidnapped daughter. The inspector is teamed up with a LAPD officer (Chris Tucker), but the two set about solving the kidnap individually; neither is successful, they often get in each other's way, and blame each other for the lack of results. Only when they decide to put their differences aside and try to collaborate, do they find that each has unique strengths that aid them in solving the kidnapping. An example of synergy from a business environment would be *Gung Ho* (Howard, 1986) in which an American car factory becomes competitive and achieves survival once the American workforce and the Japanese owners learn to work together.

Although it does not tend to feature as a whole session, the subject of *strategic intent* is a common theme within the strategy development section of the curriculum. Strategic intent is the idea that there must be a sustained obsession for winning, held at all levels of the organization, if it is to be successful. It is about stretching the organization. Although we have already noted that the two film genres of military and sport need to be used with some caution, there are examples within these categories which do address this subject matter directly, and as such their inclusion in the curriculum may be justified, as both commonly feature the importance of the group passionately believing in the strategy. One amusing example would be *Major League* (Ward, 1989), where a baseball team is turned around by a collective passion to spite their owner who wants them to lose so she can move the team. The players go to such extreme lengths to win that it becomes an obsession; they end up sacrificing a chicken in a Voodoo ceremony to help them win. However, as we mentioned earlier, there is a danger in using too many military or sporting examples as the culture of these environments is so different to most business environments.

An alternative environment is the Starship Enterprise and its five year mission "to boldly go where no one has gone before." At the time of writing, there are eleven movies in the Star Trek stable. All of these illustrate the collective obsession of the crew to "seek out new life and new civilizations" in pursing the starship's objectives. One of the interesting features of using Star Trek, especially from the Next Generation era, is that many of the management and leadership processes are reminiscent of large-company top team decision-making processes, which is particularly helpful for the strategic management educator.

Resource-Based View of the Firm

Adopting a *fit strategy* approach means studying the external environment, developing the necessary resources, formulating, and then implementing a strategy (an analogous example would be the Trojan Horse that the Greeks used to gain entry to the city of Troy in the eponymous film (Petersen, 2004)), whereas adopting a *resource-based strategy* means identifying your resources, finding a relevant industry, formulating, and then implementing the strategy (for example, Jerry (Daphne; Jack Lemmon) and Joe (Josephine; Tony Curtis) use their expertise as musicians to gain entry to a female band to escape from the mob in *Some Like It Hot* (Wilder, 1959)). A film that illustrates the movement from one strategy to another is *Chicken Run*. Loosely based on *The Great Escape* and other World War II prisoner of war escape movies, this 'claymation' film tells the story of chickens trying to escape from their farm before they are turned into chicken pies by the farmer's evil wife, Mrs. Tweedy. The film shows many early attempts to escape based on careful analysis, but all fail. Eventually a determined chicken, Ginger, realizes that they cannot go under the wire, and so must go over it. They try to learn to fly without success (i.e., a fit strategy), but eventually escape by examining their own resources and using these to construct and fly a plane (i.e., resource-based strategy).

Valuable, rare, inimitable, and imperfectly substitutable resources are the main sources of competitive advantage. There are many examples to draw upon from films, but one which illustrates the concept well is the ring ("the one ring to rule them all") in *The Lord of the Rings* trilogy (Jackson, 2001, 2002, 2003). In the lands of Middle Earth, the Dark Lord, Sauron, forged the One Ring of Power so that he could rule all the peoples and creatures of Middle Earth, but the One Ring was taken from him, and eventually given to Frodo (Elijah Wood), who has to destroy it in the fires of Mount Doom. The Ring is valuable, as it gives control over all; it is rare, as it is the 'One Ring'; it cannot be imitated hence the pursuit and attacks on Frodo to take the Ring from him; and finally, it is non-substitutable as nothing else has the same power. An alternative source, is *Charlie and the Chocolate Factory* (Burton, 2005) in which the resources are the ingenuity, invention, and innovation of Willy Wonka (Johnny Depp), the relationship between Wonka and the Oompa-Loompas, and environs of the factory.

The subject of *tacit knowledge*, which is similar to non-codified know-how, resides in action, and is difficult to communicate. This topic can be illustrated with excerpts from *Star Wars Episode V: The Empire Strikes Back* (Kershner, 1980). In this film, we see the process undertaken to become a Jedi. To become one, Luke (Mark Hamill) sets off to the Dagobah system to be trained by the best Jedi Master, Master Yoda. Yoda then teaches Luke the ways of the Force by showing him how to harness and use its power. It is not easy, but after many lessons he learns how to control the power of the force, even though he cannot explain what it is or how it works. A similar example can be found in the *Harry Potter* films in the power of magic and, in particular, Harry's awakening to his new magical powers in the first film of the series, *Harry Potter and the Sorcerer's Stone* (Columbus, 2001).

Causal ambiguity is concerned with uncertainty in understanding the links between actions and results. This is a subject that lends itself to being illustrated with films: any motion picture with complex characters allows the viewer to explore the causal ambiguity of behavior. A good example comes from *American Beauty* (Mendes, 1999). This film tells the story of Lester Burnham (Kevin Spacey), a mild-mannered 42 year-old man who diligently writes copy for an advertising magazine. The film plots his transition into a nervous breakdown and offers many triggers: his wife's infidelity, his wife's whining, his daughter's teenage angst, lust for his daughter's best friend, smoking 'weed' at a party, memories of teenage years, frustration with corporate life, and so forth. The film does not try to explain which of these influences triggered Lester's crisis, opting instead to portray complex behaviors with ambiguous roots. An alternative way of demonstrating causal ambiguity is to use films that are not shot in chronological order, that is films which begin at either the middle or end of the film, and scene-by-scene move towards the start. Recent films with distorted timelines that challenge viewers to discover the thread of causality are *Memento* (Nolan, 2000), *Pulp Fiction*, *Go* (Limon, 1999) and *Sex and Lucia* (Medem, 2001), although the content of some parts of these films may restrict their suitability for the classroom if sections for viewing are not carefully selected.

Path dependency is an isolating mechanism in which the present is the result of history, and to arrive at the same point that one organization has reached, may mean repeating that organization's history. This subject is perfectly captured in *Groundhog Day* (Ramis, 1993). In this film, television news reporter Phil Connors (Bill Murray) wakes every morning to find himself living the same day, day after day. We see how his slight change of behavior results in different outcomes. This is particularly well illustrated in a series of days where he changes his responses to questions until he is able to seduce an attractive woman. A similar narrative design, although with a different purpose, is employed in *Source Code* (Jones, 2011). An alternative illustration of path dependency comes from the *Harry Potter* films, with the scar on Harry's forehead. This scar was the result of Voldemort's murder of Harry's mother and her protection of him. The scar throbs with pain whenever Voldemort is near, thereby reminding him of Voldemort's evil and his own need for revenge and retribution.

Internal Environment

Organizational knowledge is the collective and shared experience accumulated across the organization through routines of sharing. In organizations it is not just individual knowledge that matters but the knowledge of groups of people. People come and go, but the organization preserves knowledge and behaviors over time. This is one process that is easily and appropriately illustrated with military examples. An example in which the development of organizational knowledge is a major theme is in the film *The Dirty Dozen* (Aldrich, 1967). In this film a rebellious Major is 'volunteered' to train twelve convicted military criminals for a suicide mission. Prior to the attack he uses a model of the target chateau and a rhyme to ingrain the roles of all the team. They are seen to repeatedly recite the roles of everybody so that if one fails the person before or after can take over and perform their task. An alternative way to depict organizational knowledge is to talk about the opposite situation where it is vitally important that there is no organizational knowledge so that the organization's members are protected. Many crime movies illustrate this. In *Reservoir Dogs* (Tarantino, 1991), for example, all the members of the hold-up team have fake names and know nothing about each other in case they are caught. Films about terrorists and resistance fighters portray a similar need to minimize all organizational knowledge; examples include *The Battle of Algiers* (Pontecorvo, 1965) and *Carve Her Name with Pride* (Gilbert, 1958).

On the surface, the subject of *organizational culture* – the beliefs and assumptions that are shared in an organization – would appear to be one of the simplest of all strategic management concepts to illustrate; all one has to do is to show excerpts from films set in workplaces. However, many directors who set films in the workplace do so with the deliberate intention of making a statement about contemporaneous work practices. An early example of this genre is *A nous la liberté* (Clair, 1931) in which the degrading, repetitive factory work of the early 1930s is shown in its full dehumanizing form. This theme was repeated by Chaplin in *Modern Times* (Chaplin, 1936) in which the image of the worker as a 'cog in the machine' is an abiding memory. The 1980s was another period in which directors clearly had something to say about the workplace. Films such as *Working Girl* (Nichols, 1988), *Nine to Five* (Higgins, 1980), *Glengarry Glen Ross* (Foley, 1992) all depicted the 'greed is good' mentality of aggressive capitalism. This genre reached its full expression in *Wall Street* (Stone, 1987); a film that Denzin (1995) has claimed was so powerful that it helped create the very working culture that it parodied. As a result, we recommend that if educators are using films to depict organizational culture, they should use contemporaneous films that represent current themes and issues in the workplace. Interesting examples that depict the high stress (Bunting, 2004), 'Living Dead' (Bolchover, 2005), unethical (Treviño & Brown, 2004) work cultures of today include *American Beauty, Happiness* (Solondz, 1998), *Elf* (Favreau, 2003), *Up in the Air* (Reitman, 2009), and two films in the tradition of French social realism, *Human Resources* (Cantet, 1999) and *Time Out* (Cantet, 2001). A particularly useful source on this subject is *The Corporation* (Achbar & Abbott, 2003). This documentary explores the rise of corporations and their current behavior. One section of the film focuses on oil company employees, especially the top team, and the ethical behavior of their organizations.

Despite the apparently earnest wishes of senior executives who are person-ally passionately committed to the environment and ethical behavior, they cannot prevent their corporations behaving in harmful ways.

One aspect of organizational culture that is commonly taught is *taken for granted assumptions*: that is, deeply held values and beliefs that influence behavior. Obviously there are many examples of these in films, but one humorous exemplar that clearly captures the concept comes from *Chicken Run*. There is a scene in which the farmer, Mr. Tweedy, begins to suspect that the chickens are planning to escape and so he confides in his wife. She responds:

"They're chickens, you dolt. Apart from you, they're the most stupid creatures on this planet. They don't plot, they don't scheme, and they are not organized!"

Here is a taken for granted assumption that blinds the holder to the reality and averts preventative action. Another humorous example comes from *North by Northwest* (Hitchcock, 1959) and the exchange between Rog-er Thornhill (Cary Grant) and Eve Kendall (Eva Marie Saint): Thornhill: "The moment I meet an attractive woman, I have to start pretending I have no desire to make love to her." Kendall: "What makes you think you have to conceal it?" Thornhill: "She might find the idea objectionable." Kendall: "Then again, she might not".

Methods of Development

Mergers and acquisitions feature on many strategic management curricula and are easy to illustrate with case studies. However, a criticism commonly leveled at case studies is that they project a world of rationality that promotes choices free from the minutiae of organizational functioning. Films can be helpful in showing students the impact that mergers and acquisitions have on organizational actors and the communities they occupy. Two films from the mid 1980s show this impact in sensitive and thoughtful ways. *Wall Street* depicts the takeover of an airline by an investment company who apparent-ly cares little for the existing workforce. *Gung Ho* shows the fictional post-merger integration of an American car factory into a global Japanese car manufacturer. It is particularly strong on integration complexity stemming from nationality, culture, work attitudes, and corporate style differences. An interesting contrast to *Gung Ho* is Michael Moore's debut documentary *Roger and Me* (Moore, 1989) in which the crusading filmmaker spends three years in search of General Motors (GM) chairman Roger Smith. Moore's home town, Flint, Michigan, had been the site of a GM car plant, which was closed and moved to Mexico to reduce production costs. Moore's film charts the devastation that GM's decision had on Flint and, in doing so he questions the 'greed is good' philosophy of other films in the genre.

A *strategic alliance* is an alliance in which capabilities are shared so that performance is enhanced. To be successful, it is important that there is strategic fit, capabilities fit, cultural fit, and organizational fit between the parties. We suggest a range of examples to illustrate this concept. In *The Devil's Brigade* (McLaglen, 1968), a special fighting unit is formed combining a crack Canadian outfit and a bunch of US Army misfits during World War II. Initially the men hate each other and continually bicker during training. Progressively, they stop fighting and begin to respect each other when they are deployed to Italy, where they must capture a strategic hilltop. In *The Lord of the Rings: The Fellowship of the Ring* (Jackson, 2001), Elrond (Hugo Weaving) brings together the various peoples of Middle Earth to create a team to destroy the 'one ring'. In *Star Trek VI: The Undiscovered Country* (Meyer, 1991), the crew of the *Enterprise* find themselves trying to stop a plot to break up the alliance between the Federation and the Klingons. Finally in *Dances with Wolves* (Costner, 1990), we see the formation and maturing of a strategic alliance between Lt. John Dunbar (Kevin Costner) and the indigenous Sioux to fight the encroaching 'white man.'

CONCLUSION

Strategy must surely qualify as the frustrating science. It is not only frustratingly difficult to practice: it is even more frustratingly difficult to teach. The problem with the current system is that it forces strategy into the direct and narrow approach to teaching ... A deep grasp of strategy, however, resists this approach ... The challenge of teaching strategy consists of creating a virtuous cycle in which articulation and intuition form an increasingly powerful combination. (Lampel, 2005, p. 20)

By arguing that films should become part of the strategy instructors, our intention was to broaden the range of learning styles that we employ in our strategic management classrooms. Moreover, we believe that this technique has a lot of value when teaching people with little experience of strategic decision-making and who therefore find it a struggle to comprehend and internalize these practical ideas.

Above, we have described a selection of film scenes that could be used to illustrate concepts that some students may have difficulties grasping. Many of these concepts are intangible, procedural, and as a whole, not easy to comprehend fully when one has little experience of strategy. We have argued that films can be an effective teaching and learning device and hence they are a useful addition to the strategy instructors' teaching toolbox. They help students remember course ideas, they add complexity, richness, depth, and reality. The ideas come 'alive', which increases student interaction and involvement. Using films in the strategic management classroom captures students' imagination, and this helps them study ideas in greater depth. They are intrigued and excited by the method and this creates a creative climate where learning is fun and memorable.

Finally we would like to add that because films are still unconventional teaching material, they are notably a break from case studies, and as such they allow educators to keep the concentration levels high. Students are intrigued and tend to focus. In many respects films in management classrooms are unequalled in their ability to hold and direct attention (Champoux, 2006). As films are unusual and fresh they help in motivating students (Buchanan & Huczynski, 2004). This is a rather important aspect as "the effect of instructional methods on instructional outcomes is partially mediated by learner motivation" (Burke & Moore, 2003, p. 39). This also means that films do not have to be and should not be perceived as "the entertaining sidelines of classroom gimmicks" (Buchanan & Huczynski, 2004, p. 312).

REFERENCES

Ambrosini, V., Billsberry, J., & Collier, N. (2009). Teaching soft issues in strategic management with films: Arguments and suggestions. *International Journal of Management Education, 8*(1), 63–72.

Baker, A., Jensen, P., & Kolb, D. (2005). Conversation as experiential learning. *Management Learning, 36*(4), 411–427.

Barney, J., & Hesterly, W. (2006). *Strategic management and competitive advantage*. (6th ed.). Upper Saddle River, NJ: Pearson Education.

Baruch, Y. (2006). Role-play teaching. *Management Learning, 37*(1), 43–61.

Billsberry, J., & Gilbert, L. H. (2008). Using Roald Dahl's *Charlie and the Chocolate Factory* to teach different recruitment and selection paradigms. *Journal of Management Education, 32*(2), 228–247.

Bolchover, D. (2005). *The living dead.* Chichester, UK: Capstone.

Buchanan, D., & Huczynski, A. (2004). Images of influence: *12 Angry Men* and *Thirteen Days. Journal of Management Inquiry, 13*(4), 312–323.

Bumpus, M. A. (2005). Using motion pictures to teach management: Refocusing the camera lens through the infusion approach to diversity. *Journal of Management Education, 29*(6), 792–815.

Bunting, M. (2004). *Willing slaves: How the overwork culture is ruling our lives.* London, UK: HarperCollins.

Burke, L. M. & Moore, J. E. (2003). *A perennial dilemma in OB education: Engaging the traditional student. Academy of Management Learning and Education, 2*(1), 37–52.

Champoux, J. E. (1999). Film as a teaching resource. *Journal of Management Inquiry, 8*(2), 206–217.

Champoux, J. E. (2000a). *Management: Using film to visualize principles and practices.* Cincinnati, OH: South-Western College Publishing.

Champoux, J. E. (2000b). *Organizational behavior: Using film to visualize principles and practices.* Cincinnati, OH: South-Western College Publishing.

Champoux, J. E. (2001). Animated films as a teaching resource. *Journal of Management Education, 25*(1), 79–100.

Champoux, J. E. (2003a). *At the movies: Organizational behavior.* Cincinnati, OH: South-Western College Publishing.

Champoux, J. E. (2003b). *At the movies: Management.* Cincinnati, OH: South-Western College Publishing.

Champoux, J. E. (2004). *Our feature presentation: Management.* Mason, OH: South-Western College Publishing.

Champoux, J. E. (2005). *Our feature presentation: Organizational behavior.* Mason, OH: South-Western College Publishing.

Champoux, J. E. (2006). European films as a management education teaching resource. In T. Torres-Coronas, M. Gascó Hernández, & A. Fernandes de Matos Coelho (Eds.), *Changing the way you teach: Creative tools for management educators.* Oviedo, Spain: Septem Ediciones.

Clemens, J. K., & Wolff, M. (2000). *Movies to manage by.* New York, NY: McGraw-Hill Education.

de Wit, B., & Meyer, R. (2004). *Strategy: Process, content, context* (3rd ed.). London, UK: Thomson.

Denzin, N. K. (1995). *The cinematic society: The voyeur's gaze.* London, UK: Sage.

Dess, G., Lumpkin, G., & Taylor, M. (2005). *Strategic management: Creating competitive advantages* (2nd ed.). Boston, MA: McGraw Hill.

Forrest III, S. P., & Peterson, T. (2006). It's called andragogy. *Academy of Management Learning and Education, 5*(1), 113–122.

Grant, R. (2005). *Contemporary strategy analysis* (5th ed.). Oxford, UK: Blackwell.

Greiner, L. E., Bhambri, A., & Cummings, T. G. (2003). Searching for a strategy to teach strategy. *Academy of Management Learning and Education, 2*(4), 402–420.

Hassard, J., & Holliday, R. (1998). *Organization-representation.* London, UK: Sage.

Hitt, M., Ireland, R., & Hoskisson, R. (2005). *Strategic management: Competitiveness and globalization.* New Jersey, NJ: Pearson.

Huczynski, A. (1994). Teaching motivation and influencing strategies using 'The Magnificent Seven'. *Journal of Management Education, 18*(2), 273–278.

Huczynski, A., & Buchanan, D. (2004). Theory from fiction: A narrative process perspective on the pedagogic use of feature film. *Journal of Management Education, 28*(6), 702–726.

Johnson, G., Scholes, K., & Whittington, R. (2005). *Exploring corporate strategy* (7th ed.). London, UK: Prentice Hall.

Joshi, M. P., Davis, E. B., Kathuria, R., & Weidner, C. K. (2005). Experiential learning process: Exploring teaching and learning of strategic management framework through the winter survival exercise. *Journal of Management Education, 29*(5), 672–695.

Kolb, D. A. (1984). *Experiential Learning.* Englewood Cliffs, NJ: Prentice-Hall.

Kolb, A. Y., & Kolb, D. A. (2005). *Learning styles and learning spaces: Enhancing experiential learning in higher education. Academy of Management Learning and Education, 4*(2), 193–212.

Lampel, J. (2005). New perspectives on teaching strategy. *European Business Forum, 21*(Spring), 20–21.

McCambridge, J. (2003). *12 Angry Men:* A study in dialogue, *Journal of Management Education, 27*(3), 384–401.

Mintzberg, H., & Gosling, J. R. (2002). Reality programming for MBAs. *Strategy and Business, 26*(1), 28–31.

Nadkarni, S. (2003). Instructional methods and mental models of students: An empirical investigation. *Academy of Management Learning and Education, 2*(4), 335–51.

Pfeffer, J. F., & Fong, C. T. (2002). The end of business schools? Less success than meets the eye. *Academy of Management Learning and Education, 1*(1), 78–95.

Reynolds, M., & Vince, R. (2004). Critical management education and action-based learning: Synergies and contradictions. *Academy of Management Learning and Education, 3*(4), 442–56.

Serey, T. T. (1992). Carpe Diem: Lessons about life and management from '*Dead Poets Society*'. *Journal of Management Education, 16*(3), 374–381.

Short, J. C., & Ketchen, D. J. (2005). Teaching timeless truths through classic literature: 'Aesop's Fables' and strategic management. *Journal of Management Education, 29*(6), 816–832.

Stadler, H. (1990). Film as experience: Phenomenological concepts in cinema and television studies. *Quarterly Review of Film and Video, 12*(3), 37–50.

Treviño, L. K., & Brown, M. E. (2004). Managing to be ethical: Debunking five business ethics myths. *Academy of Management Executive, 18*(2), 69–81.

White, C. (2004). *Strategic management.* Basingstoke, UK: Palgrave.

Films

Achbar, M., & Abbott, J. (Directors). (2003). *The corporation* [Motion picture]. Canada: Big Picture Media Corporation.

Aldrich, R. (Director). (1967). *The dirty dozen* [Motion picture]. United States: MGM

Burton, T. (Director). (2005). *Charlie and the chocolate factory* [Motion picture]. United States: Warner Bros.

Cantet, L. (Director). (1999). *Human resources* [Motion picture]. France: La Sept Arte.

Cantet, L. (Director). (2001). *Time out* [Motion picture]. France: Le Studio Canal+.

Chaplin, C. (Director). (1936). *Modern times* [Motion picture]. United States: Charles Chaplin Productions & United Artists.

Clair, R. (Director). (1931). *À nous la liberté* [Motion picture]. France: Société des Films Sonores Tobis.

Coen, J. (Director). (1994). *The Hudsucker Proxy* [Motion picture]. United States: Warner Brothers.

Collinson, P. (Director). (1969). *The Italian job* [Motion picture]. United Kingdom: Paramount Pictures.

Columbus, C. (Director). (2001). *Harry Potter and the sorcerer's stone* [Motion picture]. United States: Warner Bros.

Costner, K. (Director). (1990). *Dances with wolves* [Motion picture]. United States: Tig Productions & Majestic Films International.

Crichton, C. (Director). (1951). *The Lavender Hill mob* [Motion picture]. United Kingdom: Ealing Studios.

Darabont, F. (Director). (1994). *The Shawshank redemption* [Motion picture]. United States: Columbia Pictures.

Donner, R. (Director). (1987). *Lethal weapon* [Motion picture]. United States: Warner Bros.

Favreau, J. (Director). (2003). *Elf* [Motion picture]. Germany & United States: Shawn Danielle Productions, Gold/Miller Productions, Guy Walks into a Bar Productions, & Mosaic Media Group.

Fincher, D. (Director). (1995). *Se7en* [Motion picture]. United States: New Line Cinema.

Foley, J. (Director). (1992). *Glengarry Glen Ross* [Motion picture]. United States: New Line Cinema.

Gilbert, L. (Director). (1958). *Carve her name with pride* [Motion picture]. United Kingdom: Angel Productions.

Higgins, C. (Director). (1980). *Nine to five* [Motion picture]. United States: 20th Century Fox.

Hitchcock, A. (Director). (1959). *North by northwest* [Motion picture]. United States: MGM.

Howard, R. (Director). (1986). *Gung ho* [Motion picture]. United States: Paramount Pictures.

Jackson, P. (Director). (2001). *The lord of the rings: The fellowship of the ring* [Motion picture]. New Zealand & United States: New Line Cinema & Wingnut Films.

Jackson, P. (Director). (2002). *The lord of the rings: The two towers* [Motion picture]. New Zealand & United States: New Line Cinema & Wingnut Films.

Jackson, P. (Director) (2003). *The lord of the rings: The return of the king* [Motion picture]. New Zealand & United States: New Line Cinema & Wingnut Films.

Jones, D. (Director). (2011). *Source code* [Motion picture]. United States & France: Vendome Pictures & The Mark Gordon Company.

Kershner, I. (Director). (1980). *Star wars V: The empire strikes back* [Motion picture]. United States: 20th Century Fox.

Levinson, B. (Director). (1994). *Disclosure* [Motion picture]. United States: Warner Brothers.

Limon, D. (Director). (1999). *Go* [Motion picture]. United States: Sony Pictures.

Lord, P. & Park, N. (Directors). (2000). *Chicken run* [Motion picture]. United Kingdom: DreamWorks, Pathé, & Aardman Animations.

Lumet, S. (Director). (1957). *12 angry men* [Motion picture]. United States: Orion-Nova Productions.

Lurie, R. (Director). (2001). *The last castle* [Motion picture]. United States: Dreamworks.

McLagan, A. (Director). (1968). *Devil's brigade* [Motion picture]. United States: MGM.

Medem, J. (Director). (2001). *Sex and Lucia* [Motion picture]. Spain & France: Studio Canal & Canal+ España.

Mendes, S. (Director). (1999). *American beauty* [Motion picture]. United States: Dreamworks.

Meyer, N. (Director). (1991). *Star trek VI: The undiscovered country* [Motion picture]. United States: Paramount Pictures.

Moore, M. (Director). (1989). *Roger & me* [Motion picture]. United States: Dog Eat Dog Films & Warner Bros.

Nichols, M. (Director). (1988). *Working girl* [Motion picture]. United States: 20th Century Fox.

Nolan, C. (Director). (2000). *Memento* [Motion picture]. United States: Summit Entertainment.

Petersen, W. (Director). (2004). *Troy* [Motion picture]. United States: Warner Bros.

Pontecorvo, G. (Director). (1965). *The battle of Algiers* [Motion picture]. Algeria & Italy: Casbah Film & Igor Film.

Ramis, H. (Director). (1993). *Groundhog day* [Motion picture]. United States: Sony Pictures.

Ratner, B. (Director). (1998). *Rush hour* [Motion picture]. United States: New Line Cinema.

Reitman, J. (Director). (2009). *Up in the air* [Motion picture]. United States: Paramount Pictures.

Sargent, J. (Director). (2000). *The Arturo Sandoval story* [Motion picture]. United States: Home Box Office.

Siegel, D. (Director). (1979). *Escape from Alcatraz* [Motion picture]. United States: Paramount Pictures.

Solondz, T. (Director). (1998). *Happiness* [Motion picture]. United States: Good Machine & Killer Films.

Sonnenfeld, B. (Director). (1997). *Men in black* [Motion picture]. United States: Amblin Entertainment/Columbia Pictures.

Stone, O. (Director). (1987). *Wall Street* [Motion picture]. United States: 20th Century Fox.

Sturges, J. (Director). (1960). *The magnificent seven* [Motion picture]. United States: Mirsch.

Sturges, J. (Director). (1963). *The great escape* [Motion picture]. United States: Mirsch.

Tarantino, Q. (Director). (1991). *Reservoir dogs* [Motion picture]. United States: Dog Eat Dog Productions.

Tarantino, Q. (Director). (1994). *Pulp fiction* [Motion picture]. United States: A Band Apart.

Ward, M. (Director). (1989). *Major league* [Motion picture]. United States: Paramount Pictures.

Weir, P. (Director). (1989). *The dead poets society* [Motion picture]. United States: Touchstone.

Wilder, B. (Director). (1959). *Some like it hot* [Motion picture]. United States: Mirsch.

CHAPTER 14

USING FILM IN THE TEACHING OF STRATEGIC DECISION-MAKING

Peter Galvin and Troy Hendrickson

In a traditional strategy class utilizing the case method for instruction, strategic decision-making was previously covered using just another case. One case presented a hypothetical situation about a potential new product and included a series of financial projections for five different possible options. Students chose and justified their choices and we were able to have a discussion around risk, central tendency theory, the issue of framing, imperfect information, and the issues of political influences and degree of uncertainty. However, the students had no real attachment to the financial projections and they struggled to engage with the case in a way that really brought many of the interesting issues concerning strategic decision-making to the fore.

A new approach was thus sought—something that would illustrate the decision-making process and how it could potentially play out. While a few different options were available, an obvious choice was the film *Thirteen Days* (Donaldson, 2000). Covering issues from path dependency in decision-making to the role of signaling, the majority of the film relates the

Moving Images: Effective Teaching with Film and Television in Higher Education,
pages 193–207
193

processes used by the US President of the time and his senior advisors to make decisions. Students may understand the cognitive limits of humans and the biases that exist, but outside of real experience, many key issues concerning strategic decision-making remain somewhat theoretical. Given so many frameworks assume that strategic decision-makers behave rationally, the main contribution of the film is to provide a clear example of why such rationality is exceptionally difficult to achieve.

Strategic decision-making is one stage in the strategy development process. It is traditionally shown as following the analysis of environmental data (internal and external) and prior to implementation (e.g. Grant, 2007; Hill, Jones, Galvin, & Hadir, 2007). Strategic decision-making usually incorporates the formation of different alternatives and a process for choosing the most desirable path of action. It is important to note that whilst the strategy process may be shown as a series of steps it is not entirely linear in that there are interactions and feedback loops throughout the process (Mintzberg, Théorêt, & Raisinghani, 1976). It is therefore important to see that any discussion of strategic decision-making tends to take place within a strategic management context. While the breadth of issues that can be covered is significant, the most obvious points tend to occur in respect of biases, decision-trajectories, team composition, cognitive limits, the use of assumptions, the role of signaling, second-order effects and the importance of leadership.

The setting for the film *Thirteen Days* is the key 13 days during the Cuban Missile Crisis. It focuses entirely upon the US side of the event with much of the movie taking place within the White House. The movie centers on how President John F. Kennedy (JFK) and various advisors decide to respond to the central problem of nuclear missiles being placed in Cuba and the related events that occur in respect of this crisis. As the movie concentrates on the formation of responses by the US Administration, it is particularly well-suited to fostering a discussion around strategic decision-making.

BACKGROUND

The movie is particularly powerful because it is a relatively accurate depiction of many of the events surrounding the Cuban Missile Crisis. There are some minor inaccuracies in the movie such as when Kenny O'Donnell (Kevin Costner) requests that pilots do not reveal to their superiors if they are shot at in their missions over Cuba (the members of ExComm were aware that the low-flying missions were attracting ground fire), but the basic thrust of the film is accurate. In fact, many of the conversations of ExComm were taped and these formed the (edited) basis for much of the discussion shown in the movie. Similarly, a series of famous Time Life photographs were taken of JFK, his brother Robert (Bobby) Kennedy, and others such as Kenny O'Donnell around this time at the White House and the movie seeks to even recreate many of these scenes to add to the realism. While it may be that some students will have read the book *Thirteen Days* by Robert Kennedy and will identify other discrepancies such as the fact that, with the possible exception of General LeMay, the relationship between the Kennedys and the US Military was not as confrontational as presented, most of these issues simply heighten many of the key teaching points within the movie.

In using this movie in class, we ask that each student take the time to watch the entire movie in totality. While it is long—almost two and a half hours—the students we have taught have almost universally enjoyed the activity. To refresh everyone's memory on the day of the class we show a small clip covering chapters 4 and 5 of the movie (starting at 12 minutes 49 seconds and running until 24:40)[1]. To give us a variety of issues to talk about we then ask each student to write one point concerning strategic decision-making that they were able to take-away on the basis of watching the movie. Thus the following issues tend not to be covered in any particular order.

PATH DEPENDENCY AND DECISION MAKING

It is impossible to make informed decisions that are not affected by prior learning. To make anything more than a guess as to how entities or constructs will interact, we must have developed a degree of knowledge concerning similar scenarios on the basis of some past learning. This learning will be driven by past events—whether these were personally experienced or not. Over time, our experiences form the basis for mental models (discussed later) but they also form the cognitive systems and memories which preserve certain behaviors, norms and values over time (Helleloid & Simonin, 1994). In complex situations, we tend to apply our learning via analogy (Winston, 1980)—previously when X and Y occurred I needed to do Z and so therefore now that something similar in the form of A and B are occurring, I think that I should do something very similar to Z. A significant challenge for decision makers is determining which past events will serve as the analogy that reflects the prior learning. Events that are similar or historically recent tend to be used, but these are not necessarily always correct. In any case, decisions cannot be made context free due to the way learning occurs and this creates path dependencies.

The movie shows numerous examples of trying to make decisions on the basis of analogy. There are three recurring events in the movie that all get mentioned in the short clip we show at the beginning of the class—Munich, Pearl Harbor, and the Bay of Pigs. The Munich conference emboldened

---

[1] If there is time, or not enough students have watched the movie in advance I also show part of chapter 7 (26:45 until 30:50).

Hitler when the British Prime Minister simply signed a treaty to try and limit Hitler's aggression. Pearl Harbor was a surprise attack on the US Pacific Fleet in Hawaii that caught the US completely off-guard, even though subsequent analysis of data showed that information collected by US intelligence suggested such an attack was going to occur. Finally, the Bay of Pigs was a failed invasion of Cuba in 1961 that was spear-headed by the CIA.

ExComm—the team that JFK assembled to help respond to the discovery of nuclear missiles in Cuba—would invariably be influenced in their decisions by these past events. While one can approach a decision in the belief that they are being entirely rational it is simply not possible to exclude past events from our cognitive processes as they help us to define what is rational in the first place. That is, decisions take place within the context of a trajectory of past events that cannot be excluded from the decision-making process.

In this particular case, there is a general feeling that, as Dean Acheson states, "appeasement only makes the enemy stronger." It failed with Hitler in Munich and thus in this case the preference is to respond forcefully, that is, military action. With Pearl Harbor, American military strength was compromised and therefore now that the spy planes had caught the nuclear missiles in the process of being made operational, there was again the feeling that something needed to be done before the US military strength (relative to the Soviets') was compromised. Finally, the Bay of Pigs probably made many people wary of promises of guaranteed success in respect of military action, but there were probably also some in the Administration (and the military) that would like a chance to make up for the previous failure in 1961. Thus overall, there was a feeling that there needed to be a strong response and a quick response that did not allow the US's significant nuclear advantage to be compromised.

These past events make strong military action seem rational—even though it may lead to nuclear war and in excess of 100 million deaths in the US and possibly Western Europe. Rationality is therefore analyzing cause and effect relationships within a particular context and relevant past events will invariably be used to predict the effect in question within the context present—even if the events are only tenuously linked. Today for example, different events (and thus analogies) would probably be used. To counter the 'appeasement' argument, some might point to the overthrow of Saddam Hussein and the subsequent problems this created when a very strong approach was taken with an aggressor. Thus trajectories do change over time.

THE ROLE OF PAST EXPERIENCE AT AN INDIVIDUAL LEVEL

Learning tends to involve the testing, revision and acceptance of knowledge that draws upon past experiences and present events (Tsoukas, 1996). It is a highly individual process within a larger system and thus our subsequent knowledge tends to be socially constructed on the basis of our own set of personal experiences. Such an approach highlights how an individual's understanding of connections among parts of the system can enable learning (Anderson, 1999; Kallinikos, 1998). This unique set of experiences and the learning attached to them leads to different ways of solving the problem (often with quite different outcomes).

For example, LeMay, as the most 'hawkish' of the military people in Ex-Comm had devised and been in command of the strategy to undertake mass-bombings of Japan in World War 2. Faced with the current problem, his past experiences suggested to him that an overwhelming show of force was likely to be successful. In this respect, all of the military members of ExComm, given they were career military people, tended to see a military solution to the problem. In comparison, Adlai Stevenson was the US ambassador to the U.N. and as a diplomat saw the problem as requiring a diplomatic solution. The Kennedys were politicians and kept pushing for an alternative course of action as the likelihood of a nuclear exchange and massive loss of life that the military option brought and the permanent existence of nuclear missiles just 90 miles off the US coast that a diplomatic option would probably produce were both politically unpalatable options. Interestingly it was a combination of political (back-room deals to remove the missiles in Turkey and a no-invasion pledge), military (the enforcement of the blockade and the massive troop build-up indicating a seriousness to follow-through), and diplomatic efforts (support for the blockade by the Organization for American States and the critical speech in the U.N. showing that the Soviet's were lying) that all together led to the defusing of the crisis.

MENTAL MODELS

These individual experiences form the basis of mental models—an individual's personal linking of concepts and relationships into abstract cognitive structures on the basis of their past experiences to provide a basis for future decision-making (Boak & Thompson, 1998). They tend to include significant amounts of tacit knowledge such that the individual cannot clearly delineate the exact relationship between different concepts or why such a relationship exists. They do, however, have a level of understanding that helps to guide their actions (even though they may not be able to fully explain why they fully believe such a course of action is correct to others). Thus, for some, mental models may be thought of as 'gut instinct' but decisions relying upon mental models are based on a degree of understanding, even if this cannot be communicated via explicit arguments (Baddeley, 1990). A number of examples in *Blink* (Gladwell, 2005) rely upon the concept of mental models to explain how experienced people are able to make quick and correct decisions, but are unable to explain their reasoning.

A discussion of mental models is a good way to begin a discussion around one of the most powerful lines in the movie when JFK states that "there is something immoral about abandoning your own judgment". Even though JFK was largely surrounded by people from the military within ExComm and they were almost universally pushing for a military solution, he continued to delay committing to this option until absolutely every other possible option had been considered. JFK's mental model of this situation would have seemed to suggest that once the chain of events initiated by an attack on Cuba was started, nothing would be able to stop the events before it led to all-out nuclear war. Dean Acheson may have hoped "that cooler heads would prevail" before a nuclear exchange occurred, but JFK could not see this happening. His reading of the *Guns of August* concerning the inability to move beyond constantly failing strategies in World War 1, plus his involvement in World War 2 as a combat soldier (as opposed to command-level duties for most other members of ExComm) made him terribly fearful of a military option that would likely risk the lives of 100 million Americans.

Interestingly, each of the other people involved in the decision-making process would have had their own mental models. While the purely diplomatic approach favored by Stevenson would have gone against the mental models of many of the Generals, the blockade was agreed to by all, suggesting that it was seen as forceful enough by the 'hawks,' yet provided enough room for a back-down by the Soviets to be accepted by the non-military personnel. Thus there did not need to be a complete 'abandoning of judgment' by any ExComm member.

THE NEED FOR ASSUMPTIONS AND THE EVEN GREATER NEED FOR DATA

In any strategic decision it is impossible to get all of the data you would like to have. Much of the problem comes from the fact that you are dealing with the future in terms of developing a strategy today for five or more years into the future. In addition, it is not possible to know how your competitor (or supplier, buyer, etc.) will react to your various actions. Strategy textbooks highlight the need to monitor the macro environment, but the implicit message of such an approach is that the future is somewhat unpredictable and at a minimum you must try and understand the present environment as much as possible. The reality is that if you wait for virtually complete information you will be frozen by inaction, but to move too hastily and act on a large number of assumptions may prove to be just as risky.

In the scene when the President and other members of his inner-circle are being briefed about the discovery of the buildup of missiles in Cuba the presenter makes continual assumptions: "we believe", "we understand", "we assume", "most likely," and "undoubtedly". Many of these assumptions were wrong. Some missiles were actually operational already, there were 40,000

Soviet personnel (not 2–3,000 as assumed) the missiles were actually a longer range missile than initially thought etc.

Nevertheless, assumptions are an integral part of strategic decision-making. What is important is to recognize what are assumptions versus what is fact. Assumptions can then be challenged or changed. For example, if you assume a certain cost for product development, will the program still be profitable if these development costs increase by 50%?, or 100%? Too often assumptions in the movie were treated as fact and nobody played the role of devil's advocate or even simply questioned what the outcome may be if some of these assumptions were changed.

THE ROLE OF SIGNALING

In making decisions, we are not privy to what is taking place within our competitors. What are they thinking, why, what will they do next and how will they react to our particular actions? When data is not easily available we often revert to interpreting actions to try and understand the thought process of our adversary. That is, we interpret signals to help in our decision-making process and we send signals (explicitly or implicitly) that may affect the actions of the other player(s). Our ability to send and appropriately interpret signals depends upon the characteristics of the sender, the characteristics of the signal (e.g. consistency, clarity, and aggressiveness), and the characteristics of the receiver (Heil & Robertson, 1991).

In the movie, we, like all the members of ExComm, have no real idea as to what Khrushchev and his advisors are thinking. The US military interpreted the placement of missiles in Cuba as a shift towards a first strike policy (whereas in actual fact the Soviets saw it as addressing a significant imbalance in respect of nuclear capabilities and could thus be construed as a defensive act to keep the superpowers more closely balanced, that is, the signal was misinterpreted). An example of trying to read an event as a signal is when Bobby Kennedy and Kenny O'Donnell drive past the Soviet embassy on the way to meet the Soviet Ambassador. They note that there is smoke coming out of the chimneys and assume that they are burning all of their important documents as they "believe that we are going to war." The Soviets may however, have simply been cleaning out their chimneys in preparation for winter. Some signals remained unresolved as to their implications. For example, the fact that a second letter was sent from Khrushchev that was very different from the first left members of ExComm wondering if there had been a coup and hardliners had taken control of the government. In times where real information is hard to come by, we tend to rely more upon the signals from the environment, but our ability to read signals accurately and separate real signals from 'noise' is often limited.

The US purposely and inadvertently 'sent' a number of signals to the Soviets. Sometimes these were mistakes such as a nuclear test in the Pacific or a U2 spy-plane getting lost in Soviet airspace. Some such as the nuclear test and moving to Defense Condition (DefCon) 2 were 'sent' by Le May to ratchet up the tension to try and start a war. The Soviets would not have know that these were unintentional and are likely to have interpreted all actions as being aggressive in that the US was readying itself for nuclear war. The classic example of signaling in the movie comes in an exchange between Robert McNamara and the Chief of Staff of the Navy concerning the firing of what amounted to a warning shot over a Soviet freighter. McNamara makes it clear that this is JFK 'talking' to Khrushchev via signals in terms of intentions and essentially escalating or partially defusing the crisis.

SECOND ORDER EFFECTS

'How will our competitors respond to our actions?' is a question that is at the heart of competitive strategy. Firms not only seek to predict competitors' actions, but also their reactions to any actions made by them. This idea of a series of responses cycling back and forth between organizations is at the heart of game theory (Brandenburger & Nalebuff, 1995). However, not only does each action have an intended effect, there may be other flow-on effects or second-order effects. Toffler's (1980) classic *Future Shock* provided somewhat radical predictions based purely upon extrapolating existing data and asking the 'then what will happen' question to future scenarios based upon existing trends. Looking at this flow of responses and second-order effects should be a critical component of strategy—though it is rarely undertaken. For example, a price cut by an airline may seem attractive in that it may lead to increased numbers with each additional passenger adding little to the overall fixed costs. Yet if competitors all drop their prices, few additional tickets will be sold, but the margins on each ticket will be cut. The value of thinking through likely reactions and second-order effects can be clearly seen in the film. For example, after agreeing that a diplomatic solution was off-the-table, JFK asks Dean Acheson to talk him through how a military strike "will all play out." An attack on the missiles in Cuba will lead to a retaliatory response by the Soviets—"most likely Berlin". Berlin will be overrun and the US/NATO will be forced to "defeat them [the Soviets] as per our plans." These plans would involve the use of nuclear arms creating a full-scale nuclear exchange.

It is the likely response of the Soviets that makes every option being considered by ExComm so problematic. To do nothing would essentially eliminate the US's vast superiority in respect of nuclear missiles being able to hit the Soviet Union as the Americans had approximately 3,000 nuclear bombs capable of hitting the Soviet Union whereas the Soviets possessed only 40 intercontinental nuclear missiles. To attack the missiles would probably lead to a retaliatory attack against Berlin and an invasion would simply increase the likelihood of such an attack. And even a blockade was expected to be met by a similar blockade on Berlin.

While these actions, reactions, and reactions to reactions made choosing a course of action difficult, it is interesting to compare this multi-step thinking to that of LeMay. When asked what the Soviets would do if their missiles and troops were attacked in Cuba he suggests that they will do "Nothing. Because the alternative open to them is one that they can't choose". Yet, when interviewing a pilot following a low-level run to photograph the missile sites he wants to know if "they so much as shot a bee-bee gun at you" as if there was any attack by Soviet forces he would want to respond instantly.

THE ROLE OF LEADERSHIP

Decision-making does not necessarily require a hierarchical structure, but in most environments a clear hierarchical system is present, for example, in organizations, families, and sporting teams. In this context, the role of leader becomes important in terms of how they influence the decision-making process. For example, the film provides a useful overview of leader-centered versus follower-centered perspectives on leadership (Jackson & Parry, 2008). For example, JFK recognized that his presence in all ExComm meetings had the potential to limit the degree to which radical ideas were put forward. He needed to give them "room to stick their necks out". While ExComm was certainly not made up of 'yes men', there is the potential for one person who so obviously has the final say to direct (and possibly hamper) the discussion just on the basis of his responses or body language to various ideas. Staying away from many of the ExComm meetings was therefore a wise move and could be classified as a combination of transactive and generative strategy development (Hart, 1992). A film with a non-hierarchical decision-making context that could be a useful contrast is 12 Angry Men (Lumet, 1957).

While JFK was not directly involved in many of the meetings, he set the ground-rules that provided the basis for the decision-making process. He kept the focus on the course of action before the implementation ("we have to work out what we are going to do before we worry about how we are going to do it"). He nominated an informal leader to drive the process when he was away; his brother Bobby. He defined the membership such as calling in potential foes such as Dean Acheson (a Republican) and ensuring that Adlai Stevenson remained in ExComm even though he had been marginalized by the military. When he was present, he spent most of his time listening, rarely offering his opinion, but rather working through the different arguments presented and making sure he obtained as much diversity of opinion as possible.

The President showed enormous strength to be able to resist making a clear decision in favor of a military option for as long as he did. To his credit, the President gave as much time to this group to devise a solution as possible. As it turns out, this time was well used with a far superior solution being developed. Early on there was enormous pressure to make a decision and make it quickly. JFK was not a career soldier and so he relied upon the advice of his military in situations like this. This group universally supported military action and yet even after this expert opinion was provided he still did not commit. In addition, he would have been well aware that some, knowing his family's history in respect of the Munich conference would have seen him as weak as seen in the comment "Let's hope appeasement doesn't run in families. 'Cause I'm afraid that weakness does". Yet in spite of all this pressure and JFK's lack of knowledge in this area, he still recognized that there "is no wise old man. Heck. There's just us". Thus while he was inexperienced, none of ExComm had ever faced this situation and that, as the leader, he needed to move carefully and not abandon his own judgment.

ADVOCACY VERSUS INQUIRY

Garvin and Roberto (2001) introduce alternative decision-making models labeled advocacy and inquiry. Advocacy sees decision-making in a group format as a contest that involves persuading others as to the merits of your proposal, downplaying weaknesses and defending your proposal. Other proposals are attacked or dismissed and the outcome is that some groups are winners (those whose proposal is accepted) and others are losers (where the proposal is rejected). It suggests a degree of adversarial behavior. In comparison, inquiry is more about collaborative problem solving, presenting balanced arguments, critical evaluation, and the encouragement of minorities that offer diverse opinions. Rather than conceptualize the decision in terms of a win/lose scenario, the decision is collectively owned and is a combination of everyone's contribution in some way. Garvin and Roberto (2001) go on to show how these two approaches might be seen via reference to the decision-making processes relating the Bay of Pigs invasion (advocacy) relative to the Cuban Missile Crisis (inquiry).

It is probably stretching the concept a little to suggest that the Cuban Missile Crisis represents inquiry, but there are certainly elements present; particularly when the group moves towards developing a response based around a blockade. Early in the decision-making process, clear coalitions emerge that are more characteristic of advocacy. The military and Dean Acheson are clearly pushing their military option including an invasion. The politicians (JFK, Bobby Kennedy and Kenny O'Donnell) are another clear group, though they do not push a particular option. The other civilians such as Sorenson, Dillon and McNamara counsel each other, but do not push an idea until much later and Adlai Stevenson is isolated and his contributions dismissed. JFK shows good skills in being able to keep this group together and move more towards inquiry. His insistence of complete consensus makes it clear that over-riding others' opinions and just pushing one opinion will not suffice.

Similarly, it is not until later in the decision-making process that the group gains the true benefits of the diversity present in terms of testing and evaluating their options. While the military tried to present a range of options, their options of (a) a surgical air-strike against the missiles themselves, (b) a much larger strike against their air defenses and the missiles, and (c) the invasion, was in reality drop some bombs, drop more bombs, or drop lots of bombs and invade. These are not three options; they are three variants of the same option (military intervention). In the same way that company boards are encouraged to use a number of non-executive directors to ensure that they obtain a degree of diversity, effective decision-making would do well to heed the advantages that come with a heterogeneous decision-making team. Without that diversity including political, military, and diplomatic orientations, the group would have been unable to develop the successful solution eventually enacted.

TEAM MEMBERS WORKING TO UNDERMINE THE DECISION OF THE LEADER

Groups may make decisions on the basis of the preferences of the leader, by simple majority or via consensus. A common decision bias in cohesive groups with a need to make a quick unanticipated decision is the notion of groupthink (Smart & Vertinsky, 1977). This can be seen in the film at the start when no questions are raised about the potential problems with a military option. Given this issue is often covered elsewhere, we prefer to tackle something a little less discussed (but probably more common; Pina, Martinez, & Martinez, 2008), which is undermining of decisions either directly or indirectly by the actions of others. How one deals with such scenarios is part of the overall issues concerning strategic decision-making.

In the movie, General LeMay seemed to be constantly pushing the boundaries in terms of how he could escalate the situation without directly defying JFK. He moved Strategic Air Command to DefCon 2 for the first time ever since the system had been developed (which involved putting B-52 bombers on airborne alert ready to strike targets in the Soviet Union). While he had the authority to do this, given the situation at the time, he would have done well to talk to his commander about taking such a move. This move would have been noted by the Soviet Union and could potentially escalate the situation. Similarly, as previously discussed, he was constantly looking for a way to attack Soviet/Cuban forces. Ground attacks on US aircraft flying over Cuba would have been one possible justification for doing so without breaking the rules of engagement set by the Kennedys. Mistakes were also made by the Soviets with the most significant being the downing of a U2 spy-plane, something that had not been authorized and it was only JFK's restraint that ensured that this did not lead to retaliatory military action.

There is often someone with their own agenda that will make implementing a decision difficult. In this case it was LeMay. However, JFK did not replace him or move him aside. To do so would have sent a signal to the Soviet Union that there was dissention within the key decision-making body and that this lack of unity could be pressured. Thus JFK kept LeMay on the team and just tried to manage him as best he could whilst keeping his own strategy in place. JFK is quoted as saying "If anybody is around to write after this, they are going to understand that we made every effort to find peace and every effort to give our adversary room to move. I am not going to push the Russians an inch beyond what is necessary" (Kennedy & Schlesinger, 1969, p. 127).

COGNITIVE PROCESSES

While strategy development assumes rationality, a strand of literature clearly recognizes the cognitive limits that exist. At best, individuals rely upon schemas and cognitive maps to develop solutions (Dutton & Jackson, 1987) and along with heuristics and biases in judgment (Schwenk, 1984) the ability for most people to be rational is limited. Leading on from this, a slightly lighter topic is how the decision makers further impaired their judgment with particular actions. Impairing the brain via alcohol or sleep deprivation will lessen the brain's ability to process information and respond to complex scenarios. Various occupations have strict guidelines concerning the consumption of alcohol such as pilots who cannot drink at least eight hours before flying (and some airlines have a 12-hour restriction). Sleep deprivation is harder to measure, but having less than five hours core sleep for more than one night will significantly impede cognitive abilities. Staying awake for a 24 hour period is the equivalent of having a Blood Alcohol Content (BAC) of 0.10%—or twice the legal limit to drive a car in many countries (Lamond & Dawson, 1998).

Yet many of the key decision makers including JFK were sleep deprived for a variety of reasons ("Sleep is for the weak Mr. President"—Ted Sorenson). They were working all day, staying up late, drinking scotch to calm them down and taking medication (with scotch to wash it down) to overcome pain (in the case of JFK). These were obviously less than optimal conditions; especially given they were making decisions that could potentially lead to the deaths of 100 million Americans.

TIME

Given that strategy development involves scanning the environment (internal and external), developing options and evaluating the consequences of such options, it is inevitably a time consuming process. The challenge is thus how it can be done in fast moving environments. In the film, the actual crisis resolved itself in less than two weeks. For most organizations it is unlikely that any strategic decision is going to be quite so rushed. Yet right from the first day of the movie there was pressure being placed on the President to make a decision quickly. Interestingly, Eisenhardt (1989) has shown that fast decision-making does not mean poor decision-making; rather that the decision-making process is the key determinant. The Generals in the movie were simply using their numbers and experience to push for their desired option with time pressures being a point of leverage. As General Taylor commented, "We have a rapidly closing window of opportunity". JFK shows considerable character to be able to avoid getting caught up in this mild level of panic. Rather he takes his time, asks questions, and does not commit to a course of action until he is convinced. He is well aware that this may lead to many people thinking that he was indecisive such as when he leaves the room at the end of the first day of discussions without making any decision. JFK: "You know they think I froze in there." K. O'Donnell: "You didn't freeze. You did what you had to. You stayed out of the corner."

In discussing with the class the way that strategic planning occurs in their decisions, the common experience is one where strategy tends to occur once a year and needs to be done within a set timeframe. Where strategic decisions are made out of this cycle, meetings are often scheduled for less than optimal lengths of time so that everyone involved can get back to their 'real work' (Mintzberg, 1994). In essence, artificial time limits are being placed upon some of the most important decisions being made by the organization. If JFK could keep asking questions and pressing for answers in an environment where he was continually being pressed for a decision and where there were real time considerations, then most organizations should be able to take the time to spend to give due consideration to the relevant issues and ensure that they make the best possible decisions rather than wrapping everything up prematurely so in fits into the pre-arranged schedule.

CONCLUSION

We have found that using *Thirteen Days* to teach strategic decision-making has been particularly successful. It does require students to watch the entire movie in advance, but with only a short clip being shown in class, the subsequent discussion can easily extend to well over two hours in length. The historical accuracy of the film sets the scene for an engrossing analysis of how strategic decision-making may often play out, including many of the common issues that typical organizations face. While the issues of path dependency, second order effects, mental models, integration of assumptions, and the notion of advocacy versus inquiry are probably the most important points to touch upon; longer discussions can have fun covering additional issues such as the different signals that were being sent and received at different times and the effect of sleep deprivation, long hours, and drinking (scotch) would have had upon the cognitive abilities of the decision-making team.

The film does not easily allow a thorough investigation of different decision-making models such as logical incrementalism (Quinn, 1980) and the search for error (Collinridge, 1980) and thus the movie needs to be supplemented by some specialized readings (as well as the Garvin & Roberto, 2001) article to cover these missing issues. Incomplete coverage of any topic is not uncommon in any standard case study, but using this film breaks up a more case-oriented series of classes and allows students to engage for more deeply with the theoretical material than has been possible with any case we have used. In this respect, we have found that this class is always well received and effective in delivering the requisite materials. Finally, some students have found the material so interesting they ask for additional material to read. *Blink* by Malcolm Gladwell (2005) is a suitable recommendation. A more detailed interpretation of particular decisions is *Fateful Choices* (2008) by Ian Kershaw. This book describes ten decisions that 'changed the world' and it tracks each decision through to its conclusion, including looking at how it got to the point of no return.

REFERENCES

Anderson, P. (1999). Complexity theory and organization science. *Organization Science, 10*(3), 216–232.

Baddeley, A. (1990). *Human memory: Theory and practice*. Hove, UK: Lawrence Erlbaum Associates.

Boak, G., & Thompson, D. (1998). *Mental models for managers: Frameworks for practical thinking*. London, UK: Century Business Books.

Brandenburger, A. M., & Nalebuff, B. J. (1995). The right game: Using game theory to shape strategy. *Harvard Business Review, 73*(4), 57–71.

Collinridge, D. (1980). *The social control of technology*. Buckingham, UK: Open University Press.

Dutton, J. E., & Jackson, S. E. (1987). Categorizing strategic issues: Links to organizational action. *Academy of Management Review, 12*(1), 76–90.

Eisenhardt, K. M. (1989). Making fast strategic decisions in high-velocity environment. *Academy of Management Journal, 32*(3), 543–576.

Garvin, D. A., & Roberto, M. A. (2001). What you don't know about making decisions. *Harvard Business Review, 79*(8), 108–116.

Gladwell, M. (2005). *Blink*. New York, NY: Back Bay Books.

Grant, R. M. (2007). *Contemporary strategic analysis* (6th ed.). Oxford, UK: Blackwell Publishing.

Hart, S. L. (1992). An integrative framework for strategy-making processes. *Academy of Management Review, 17*(2), 327–351.

Heil, O., & Robertson, T. (1991). Toward a theory of competitive market signaling: A research agenda. *Strategic Management Journal, 12*(6), 403–418.

Helleloid, D., & Simonin, B. (1994). Organizational learning and a firm's core competence. In G. Hamel & A. Heene (Eds.) *Competence-Based Competition* (pp. 213–239). Chichester, UK: John Wiley & Sons.

Hill, C., Jones, G., Galvin, P., & Hadir, A. (2007). *Strategic management: An integrated approach*, (2nd ed.). Brisbane, Australia: John Wiley & Sons.

Jackson, B., & Parry, K. W. (2008). *A very short, fairly interesting and reasonably cheap book about studying leadership.* London, UK: Sage.

Kallinikos, J. (1998). Organized complexity: Posthumanist remarks on the technologizing of intelligence. *Organization, 5*(3), 371–396.

Kennedy, R. F., & Schlesinger, A. (foreword) (1969). *Thirteen days: A memoir of the Cuban missile crisis.* New York, NY: W. W. Norton and Company.

Kershaw, I. (2008). *Fateful choices: Ten decisions that changed the world 1940–1941.* London, UK: Penguin Books.

Lamond, N., & Dawson, D. (1998). Quantifying the performance impairment associated with sustained wakefulness. The Centre for Sleep Research, The Queen Elizabeth Hospital, South Australia. Accessed at: *http://cf.alpa.org/internet/projects/fldt/backgr/Daw_Lam.html* on Friday 30 May, 2008.

Minztberg, H. (1994). The rise and fall of strategic planning. *Harvard Business Review, 72*(1), 107–114.

Mintzberg, H., Théorêt, A., & Raisinghani, D. (1976). The structure of the unstructured decision making process. *Administrative Science Quarterly, 21*(2), 246–275.

Pina, M. I. D., Martínez, A. M. R., & Martínez, L. G. (2008). Teams in organizations: A review on team effectiveness. *Team Performance Management, 14*(1), 7–21.

Quinn, J. B. (1980). *Strategic change: Logical incrementalism.* Homewood, IL: Richard D. Irwin Press.

Schwenk, C. (1984). Cognitive simplification processes in strategic decision-making. *Strategic Management Journal, 5*(2), 111–128.

Smart, C., & Vertinsky, I. (1977). Designs for decision crisis units. *Administrative Science Quarterly, 22*(4), 640–657.

Toffler, A. (1970). *Future shock.* New York, NY: Bantam Books.

Tsoukas, H. (1996). The firm as a distributed knowledge system: A constructionist approach. *Strategic Management Journal, 17* (Winter Special Issue), 11–25.

Winston, P. H. (1980). Learning and reasoning by analogy. *Communications of the ACM, 23*(12), 689–703.

Films

Donaldson, R. (Director). (2000) *Thirteen days* [Motion picture]. United States: New Line Cinema, Beacon Communications, & Tig Productions.

Lumet, S. (Director). (1957). *12 angry men* [Motion picture]. United States: Orion-Nova Productions.

CHAPTER 15

USING VISUAL MEDIA TO TEACH RECRUITMENT AND SELECTION

Jon Billsberry

Few management topics are as amenable to visual media as recruitment and selection. Whether the teaching goal is to help selectors make better decisions, or to help applicants perform better, or to facilitate a critical awareness of the process, visual media has a role to play. In the first section of this paper, I describe how visual media can be used to develop recruitment and selection skills. The second section is devoted to an identification of film clips that can be used to illustrate particular recruitment and selection processes in the lecture theatre. In the final section, I highlight films that can be used as extended case studies for the critical discussion of recruitment and selection themes.

SKILL AND AWARENESS DEVELOPMENT

Images, both still and moving, play a significant role in teaching the practical elements of recruitment and selection. These include the exploration of discriminatory attitudes and behavior for training interviewers and they can

Moving Images: Effective Teaching with Film and Television in Higher Education,
pages 209–222

be used to develop applicants and improve their interviewing skills. I will briefly look at these three different uses of images showing how they can be used for different aspects of recruitment and selection training.

Still Images

When I first joined The Open University some sixteen years ago, there was a strong relationship with the BBC. This relationship was so strong that the BBC had studios on the campus as well as staff to run them. Amongst the benefits this brought were the inevitable and suitably infamous BBC canteen and a BBC wardrobe department. Apart from the benefits shooting course videos, these facilities gave us an extra benefit when we were developing the recruitment and selection material for a new Certificate in Management. One of our learning objectives was for students to surface their prejudices and biases. In a preliminary exercise, students were shown four images of applicants to a job. They were asked to record their first impressions of the four people and their assessment of each person against the vacancy. The 'trick' in the exercise was that the four images were those of the same person 'made up' by the BBC's wardrobe department. For students who were new to recruitment and selection, the exercise was very powerful and forcibly made the points that applicants' appearances are largely irrelevant for objective assessment and selectors' initial assessments of applicants are influential and irresistible.

Video Disks

When video disks first appeared in the mid 1990s, there were many experiments with the format. One interesting idea was to use their interactive facility to train people in managerial processes such as selection interviewing. The idea was that you could choose what question to ask from a list. These would be put to the applicant who would supply an answer. This process would repeat until you felt confident to make your selection decision. The smarter versions would have an 'intelligent' brain that would eliminate questions and alter answers depending on the sequence of questions and answers. These disks were fun, but they had many problems. They were expensive to produce, required high production qualities, and excellent acting. In addition, they were very constraining and overly rational. Consequently, they have largely disappeared from the market. Nowadays, most recruitment and selection training DVDs have a simpler less interactive format, but they exist for both applicants and selectors.

Video Cameras

Video cameras have an important role to play in both improving applicants' performance in interviews and in helping selectors with their interview technique. Their main use is to record role-playing sessions to let the participants see how they come across. The videos allow them to critique their own performance and, more importantly, to understand the advice of instructors. They make feedback specific and focus on behavior and impressions. However, the power of the approach also makes it quite challenging and many learners may be overwhelmed by the process. It requires careful handling and experienced facilitators. Recent developments in video technology, especially High Definition and hard disk digital recording, have made the format much quicker, more powerful, and easier to use.

DEPICTIONS OF RECRUITMENT AND SELECTION

Of all management and leadership topics, few feature more prominently and regularly in feature films as recruitment and selection. There are many reasons for this common appearance. These include the dramatic nature of recruitment and selection, the way that recruitment and selection is often a hinge that changes the direction of people's lives, selection is an episode of rapid information exchange that directors can use to convey character's nature, and passing a selection test can legitimize a hero or their success. As result, feature films are a rich landscape from which to draw material to illustrate key recruitment and selection ideas in the lecture theatre.

Preliminary Stages

In most textbooks, recruitment and selection is portrayed as a linear and rational decision making process. The paradigm is based on analyses of needs and the knowledge, skills, and abilities required to perform well in the role. These form the criteria by which applicants are assessed. A mistake made at this point will cascade down through the whole decision making process and make finding a good employee a matter of chance. Given this crucial role, job analysis and the formation of selection criteria might be expected to feature strongly in cinematic depictions of recruitment and selection. But they don't. In fact, I couldn't find a single example, although there is a mention of the characteristics of a suitable 'applicant' in *Ôdishon* (*Audition*; Takashi, 1999); see later. A related episode that might be useful for instructors can be found in the Arthurian tale, *Excalibur* (Boorman, 1981). According to legend, the man who can draw the great sword, Excalibur, from the stone will be the true King of England. Knights compete in a joust to earn the right to drawing out the sword; heaven knows why if there is only one person in the Kingdom who can release the sword. By accident, Arthur withdraws the sword. He puts it back and allows knights to attempt to withdraw it, but they fail. Arthur tries again and, again, is successful. Despite the clarity of the legend, opinion is divided on whether Arthur is the true King and this starts a war. This is an interesting example of how politics, personal ambition and disappointment can compromise even the clearest of selection criteria.

CV and Application Forms

Let's be honest, the filtering of CVs application forms is not the most cinematic process. Nevertheless, there is an excellent example of this phase in the aforementioned, *Ôdishon*. This is a poignant story of a man who is looking for companionship many years after his wife passed away. He is involved in films and TV and his producer friend suggests holding auditions for someone matching his criteria under the guise of casting for a new TV show. When the application forms come in, we see the hero going through these very carefully. But despite his rigor, it is the unusual qualities of one applicant that stands out and these cause him to ignore all other applicants during the auditions in anticipation of his preferred 'applicant.' I must issue a word of warning with this film; it is infamous for being one of the most shocking films in movie history. Even hardened film critics found the end too shocking with some of their number throwing up in the aisles and running for the exits at an infamous press screening. Even cover notes have their role in films. In *La Tourneuse de Pages* (*The Page Turner*, Dercourt, 2006), we see how a made up cover note gets someone a job.

Selection Interviews

Whilst there are very many examples of selection interviews in films, almost every one I have spotted has an unstructured nature. I have not yet found an example of a properly structured interview yet, but there are some spectacular unstructured ones. My favorites include the interview of Eileen Wanous in *Monster* (Jenkins, 2003; if only the interviewer knew to whom he was talking!), Spud's interview in *Trainspotting* (Boyle, 1996), the shrunken interview in *Being John Malkovich* (Jonze, 1999) and the series of interviews in *Mrs. Doubtfire* (Columbus, 1993).

Personality Tests

Anyone who has been subjected to a personality test will know how desperately dull they are. So it isn't surprising that they don't feature strongly in feature films. Nevertheless, I do have one example; the sorting hat in the first Harry Potter film, *Harry Potter and the Philosopher's Stone* (aka *Harry Potter and the Sorcerer's Stone*, Columbus, 2001). When the young wizards attend Hogwarts School for Wizards for the first time, they are allocated to one of the four houses. This allocation is performed by the sorting hat; a large hat that is placed on each new student in turn. The hat has the ability to read and communicate with the *mind* of the person wearing the hat. Through these conversations, the hat is able to discover the real nature of the students and allocate them to the house that best suits them. These conversations are better covered in the book and I would recommend using both sources to convey the way the hat can discover the true nature of the students, especially Harry.

Intelligence Tests

I have been unable to find an example of a typical paper and pencil intelligence test in a film. This absence is somewhat ironic given that intelligence tests have been shown to be one of the most effective selection techniques. Examples of where intelligence tests may be being used, but not explicitly, are *Men in Black* (Sonnenfeld, 1997) during Agent Jay's formal assessment (motor skills, concentration, and stamina), which also features an excellent example of the importance of administrating tests correctly, an analogous test in a firing range, and trying to convince someone to take an unusual job, and amongst the battery of physiological assessments of potential astronauts in *The Right Stuff* (Kaufman, 1983).

Work Record/Portfolio

The assessment of a portfolio or prior track record is depicted in *Kramer vs. Kramer* (Benton, 1979). In this film, advertising man Ted Kramer must quickly find a job in order to get custody of his son in an acrimonious divorce. When attending interviews, he takes his portfolio of past work with him. This impresses so much that the interviewer changes the recruitment process. Also, Kramer is able to demand a decision there and then, which is vital if he is to keep custody of his son. Another example of portfolio assessment comes from *La Mala Educación* (*Bad Education*; Almodóvar, 2004). In contrast to *Kramer vs. Kramer*, a portfolio is ignored because of prior knowledge of the applicant.

Assessment Centers

Assessment centers are herein defined as occasions when multiple selection methods are deployed on applicants, usually back-to-back or without leaving the selection venue. Defined as such, there are many examples of assessment centers in film. Elsewhere (Billsberry & Gilbert, 2007), I have deconstructed *Charlie and the Chocolate Factory* (Burton, 2005) and shown that the factory tour can be viewed as an assessment center used to select a new factory manager. Other prominent examples of assessment centers include *Top Gun* (Scott, 1986), possibly the most expensive assessment centre in the world, and *The Right Stuff*, which contains material that can also trigger a discussion about the ethical limits of selection practice.

Job Trials

Job trials come in shapes and sizes and many sports films, in particular, have some sort of trial as part of the genre. But my favorite job trial comes from *Boogie Nights* (Anderson, 1997). This film is a fictional depiction of the Californian porn industry of the 1970s and 1980s. Budding porn star, Eddie Adams (aka Dirk Diggler), has to demonstrate his abilities to do the job under lights and in front of a camera and an audience. A slightly less risqué film to use in the management classroom to illustrate a job trial would be James Clayton's recruitment as an elite CIA undercover agent in *The Recruit* (Donaldson, 2003). Interesting alternative examples of job trials are those where the person being observed does not realize their performance is being assessed such as in *Men in Black.*

Letters of Reference

Reference letters are requested in almost every 'real' recruitment and selection process, but they have a strange place in cinematic portrayals of the process. Rather than being used to legitimize the selection of a preferred candidate, they appear when something goes wrong with the recruitment process. In *Modern Times* (Chaplin, 1936), the star is appointed as a hopeless night watchman on the strength of his references. In *Marnie* (Hitchcock, 1964), we see how the eponymous heroine's good looks cause an employer to fail to take up references with dire consequences. In *I Love You Phillip Morris* (Ficarra & Requa, 2009), conman Steven Russell (Jim Carrey) supplies his own telephone number as a fake referee's one and gives himself a fake telephone reference to get a job as a Chief Financial Officer (something that must be a lot easier to do nowadays with the omnipresence of mobile phones).

Graphology

I must admit that I didn't expect to find an example of graphology in the movies. Not only is it a rarely used technique, but it is also completely discredited and unexciting from a cinematic perspective. So I was quite surprised when I found an example and it is one of the most dramatic of all recruitment and selection scenes. The scene occurs in the fourth film of the Harry Potter series, *Harry Potter and the Goblet of Fire* (Newell, 2005). The Goblet of Fire, it turns out, is a personnel selection device. Eighteen year-old wizards who wish to take part in the TriWizards Tournament have to write their names on a piece of paper and put it in the Goblet of Fire. On the appointed hour, the Goblet uses magic to determine which wizards will complete. And, of course, this scene is highly symbolic because magic is the only way that graphology works.

Auditions

The recruitment literature has not devoted many column inches to auditions. But they are a staple of recruitment and selection in films. Auditions are inherently dramatic and *A Chorus Line* (Attenborough, 1985) is structured around an audition. Other films featuring auditions include *Billy El-*

liot (Daldry, 2000), *Tootsie* (Pollack, 1982), *Ôdishon, Fame* (Parker, 1980), *The Commitments* (Parker, 1991), and *The Full Monty* (Cattaneo, 1997).

Elections

Although the recruitment and selection textbooks seem to have forgotten it, many people are selected via an election. Obviously, in the movies, almost every conceivable angle of elections has been covered. These typically divide into micro, High School type elections (e.g. *Election* [Payne, 1999] and *Carrie* [De Palma, 1976]), and those on a national stage particularly for the US Presidency. Two worth mentioning are *All the President's Men* (Pakula, 1976) which forensically explores the way that an election can be hijacked, and *The Ides of March* (Clooney, 2011), which shows the politics behind the politics.

Induction and Orientation

Once selected, there follows the discussion of terms and conditions and, if that is successful, the induction of the favored applicant to the organization. A rich example of the negotiation stage can be found in *Charlie and the Chocolate Factory*. The ending of this film adaptation of Roald Dahl's classic children's tale was changed by the director, Tim Burton. In this version, Charlie rejects Willy Wonka's offer of life in the chocolate factory if it means leaving his family. Initially, Wonka cannot understand his decision, but he reflects and comes to understand Charlie better. A satirical example of induction in an organizational setting can be found in *The Hudsucker Proxy* (Coen, 1994). The first half of the film, *Full Metal Jacket* (Kubrick, 1987), is devoted to the intense induction of raw recruits to the US marines during the Vietnam War.

FILM CASE STUDIES: HIGHLIGHTING CRITICAL ISSUES

In addition to the inclusion of recruitment and selection scenes in feature films, some films are all about recruitment and selection. Sometimes this is a main plot line; other times it is the central purpose of the film. Such films are useful tools for instructors as they can be used as extended case studies. These video case studies allow the exploration of different aspects of the process in a detailed and multifaceted way. These are films that are rich in detail, subtle and sufficiently complex to allow different and critical 'readings' of recruitment and selection.

The first recruitment and selection theme that films have been constructed around is desperation, particularly the desperate lengths that people will go to in order to find work. The desperation of the unemployed is depicted in *Ladri di Biciclette* (*The Bicycle Thieves*; De Sica, 1948) in post-war Italy. Here men queue outside employers hoping to be picked from the crowd to get work for the day; a similar scene can be seen in *Cinderella Man* (Howard, 2005). The hero has a bicycle and this is crucial in him getting a job putting posters up. When his bicycle is stolen he goes to desperate lengths to find it. *The Bicycle Thieves* has been remade in China as *Shiqi Sui de Dan Che* (*Beijing Bicycle*, Wang, 2001) where the bicycle is crucial to a teenager's employment. Similar endemic employment problems are the subject of Michael Moore's documentary *Roger & Me* (Moore, 1989), in which the filmmaker goes in search of General Motor's CEO, Roger Smith, to quiz him about the closure of manufacturing in Flint, Michigan and its transfer to Mexico. A quantum leap in an industry that challenges the position of all employees is depicted in *Singin' in the Rain* (Donen & Kelly, 1952) where actors and filmmakers are all caught in cinema's sound revolution.

A subtheme within this desperation theme revolves around people prepared to cross-dress such is their desperation to find work. Examples of men dressing as women to get jobs include *Tootsie, Mrs. Doubtfire*, and *Some Like It Hot* (Wilder, 1959). Examples of women dressing as men include *Shakespeare in Love* (Madden, 1998) and *Victor Victoria* (Edwards, 1982). *Tootsie* is a particularly rich recruitment and selection case study. The film begins with a rat-a-tat-tat series of glimpses of the hero's failed auditions interwoven with his teaching, which is how he makes a living. He finds it so difficult to find acting parts that he is prepared to deceive others by dressing as a woman to get a role.

Headhunting is another theme around which some films have been structured. When I say 'headhunting,' I am defining the term loosely and referring to a selector's identification of talent which he or she then tries to recruit. A good example is *Men in Black* and its sequel, *Men in Black II* (Sonnenfeld, 2002). Both films are about the identification of someone who can do a particular job followed up by convincing the person to do the job and then inducting them into the role.

Headhunting also plays a role in perhaps the richest source of films centered on recruitment and selection; namely, *Shichinin no Samurai* (*Seven Samurai*, Kurosawa, 1954) and the plethora of remakes, reimaginings, and references. The plot is uncomplicated. A Japanese village is being terrorized by bandits. As they do not have the skills needed to defend themselves, they decide to combine their miniscule assets and use these to hire a samurai to defend them. They spot an out of work samurai and approach him. They do not have much money and appeal to his sense of honor. He accepts and he recruits a further six samurai to help. The film shows the different ways he recruits them. Some he knows and respects, others he tests. They go to the village, they train the villagers, they fight and some die, but they win and free the village from its torment. The most well-known remake of the classic film is the almost-as-brilliant *The Magnificent Seven* (Sturges, 1960), which sets the story as a western and a Mexican village's attempt to save themselves from rampaging bandits. This version rigorously copies the original which means that the same focus on the various recruitment and selection episodes exists. I should note that *The Magnificent Seven* spawned three sequels which feature similar plots (*The Return of the Seven* (Kennedy, 1966), *Guns of the Magnificent Seven* (Wendkos, 1969), *The Magnificent Seven Ride!* (McCowan, 1972). Two other well-known remakes are *Tampopo* (Itami, 1985) in which the owner of a fast-food noodle shop is helped by a trucker (this film owes as much to *Shane* [Stevens, 1953] as it does to *Shichinin no Samurai*) and *A Bug's Life* (Lasseter & Stanton, 1998) in which ants need help to fight off grasshoppers in an animated version. Less well-known remakes include *Kill a Dragon* (Moore, 1967) in which villagers hire karate experts to defend themselves against gangsters, *Liu He Qian Shou* (*The Scorpion*; Yang, 1979) in which martial arts masters are recruited to fight a Japanese karate expert who is terrorizing a Chinese martial arts community, *Battle Beyond the Stars* (Murakami, 1980), a version set in space, *I Sette Magnifici Gladiatori* (*The Seven Magnificent Gladiators*; Fragasso & Mattei, 1983), a sword and sorcery version, *Dune Warriors* (Santiago, 1990) which has an end of the world scenario and a lot of Kung Fu, *Dikiy Vostok* (*The Wild East*; Nugmanov, 1993) which is about a group of dwarves who leave the circus and set themselves up in the Kazak wilderness and find themselves terrorized by a gang of bikers, and the Bollywood version, *China Gate* (Santoshi, 1998).

There are a group of films that explore issues of social engineering. To what extent is it possible to transform 'someone from the gutter' and make them a 'respectable' member of society? In *Pygmalion* (Asquith & Howard, 1938) and its musical remake, *My Fair Lady* (Cukor, 1964), a 'guttersnipe,' Eliza Doolittle, is intensively and successfully trained to adopt the speech and manners of 'a lady' by a misogynistic phonetics professor, Henry Higgins. Doolittle accepts the abuse because she wants to get a job in a florist rather than continue selling flowers from a basket in the street. But none of the participants had anticipated how this training would influence her ambitions and the conversion leaves her stranded socially. *Trading Places* (Landis, 1983) is about a wicked pair of rich commodity-broking brothers, Mortimer and Randolph Duke, who wonder whether it is possible to take someone from the streets and make him successful in business and also whether a successful business person can cope with unemployment and loss of assets. They engineer these changes and watch the impact on the two individuals. These social engineering films are particularly relevant to recruitment and selection because they explore the image vs. substance issue. To what extent is appearance important? Or experience? Or background? Or skills? The premise in *Pygmalion* and *My Fair Lady* is that image is everything, but in *Trading Places* the suggestion is that environments shape behavior and that previous skills and experience may be relatively unimportant for success.

Deciding whom to send into space is a central plot of a number of films. This is an important decision because astronauts are representatives of nations or the entire planet. In addition, huge amounts of money are invested in the projects. Hence, these are highly politicized and thorough decisions. The political side of such decisions is the main theme in *Contact* (Zemeckis, 1997). The decision of who should fly is even more important when the future of humanity is at stake, as in *When Worlds Collide* (Maté, 1951). The expense and detailed nature of astronaut selection and training is the subject of *The Right Stuff*, which also has political dimensions. Less elaborated examples of this theme can be found in *Armageddon* (Bay, 1998), *Star Trek: The Motion Picture* (Wise, 1979), *Deep Impact* (Leder, 1998), *Space Cowboys* (Eastwood, 2000), and *Another Earth* (Cahill, 2011).

Finally, I offer a collection of films whose recruitment and selection themes are not connected. *Catch Me If You Can* (Spielberg, 2002) is the 'true' story of how the FBI recruited Frank Abagnale Jr. as their expert on the forgery of bank notes. Most of the film, which is a homage to Hitchcock, concentrates on the criminal life of Abagnale and how he was hunted down. His expertise as a forger made him the best qualified person to track down others and the FBI made use of his eminence in the field.

I Was Monty's Double (Guillermin, 1958) also tells a 'true' story. This one relates the experience of M. E. Clifton-Jones, who was the spitting image of Field Marshall Montgomery. The film shows how he was spotted, recruited, and trained to stand-in for Montgomery and how his involvement mislead the Germans about the location of the invasion of Europe.

A Matter of Life and Death (Powell & Pressburger, 1946) is a fantasy about a Royal Air Force pilot, Peter Carter, who is shot down and should die. But the angel misses the pickup and Carter does not die. Instead he carries on his life and falls in love. The angels recognize the mistake and send someone down to get him. Carter argues that he should not die as it was not his fault he did not die and now there are others who would be affected by his death. He wins a stay of execution and has to present his case to a heavenly court. His selection decision revolves around who should represent him in this matter of life and death.

Speaking of life and death, *The Boy in the Striped Pyjamas* (Hermon, 2008) looks at the Holocaust from a child's perspective. The child of the title is the son of an SS officer who is given the command of a death camp. The boy does not wish to leave Berlin, where he has many friends. He sulks terribly but eventually finds a friend, a Jewish boy in the death camp, with tragic consequences. It is a moving film that beautifully captures the impact of a job change necessitating a geographical relocation on the new recruit and his or her family.

CONCLUDING THOUGHTS

In writing this chapter, I have tried to show the myriad of ways in which moving images can be used in the teaching of recruitment and selection. Perhaps more than any other management topic, recruitment and selection lends itself to the use of such methods. Videotaping trainees in development sessions is a crucial element in helping applicants and interviewers improve their interview technique. Showing trainees how people perceive them is the first step in helping them appreciate their strengths and weaknesses. Then, during the development work, they can see the improvements and get personalized feedback on their efforts.

I have also tried to identify some scenes from feature films that can be used to illustrate recruitment and selection processes and also whole films that can be used as extended case studies. But these examples are just the tip of the iceberg and you will surely know of other films that depict these processes. The purpose of highlighting these examples is not just to help instructors locate sources; it is also to demonstrate the hugeness of possibility. Films focus on life-changing events and job switches often symbolize the start or end of these episodes; passing a selection test begins the adventure or marks its completion. It seems certain, therefore, that recruitment and selection will continue to be included in films thereby providing a rich seam of new material for instructors to mine.

REFERENCE

Billsberry, J. & Gilbert, L. H. (2008). Using Roald Dahl's *Charlie and the Chocolate Factory* to teach different recruitment and selection paradigms. *Journal of Management Education, 32*(2), 228–247.

Films

Almodóvar, P. (Director). (2004). *La mala educación (Bad education)* [Motion picture]. Spain: Canal+ España, El Deseo, & Televisión Española.

Anderson, P. T. (Director). (1997). *Boogie nights* [Motion picture]. United States: New Line Cinema.

Asquith, A., & Howard, L. (Directors). (1938). *Pygmalion* [Motion picture]. United Kingdom: Gabriel Pascal Productions.

Attenborough, R. (Director). (1985). *A chorus line* [Motion picture]. United States: Embassy Films Associates, Polygram Pictures, & Feuer and Martin Productions.

Bay, M. (Director). (1998). *Armageddon* [Motion picture]. United States: Touchstone Pictures.

Benton, R. (Director). (1979). *Kramer vs. Kramer* [Motion picture]. United States: Columbia Pictures.

Boorman, J. (Director). (1981). *Excalibur* [Motion picture]. United States & United Kingdom: Orion Pictures.

Boyle, D. (Director). (1996). *Trainspotting* [Motion picture]. United Kingdom: Channel Four Films.

Burton, T. (Director). (2005). *Charlie and the chocolate factory* [Motion picture]. United States: Warner Bros.

Cahill, M. (Director). (2011). *Another earth* [Motion picture]. United States: Artists Public Domain.

Cattaneo, P. (Director). (1997). *The full Monty* [Motion picture]. United Kingdom: Redwave Films, Channel Four Films, & Twentieth Century Fox.

Chaplin, C. (Director). (1936). *Modern times* [Motion picture]. United States: Charles Chaplin Productions & United Artists.

Clooney, G. (Director). (2011). *The ides of march* [Motion picture]. United States: Cross Creek Pictures, Exclusive Media Group, Smoke House, & Crystal City Entertainment.

Coen, J. (Director). (1994). *The Hudsucker proxy* [Motion picture]. United States: Warner Brothers.

Columbus, C. (Director). (1993). *Mrs. Doubtfire* [Motion picture]. United States: Blue Wolf & Twentieth Century Fox.

Columbus, C. (Director). (2001). *Harry Potter and the philosopher's stone* (*Harry Potter and the sorcerer's stone*) [Motion picture]. United States: Warner Bros.

Cukor, G. (Director). (1964). *My fair lady* [Motion picture]. United States: Warner Bros.

Daldry, S. (Director). (2000). *Billy Elliot* [Motion picture]. United Kingdom & France: Arts Council of England, BBC Films, Studio Canal, Tiger Aspect Productions, WT2 Productions, & Working Title Films.

De Palma, B. (Director). (1976). *Carrie* [Motion picture]. United States: Redbank Films.

Dercourt, D. (Director). (2006). *La tourneuse de pages* (*The page turner*) [Motion picture]. France: Diaphana Films & France 3 Cinéma.

De Sica, V. (Director). (1948). *Ladri di biciclette* (*The bicycle thieves*) [Motion picture]. Italy: Produzioni De Sica

Donaldson, R. (Director). (2003). *The recruit* [Motion picture]. United States: Touchstone Pictures, Spyglass Entertainment, & Epsilon Motion Pictures.

Donen, S. & Kelly, G. (Directors). (1952). *Singin' in the rain* [Motion picture]. United States: Loew's, Metro-Goldwyn-Mayer (MGM), & RKO-Pathe Studios.

Eastwood, C. (Director). (2000). *Space cowboys* [Motion picture]. United States & Australia: Clipsal Films, Mad Chance, Malpaso Productions, Village Roadshow Pictures, & Warner Bros. Pictures.

Edwards, B. (Director). (1982). *Victor Victoria* [Motion picture]. United Kingdom & United States: Artista Management, Blake Edwards Entertainment, Ladbroke, Metro-Goldwyn-Mayer (MGM), & Peerford.

Ficarra, G., & Requa, J. (Directors). (2009). *I love you Phillip Morris* [Motion picture]. France & United States: Europa Corp. & Mad Chance.

Fragasso, C., & Mattei, B. (Directors). (1983). *I sette magnifici gladiatori* (*The seven magnificent gladiators*) [Motion picture]. Italy: Cannon Italia.

Guillermin, J. (Director). (1958). *I was Monty's double* [Motion picture]. United Kingdom: Film Traders & Setfair Productions.

Hermon, M. (Director). (2008). *The boy in the striped pyjamas* [Motion picture]. United Kingdom & United States: Miramax Films, BBC Films, & Heyday Films.

Hitchcock, A. (Director). (1964). *Marnie* [Motion picture]. United States: Universal Pictures.

Howard, R. (Director). (2005). *Cinderella man* [Motion picture]. United States: Universal Pictures, Miramax Films, & Imagine Entertainment.

Itami, J. (Director). (1985). *Tampopo* [Motion picture]. Japan: Itami Productions & New Century Productions.

Jenkins, P. (Director). (2003). *Monster* [Motion picture]. United States & Germany: Media 8 Entertainment, Newmarket Films, DEJ Productions, K/W Productions, Denver and Delilah Films, VIP Medienfonds 2, & MDP Worldwide.

Jonze, S. (Director). (1999). *Being John Malkovich* [Motion picture]. United States: Gramercy Pictures, Propaganda Films, & Single Cell Pictures.

Kaufman, P. (Director). (1983). *The right stuff* [Motion picture]. United States: The Ladd Company.

Kennedy, B. (Director). (1966). *The return of the magnificent seven* [Motion picture]. United States & Spain: Mirisch & C. B. Films.

Kubrick, S. (Director). (1987). *Full metal jacket* [Motion picture]. United Kingdom & United States: Natant, Stanley Kubrick Productions, & Warner Bros.

Kurosawa, A. (Director). (1954). *Shichinin no samurai (Seven samurai)* [Motion picture]. Japan: Toho Company.

Landis, J. (Director). (1983). *Trading places* [Motion picture]. United States: Cinema Group Ventures & Paramount Pictures.

Lasseter, J., & Stanton, A. (Directors). (1998). *A bug's life* [Motion picture]. United States: Pixar Animation Studios & Walt Disney Pictures.

Leder, M. (Director). (1998). *Deep impact* [Motion picture]. United States: Paramount Pictures, DreamWorks, Zanuck/Brown Productions, & Manhattan Project.

Madden, J. (Director). (1998). *Shakespeare in love* [Motion picture]. United States & United Kingdom: Universal Pictures, Miramax Films, & Bedford Falls Productions.

Maté, R. (Director). (1951). *When worlds collide* [Motion picture]. United States: Paramount Pictures.

McCowan. (Director). (1972). *The magnificent seven ride!* [Motion picture]. United States: Mirsch.

Moore, M. D. (Director). (1967). *Kill a dragon* [Motion picture]. United States: Aubrey Schenck Productions.

Moore, M. (Director). (1989). *Roger & me* [Motion picture]. United States: Dog Eat Dog Films & Warner Bros.

Murakami, J. T. (Director). (1980). *Battle beyond the stars* [Motion picture]. United States: New World Pictures.

Newell, M. (Director). (2005). *Harry Potter and the goblet of fire* [Motion picture]. United Kingdom & United States: Warner Bros. Pictures, Heyday Films, & Patalex IV Productions.

Nugmanov, R. (Director). (1993). *Dikiy vostok (The wild east)* [Motion picture]. Kazakhstan: Studio Kino.

Pakula, A. J. (Director). (1976). *All the president's men* [Motion picture]. United States: Warner Bros. & Wildwood.

Parker, A. (Director). (1980). *Fame* [Motion picture]. United States: Metro-Goldwyn-Mayer (MGM).

Parker, A. (Director). (1991). *The commitments* [Motion picture]. Ireland, United Kingdom, & United States: Beacon Communications, Dirty Hands Productions, & First Film Company.

Payne, A. (Director). (1999). *Election* [Motion picture]. United States: Bona Fide Productions, MTV Films, & Paramount Pictures.

Pollack, S. (Director). (1982). *Tootsie* [Motion picture]. United States: Columbia Pictures.

Powell, M. & Pressburger, E. (Directors). (1946). *A matter of life and death* [Motion picture]. United Kingdom : The Archers.

Santiago, C. H. (Director). (1990). *Dune warriors* [Motion picture]. Philippines & United States: Concorde-New Horizons & New Horizon Picture Corp.

Santoshi, R. (Director). (1998). *China gate* [Motion picture]. India: Santoshi Productions.

Scott, T. (Director). (1986). *Top gun* [Motion picture]. United States: Paramount Pictures.

Sonnenfeld, B. (Director). (1997). *Men in black* [Motion picture]. United States: Amblin Entertainment & Columbia Pictures.

Sonnenfeld, B. (Director). (2002). *Men in black II* [Motion picture]. United States: Amblin Entertainment, Columbia Pictures, & MacDonald/Parkes Productions.

Spielberg, S. (Director). (2002). *Catch me if you can* [Motion picture]. United States & Canada: DreamWorks.

Stevens, G. (Director). (1953). *Shane* [Motion picture]. United States: Paramount Pictures.

Sturges, J. (Director). (1960). *The magnificent seven* [Motion picture]. United States: Mirsch.

Takashi, M. (Dirctor). (1999). *Ôdishon (Audition)* [Motion picture]. Japan: AFDF, Creators Company Connection, & Omega Project.

Wang, X. (Director). (2001). *Shiqi sui de dan che (Beijing bicycle)* [Motion picture]. France, Taiwan, & China: Pyramide Productions, Arc Light Films, Public Television Service Foundation, Eastern Television, Asiatic Films, & Beijing Film Studio.

Wendkos, P. (Director). (1969). *Guns of the magnificent seven* [Motion picture]. United States: Mirsch.

Wilder, B. (Director). (1959). *Some like it hot* [Motion picture]. United States: Mirsch.

Wise, R. (Director). (1979). *Star trek: The motion picture* [Motion picture]. United States: Century Associates & Paramount Pictures.

Yang, C. (Director). (1979). *Liu he qian shou (The Scorpion)* [Motion picture]. Hong Kong: Goldig Film Company.

Zemeckis, R. (Director). (1997). *Contact* [Motion picture]. United States: Warner Bros.

CHAPTER 16

USING MOVIES TO TEACH BUSINESS AND LEADERSHIP PRINCIPLES

Troy Hendrickson and Peter Galvin

THE RATIONALE FOR USING MOVIES TO TEACH

Utilizing film as an active medium for teaching and conveying various perspectives about business topics in a learning environment has great merit for people involved in a teaching capacity. This is because it naturally appeals to a wider variety of learning style preferences that are not often addressed during the typical passive 'lecture style' of instruction (Knowles, Holton, & Swanson, 2005). Additionally, it is normally a welcome change for students to experience vicariously the moods, messages, and concepts that are depicted in scenes which have been carefully crafted in a specialized manner for that particular film. Most scenes within contemporary films have had the luxury of significant budgets and professional actors that strive to capture the exact circumstances that contribute to the overarching plot. In addition, contemporary films typically pay meticulous attention to lighting, props, background music, and setting; as well as various nonverbal

Moving Images: Effective Teaching with Film and Television in Higher Education,
pages 223–238

and verbal messages that are woven into the scenes. The approach must be both strategic and deliberate in order to justify the massive budgets that are spent for the creation of these films. Careers are often determined by whether the final result is successful or not. All of these things are focused upon with the objective of completely engaging the viewer and maintaining their attention by arousal and stimulation of a variety of emotional states during the course of the film. Obviously with such a large financial investment at stake, films must be made with great attention to detail. Today's audiences are very discerning (*and unforgiving at the box office*), and usually will not settle for anything less than a convincing plot and impressive performances by the actors.[1*]

Most films are made with the ultimate goal of being an entertainment medium that allows the viewer to escape from his or her normal reality. Therefore, directors must be mindful of creating them in a way which thoughtfully considers plot development *and* the depiction of character relationships in a comprehensive and believable manner. Furthermore, the related in-depth dynamics of the characters must be portrayed in a calculated fashion with the aim of providing thought-provoking insights, meaningful lessons, and support for the viewer that allows them to empathize with the circumstances that are taking place. All of this precise attention to detail is necessary in order to sustain an engaging and enjoyable story line. A film is seldom successful if it does not accomplish these things in the 21st century, where competition has increased greatly due to technological enhancements as well as easier access to filmmaking equipment for professionals and amateurs alike. In the extremely competitive environment of cinematography, being mediocre is rarely acceptable or tolerated. One could argue that these are the trends that have improved the quality of films for audience members over the past several decades.

Our goal throughout this chapter is to provide a few practical illustrations of how movies and films can be incorporated into lectures. We will do this by highlighting examples of film clips that we have actually integrated into our teaching. It needs to be stated that we are not 'replacing' the teaching of important business concepts by using films in the classroom setting. Instead, the goal is to reinforce the various business and leadership principles in practice by using the character portrayals that are captured so well within selected film scenes. Films can clearly provide an augmentation to the overall teaching and learning strategy, rather than just 'a way to pass time' in the classroom. Unfortunately, this may have been the cynical view of this practice in the past, as some instructors historically did not take

---

[1] If you question whether this is true, consider asking Kevin Costner about the discriminating viewers who were shrewd and intolerant of the movie *Waterworld* (Reynolds, 1995) which corresponded in a dismal box office performance despite the $150 million *investment* spent to create the movie.

the time to tease out important messages for the sake of learning. Without delving deeply into adult learning modalities or retention percentages, it is worth citing a study done by Montgomery (1995) that succinctly reveals some relevant statistics that relate to this discussion. This type of research provides further support for the rationale of using films as a teaching tool in the academic environment (Montgomery, 1995). This study revealed that:

- 67% of the students learn best actively, yet lectures are typically passive;
- 57% of the students are sensors, yet we teach them intuitively;
- 69% of the students are visual, yet lectures are primarily verbal;
- 28% of the students are global, yet we seldom focus on the "big picture."

We are not suggesting that using films in the classroom is a panacea that guarantees effective learning of all concepts, but our experience using this medium has been powerful and productive enough to make us believe that it is clearly a step in the right direction. Like anything that is new and different, the incorporation of films in teaching is something that must be planned methodically with preparation being paramount. However, with practice it can become a seamless part of the instruction process that is unique, enjoyable, and effective.

This is also the premise that allows films and film clips to be a powerful forum to examine, dissect, and question a variety of principles that are associated with business and leadership. We feel that it accomplishes the teaching and learning goals in a manner that is much more dynamic than mere classroom discussion or lectures alone. With the enhancements in equipment and technology to show the films, as well as relatively easy access to obtain these films, it makes their use a more viable (and arguably necessary) option to incorporate into the teaching and learning environment (Rohm, 1979). In many ways, we believe that there is now almost an expectation from students to use visual methods as a teaching tool, to the extent that learners are now surrounded by more sensory experiences in every other aspect of their lives. Furthermore, bringing the cinema into the classroom often bridges a degree of comfort and familiarity for the students as they watch films that they often already know, but have perhaps never considered viewing through the lens of key business principles.

Although the main focus for incorporating progressive teaching methods should always be for the benefit of the students' learning, our experience in teaching postgraduates is that incorporating films into teaching has also enhanced our instructional method. Learners often appreciate the willingness to break traditional "norms" by instructors who are trying to convey messages and strengthen the learning, relevance and application of important concepts in a creative fashion. This is something that film utilization accomplishes.

A good reminder for us as educators is this, "Effective teaching is occurring where the majority, preferably all the students, learn most of what the teacher intended. The students want to learn and do not have to be made to do so" (Montgomery, 1999). We argue that using films effectively in the classroom assists in creating a desire to learn by engaging the brain in a more creative way than by simply using PowerPoint slides accompanied by the standard 'prepared lecture.' We find that our students will make reference to film clips used previously during the semester, while also citing their impact in the final 'end of term teaching evaluations.' In our view, this clearly reinforces the argument that movies are both memorable and effective as a means of conveying key messages in the classroom (or in any educational setting for that matter). This practice also nicely coincides with Kolb's (1984) work in experiential learning (Kolb, 1984). The experience of watching the film followed by thoughtful reflection and consideration of its application allows students a unique opportunity for them to understand and then own the concepts being highlighted.

There are many research projects in the fields of neuroscience and adult learning which further support why film clips aid retention and recall. However, this chapter is not trying to comprehensively defend the use of films or provide a literature review on learning modalities. Therefore, in this next section we turn to a discussion of a few selected films and specific clips that we have found effective, particularly in relation to the teaching of leadership principles. We then provide some guidelines for discussion which we hope will spark more ideas that will allow you to customize the debriefing and discussions to better suit the needs and unique environment of your classroom settings.

The concepts that are highlighted in these film clips will reinforce a variety of relevant theories and seminal research that has been done on these leadership and organizational behavior principles. It is worth noting that there are some great discussions surrounding gender and other diversity issues that also deserve to be considered when utilizing film clips. In our experience, there is a very strong portrayal of men in films, which warrants further discussion with students about important issues relating to the influence that this may have on the broader societal matters.

ALIVE (MARSHALL, 1993)

Brief Summary and Context

This movie is based on the true story of the plane crash involving a rugby team from Uruguay. Whilst they were traveling to a game, they experienced bad weather and their plane went down in the Andes mountain ranges.

Although a total of 29 people perished, 16 passengers actually survived for over two months after the plane crashed, relying only on the remnants of the plane's contents, innovative thinking, and the encouragement of each other. In desperation (after several weeks had passed), they felt they had no choice but to ultimately turn to cannibalism in order to survive. They had to overcome numerous adversities with limited resources at their disposal. The entire storyline is gripping and dramatic, especially when one considers that it is based on a true occurrence. The film's tagline captures this: *"They survived the impossible … by doing the unthinkable."*

Scenes Used for Teaching Purposes

Chapter 1 and Chapter 2 (2:15–11:00) This portion of the movie shows the extreme shift in mood as a result of a horrific turn of events during the plane ride. At the beginning of the film, the team members and passengers are joking, laughing, and anticipating their arrival to the destination where the game will be played. However, the tension builds and emotions shift as the plane experiences turbulence. Within no time the mood and stress levels are quite apparent as the plane flies over the Andes mountains, almost colliding with the mountain peaks. The tension builds, and the climax is when a loud "thud" is heard and experienced by the characters (as well as those viewing the film). During this dramatic incident, the plane's fuselage is severed and the plane crashes into a mountain. Some graphic and stressful moments follow, during which the viewer experiences a variety of emotions including: joy, tension, stress, panic, fear, relief, and then uncertainty all in the course of about nine minutes!

Ultimately, by the eleventh minute of the clip, it is clear that there are some survivors who are going to have to deal with a very difficult situation. There are several people marooned in the middle of a mountain range in extreme cold winter weather, followed by many graphically portrayed challenges including an avalanche, death of fellow passengers, several bouts of extreme sickness and hypothermia, and high levels of physical and mental stress.

Chapter 15 and Chapter 16 (1:52:38–1:57) Although watching this clip does not adequately capture all of the hardship that was experienced during the sixty days while the survivors were stranded in the Andes, it does provide some 'closure' for the students in terms of a positive ending to a tragic situation. Nando and Canessa (two of the rugby players) take off on a trek to reach civilization to get help. However, they have no way of communicating with those left stranded with the fuselage to let them know of their safety or progress. This final scene depicts the elation that the group experiences, as two helicopters appear over the peaks of the mountain to bring the survivors back to civilization. They are finally rescued and attempt to go back to living a 'normal' life having experienced a tremendous amount of trauma and having compromised some of their own values in order to stay alive.

Relevant Concepts: Leadership, teamwork, stages of team development, decision-making, dealing with stress, conflict management, survival under pressure, ethical dilemmas, utilization of minimal resources, values, emotions felt versus emotions displayed, and staying motivated amidst conditions of extreme uncertainty.

How to Use this Film in a Teaching Capacity

While it is not practical to show the entire film in the classroom, it is probably a wise option to have students view the entire movie at home and then "revisit" these relevant sections of the movie in the classroom. If this is not possible, then it is worthwhile to summarize some of the key points of the movie in terms of the decisions that had to be made by the characters in order to stay alive (especially the controversy of eating some of the deceased in order to avoid starvation). The first clip shown to the class aims to give students a real sense of the extreme conditions that the survivors are faced with in the middle of mountain ranges. It allows them to experience vicariously having to spend two months in these severe circumstances and gives them a real sense of the climate conditions as well.

This is a great opportunity for students to reflect on and discuss some of the extreme conditions in which leadership is required. This film can generate a robust dialogue about teamwork and stages of team development amidst extreme conditions. There are also some conversations to have around ethical decision-making and the need to make choices that may contradict personal value systems. From a leadership perspective, the notion of looking after each other, staying calm under pressure, displaying emotions, motivating each other, and making very difficult decisions are obvious areas of discussion. When one considers that in this true life situation, it gives students a chance to get a sense of perspective about the relative severity of problems that they face in the workplace.

Kouzes and Posner's (2002) work on the *Five Practices of Exemplary Leadership* is a good framework within which to set up a discussion. How did the film demonstrate the following?

- Model the Way
- Inspire a Shared Vision
- Challenge the Process
- Enable others to Act
- Encourage the Heart

Some Discussion/Debrief Questions to Generate Thought

- What is the most extreme circumstance that you have experienced where you had to rely on other "team members" to achieve an outcome?
- During times of crisis, is it best to appoint a leader, or do leaders often just "emerge" as the situation progresses? How would you have dealt with a situation that was as extreme as this?
- Do stressful situations tend to make people more creative? Explain.
- How are decisions made typically in your workplace? Do the consequences of the decisions change the decision making procedures?
- How do you deal with having to manage limited resources? Give some examples of times when you had to "make do." What were the stakes in these situations.
- In terms of moral and ethical decision making, do you think it was wrong to turn to cannibalism and eat the fellow passengers? Does the issue of survival complicate the moral and ethical boundaries that people live by? Can you think of times where you have had to make ethical decisions where the lines were blurred because of circumstances?
- In a leadership position, how do you manage to keep people motivated when sometimes the "signs" and "messages" that surround you seem pretty bleak?
- It's easy to watch a movie when you know the outcome and you have an idea of how the story ends, but imagine that you were in their shoes and stuck in those circumstances, how would you have coped? Have you been in positions of uncertainty? How important is it for leaders to deal with uncertainty?
- Do you think leadership is best showcased when there are extreme circumstances that must be dealt with? Are leaders best defined only by how they cope with difficult situations or can a person be a great leader when things are calm, cool, and collected?
- By extension, a discussion of the 9/11 attacks on the Twin Towers and how it was dealt with under conditions of such extreme emotion and pressure is possible.
- "Character is not created during crisis, it is revealed." Discuss and debate.

BRAVEHEART (GIBSON, 1993)

Brief Summary and Context

This movie is based on the partly historical, partly mythological story of William Wallace, a Scottish common man who fought for his country's freedom from English rule at the end of the 13th century. Wallace leads his people in a rebellion against the tyranny of the English King who has granted the English nobility in Scotland "Prima Nocta," which is the right to take all new brides for the first night. Wallace (Mel Gibson) courageously defends the rights of his countrymen and provides leadership through his charisma, strategic direction, and perseverance. Throughout the movie, there are many dramatic (and graphic) fighting scenes as well as moments of intense emotion for the viewer to experience as 'the underdog' fights for a purpose, defying the odds against the much larger English army. There are many well-known lines in the film, not least of which is the main tagline, *"All men die, but not every man truly lives!"*

Scenes Used for Teaching Purposes

Chapter 11 (58:46–1:11:50) This clip of the movie shows a dramatic shift in the emotions of the Scottish commoners as they are faced with the daunting prospect of fighting the intimidating and significantly larger English army. Many of the Scots are overcome by the awesome sight of the English army who are assembling across the large, open field. Not surprisingly, they are tempted to surrender or retreat home. At this dramatic point, Wallace makes an entrance on horseback and gives a powerful speech which dramatically shifts the attitudes of the people. He inspires them with a unifying vision with such words as, "What will you do without freedom?!!" Upon creating a shared vision and giving the Scots a sense of purpose, he helps create an environment laced with motivation and inspiration that allows the Scots to embrace the possibility of fighting against the English despite the odds being stacked against them. The twelve minute clip produces emotions such as doubt, uncertainty and fear, slowly shifting to feelings of excitement and enthusiasm as the ensuing battle is anticipated. Whilst there are a variety of scenes throughout the film that are useful, this particular section captures the essence of a charismatic leader. He instills a sense of vision and purpose amongst a large group of people and gives them a figurehead to believe in and follow. Wallace's enthusiasm and passion are both very convincing and stirring.

Relevant Concepts: Leadership, teamwork, charisma, creating a unifying vision, instilling a sense of purpose, strategic thinking, negotiation, motivation, and communication.

How to Use this Movie in a Teaching Capacity

It is not necessary to show the entire film as the storyline is rather long and drawn out. Inevitably, students will want to watch more because the clip is such an intense section of the film. We would advise explaining the background and history that has taken place prior to this scene, in order to help students get a sense of the factors motivating William Wallace's passion and sense of purpose. Additionally, it is useful to have students take notice of the various shifts in emotion and the factors which actually influence these shifts. The power of articulation and charisma are clearly demonstrated, as well as the notion of creating a vision for the future that people can relate to and want to be a part of. Ultimately, this is a real testament to the idea that people support what they have helped to create.

Throughout this film, the driver for the Scots' perseverance is a better life; free from English rule. In the classroom it is useful to encourage students to put themselves in the shoes of the Scots, where the future looked quite bleak unless they took a stand and were willing to fight. There is a good opportunity to ask students to "compare, contrast, and consider" the numerous rebellions and revolutions that have taken place throughout history and which have produced both successful and unsuccessful outcomes. For instance, the 'revolt' that Gandhi led was dramatically different to the approach of William Wallace. Such different environments and approaches warrant discussion and debate. There is also an opportunity to discuss masculinity and leadership. Could other approaches and styles of leadership produce similar or better outcomes? What role does the context of a situation play in highlighting the most effective approach to leadership?

Some Discussion/Debrief Questions to Generate Thought

How important is it for leaders to create a unifying vision that people can relate to and believe in? What are the drawbacks of having, or not having, a defined vision?

How important is it to communicate that vision? Does good communication of the vision increase the likelihood of others supporting the vision?

How important is it to be a good communicator when in a leadership role? Is it necessary to display the same type of charisma as William Wallace?

How do leaders make sure that what they are communicating is resonating with 'the followers' who are receiving the message?

In general, does passion and enthusiasm motivate people? What are the potential dangers of creating too much enthusiasm? Does passion always get communicated in the same manner? What are other ways to demonstrate passion? Was Anita Roddick 'passionate' in the same manner as William Wallace?

Who is the most inspirational and motivational person that you have been associated with? Why? What did they do to make you feel "inspired?"

Have you had any situations where you have had to take a stand on an issue and make it be known that "enough is enough" and that you were not willing to succumb to the present circumstances?

How much influence do you think one person can have amongst a large group of people? How do *you* exert *your* influence? Do you think you are effective or ineffective? How do you know? What things could you do to make more of an impact in your workplace?

Have you felt intimidated by other people or maybe competitors in the business world? How do you overcome that in a productive and positive manner?

How important is achievement of the "task" versus the "process" and the "people" when you are in a leadership position? Do you think great leaders are only remembered for their positive outcomes and contributions?

What role does humility play in leadership? How is it demonstrated without appearing 'weak' in the eyes of others?

COACH CARTER (CARTER, 2005)

Brief Summary and Context

This movie is based on the true story of Coach Ken Carter, a controversial high school basketball coach played by Samuel L. Jackson. Carter accepted the position of coach with the understanding that he could lead the team according to his rules, which included the importance of not just being a great athlete, but also being a good student. He believed that the players had to maintain solid grades in the classroom or he would not allow them to play for the basketball team. He even had the players sign a contract at the beginning of the season forcing them to agree to these terms. The team was undefeated and on their way to the State Championship in 1999, when Coach Carter was made aware that some of the players were not holding true to the agreement. Being a strict disciplinarian and holding true to his word, Coach Carter received national media attention when he locked the gymnasium and benched the entire team for having poor grades. Despite having a very talented and athletic team on the basketball court, Coach Carter was determined to send the message that success in life would be related more to their commitment and intelligence in the classroom than their success in the gymnasium. Coach Carter was criticized greatly by the community because the team was performing so well that season, but he held strong to his beliefs. Ultimately the team members pulled together and became committed to their obligations as students. The story is powerful in many ways and reveals messages about keeping priorities in order and standing by principles even when there is tremendous pressure to cave in and succumb to the pressure by outsiders. The main tagline for the movie is *"You don't perform in the classroom; you don't play in the game!"*

Scenes Used for Teaching Purposes

Chapter 3 (9:30–15:30) and Chapter 17 (1:19–1:28) There are many scenes that are worth showing during this film but showing these two clips gives viewers a "taste" of the leadership approach that was taken to establish respect with a group of very undisciplined young men. The first scene shows Coach Carter coming into his new role with players that had previously been quite unmanageable *and* unsuccessful. Not only did the coach have to establish what the 'operating procedures' were going to be, he also had to generate enough respect from the players in order to achieve these. This first scene shows how he establishes his credibility and then clearly sets the level of expectation. The second scene captures the outrage that the players have toward him because of his stance. However, they then stand behind his expectation about good performance both in and out of the classroom. Despite the pressure from the community and other school officials, Coach Carter refuses to allow the team to be "great" only on the basketball court. He even forfeits the games that were scheduled due to the players not holding true to their side of the "contract." He repeatedly states that he will do anything he can to make sure the players have a better life. His seemingly harsh decision not to allow them to play basketball is because he wants to send a message about the importance of getting an education, rather than relying on athletic ability alone.

These two scenes do not completely capture all of the "success" that the athletes experience as basketball players throughout the film. It is useful therefore to set the scene for your students that Coach Carter's basketball team is undefeated when he decides to lock the doors to the gym. This decision is not only unpopular, but many people criticize Coach Carter for being too harsh and feel that the penalty doesn't fit the crime.

Relevant Concepts Leadership, teamwork, stages of team development, credibility, conflict management, negotiation, decision-making, respect versus rapport, celebrating success, staying true to your word, dealing with pressure, dealing with difficult people, consequences for behavior, and conflict management

How to Use this Film in a Teaching Capacity

This is one of those movies that could be beneficial for students to watch on their own so that they can really get a sense of the anger that was generated when Coach Carter took his harsh stance. If the students watch the whole movie, it really drives home the intense pressure that the coach was up against when he held true to his word. From a teaching perspective, there are many engaging discussions that can be generated around dealing with the pressures of a leadership position as well as not compromising or giving in when a critical (and controversial) stance is taken on an issue.

There are also a lot of positive aspects in the film which can be used for teaching purposes around motivation and teamwork, as well as the necessity for a stern leadership approach at times. Holding people to be accountable to their commitments is a good theme to explore in discussion. There are some useful scenes in the film that can be referred to that clearly show people making a commitment, but then not honoring that commitment. As a leader, Coach Carter has to deal with some difficult situations without showing bias or special treatment to any team member despite circumstances sometimes warranting such behavior. This film has themes of both a positive and negative nature woven through it that highlight the importance of consequences as well as the significance of being disciplined and working together as a team to achieve goals that are going to be of greater benefit in the future than the present.

Some Discussion/Debrief Questions to Generate Thought

- In terms of Situational Leadership, do you think Coach Carter's style was appropriate for the situation in the early part of the movie? Did it change during the course of the film?
- What other styles of leadership and leadership theories were present?
- How important is credibility when you are in a leadership position? How do you gain credibility? How do you lose it? What is the relationship of trust with credibility?
- Have you ever had to take a stance on something that went against 'popular opinion' and had to defend that stance? How did you handle it? In leadership positions, how important is it to be able to do this?
- In the movie, Coach Carter was driven by the 'higher purpose' of wanting to see these young men be successful in life long after their basketball careers are over. Do you think the players realized that he was actually looking after their needs by taking such a strong stance? For those of you that have children, do you have any circumstances that relate to this difficult position, or perhaps you may have experienced it yourself in some capacity. Please share with the class.
- How important is it to hold people accountable to things that they have agreed to do? How would you have dealt with the same scenario if you were in Coach Carter's shoes? In leadership positions, do you think the situation is any different?
- How do you handle conflict? Do you think there are times when your approach does not allow you to achieve the best results? Explain.
- How do good leaders show sensitivity and understanding about diversity? How prominent are diversity issues in your workplace? Do they get handled well or poorly?

SUMMARY

We have provided three in-depth examples to supply a taste of how film clips can be used to demonstrate some key business and leadership principles in practice. This is only one of many ways that films can be incorporated into the learning process. The opportunities and options are virtually endless when one considers the number of films that are accessible. We must emphasize that it is extremely important to discuss the shortcomings of the films as well. For instance, there needs to be discussions about the roles of masculinity and femininity in leadership and the archetypes that are frequently portrayed. Sometimes the *absence* of a particular concept or principle being displayed warrants discussion, and can prove to be even more insightful for students in considering stereotypes that exist and the impact these issues may have in practice.

There are *many* other good films that should also be considered such as these in the following list:

- *Apollo 13* (Howard, 1995)
- *Erin Brockovich* (Soderbergh, 2000)
- *Finding Nemo* (Stanton & Unkrich, 2003)
- *Master and Commander: The Far Side of the World* (Weir, 2003)
- *Mr. Holland's Opus* (Herek, 1995)
- *Norma Rae* (Ritt, 1979)
- *North Country* (Caro, 2005)
- *October Sky* (Johnston, 1999)
- *Pay it Forward* (Leder, 2000)
- *Remember the Titans* (Yakin, 2000)
- *The Pursuit of Happyness* (Muccino, 2006)

Obviously, this list is far from exhaustive. In fact, once you become comfortable using films and looking for the messages that they contain, you will be amazed at just how frequently you can pull out some meaningful clips to demonstrate key principles when you are teaching in the classroom. Additionally, we have provided a method/template for breaking down the scenes into robust discussion topics in the classroom. We have also highlighted the use of the scenes as the primary teaching option, but what is unique about using films in the classroom is that you can analyze them from many different angles. For instance, at a deeper meta-cognitive level, it is very worthwhile having students examine the similarities between leadership and film production in a general sense. Successful leaders are expected to articulate an organization's vision; which is not dissimilar to the way a film director must endeavor to express a script of words into visual images or translate a vision into reality. Getting students to consider some of the many elements of making a film can generate some discussion about similarities and differences between leadership in an organization, and the elements of leadership necessary to create a film. The point is that the use of the chosen film itself can demonstrate key leadership principles while at another deeper level of analysis, the act of discussing the construction of the film provides an opportunity for exploring practical business and leadership principles.

CONCLUSION

Films have served to captivate and mesmerize audiences for years allowing storylines to be viewed that transcend race, gender, age, culture, nationality, peace, war, suspense, comedy, and drama amongst other things. Films such as *Hotel Rwanda* (George, 2004), *In Good Company* (Weitz, 2004), *Mona Lisa Smile* (Newell, 2003), and *Erin Brockovich* are a few examples that touch on some of these other important areas. We are suggesting that this powerful medium can be incorporated into your lectures as yet another educational tool and valuable part of the learning process when teaching topics such as business and leadership. Although it requires diligent planning in order to amalgamate them into the classroom setting to avoid being a disruption, we believe that the results will more than justify the effort.

Films can clearly be educational, engaging, energizing, and entertaining, which, not surprisingly, are the same types of labels that we should logically be striving to achieve as educators. When used in a skillful manner and done with preparation and forethought, the use of films in the classroom will be another valuable resource in your toolkit of instructional methods that the learners will appreciate and you will find delight in. So, lights, camera, action!! Films can help create a mindset while also highlighting leadership skill sets. Let the learning be enhanced as you begin to explore the benefits of using movies in your teaching. Best of luck!

For further readings related to this chapter and subject matter please refer to Felder and Silverman (1988), Graham, Sincoff, Baker, and Ackermann (2003), Harb and Terry (1992), Stice (1987), and Qasem and Mohamadian (1992).

REFERENCES

Felder, R. M., & Silverman, L. K. (1988). Learning and teaching styles in engineering education. *Engineering Education, 78*(7), 674–681.

Glickman, C. D., Gordon, S. P., & Ross-Gordon, J. M. (2001). *SuperVision and instructional leadership* (5th ed.). Needham Heights, MA: Allyn & Bacon.

Graham, T. S., Sincoff, M. Z., Baker, B., & Ackermann, J. C. (2003). Reel leadership: Hollywood takes the leadership challenge. *Journal of Leadership Education, 2*(2), 37–56.

Harb, J. N., & Terry, R. E. (1992). A look at performance evaluation tools through the use of the Kolb Learning Cycle. *Proceedings of the Annual ASEE Conf.* (pp. 1124–7). Toledo, OH, June.

Knowles, M. S., Holton, E., & Swanson, R. A. (2005). *The adult learner: The definitive classic in adult education and human resource development* (6th ed.). Amsterdam, The Netherlands: Elsevier.

Kolb, D. A. (1984). *Experiential learning: Experience as the source of learning and development.* Englewood Cliffs, NJ: Prentice-Hall.

Kouzes, J. M., & Posner, B. Z. (2002). *The leadership challenge* (3rd ed.). San Francisco, CA: Jossey-Bass.

Montgomery, D. (1999). *Positive teacher appraisal through classroom observation.* London, UK: David Fulton.

Montgomery, S. (1995). *Addressing diverse learning styles through the use of multimedia.* University of Michigan, Michigan, USA. Retrieved June 2nd, from http://www.vpaa.uillinois.edu/reports_retreats/tid/resources/montgomery.html

Qasem, I., & Mohamadian, H. (1992). Multimedia technology in engineering education. *Proceedings of IEEE Southeastcon '92* (Cat. No. 92CH3094-0), New York IEEE, 46–49.

Rohm, R. (1979). *Teaching with media, filmstrip.* Chicago, IL: Society for Visual Education.

Stice, J. E. (1987). Using Kolb's learning cycle to improve student learning. *Engineering Education,* 77(5), 291–296.

Films

Caro, N. (Director). (2005). *North country* [Motion picture]. United States: Warner Bros.

Carter, T. (Director). (2005). *Coach Carter* [Motion picture]. United States & Germany: Coach Carter, MTV Films, MMDP Munich Movie Development & Production, & Tollin/Robbins Productions.

George, T. (Director). (2004). *Hotel Rwanda* [Motion picture]. United Kingdom, United States, Italy, & South Africa: United Artists, Lions Gate Entertainment, Industrial Development Corporation of South Africa, Miracle Pictures/Seamus, Inside Track Films, Mikado Film, & Endgame Entertainment.

Gibson, M. (Director). (1993). *Braveheart* [Motion picture]. United States: Icon Productions, Ladd Company, & B. H. Finance.

Herek, S. (Director). *Mr. Holland's opus* (1995). [Motion picture]. United States: Hollywood Pictures, Interscope Communications, Polygram Filmed Entertainment, & The Charlie Mopic Company.

Howard, R. (Director). (1995). *Apollo 13* [Motion picture]. United States: Universal Pictures & Imagine Entertainment.

Johnston, J. (Director). (1999). *October sky* [Motion picture]. United States: Universal Pictures.

Leder, M. (Director). (2000). *Pay it forward* [Motion picture]. United States: Warner Bros., Bel Air Entertainment, & Tapestry Films.

Marshall, F. (Director). (1993). *Alive* [Motion picture]. United States: Film Andes, Kennedy/Marshall, Paramount Pictures, & Touchstone Pictures.

Muccino, G. (Director). (2006). *The pursuit of happyness* [Motion picture]. United States: Columbia Pictures, Relativity Media, Overbrook Entertainment, & Escape Artists.

Newell, M. (Director). (2003). *Mona Lisa smile* [Motion picture]. United States: Revolution Studios & Red Om Films.

Reynolds, K. (Director). (1995). *Waterworld* [Motion picture]. United States: Universal Pictures.

Ritt, M. (Director). (1979). *Norma Rae* [Motion picture]. United States: Twentieth Century Fox.

Soderbergh, S. (Director). (2000). *Erin Brockovich* [Motion picture]. United States: Jersey Films.

Stanton, A. & Unkrich, L. (Directors). (2003). *Finding Nemo* [Motion picture]. Australia & United States: Walt Disney Pictures & Pixar Animation Studios.

Weir, P. (Director). (2003). *Master and commander: The far side of the world* [Motion picture]. United States: Twentieth Century Fox, Miramax Films, Universal Pictures, & Samuel Goldwyn Films.

Weitz, P. (Director). (2004). *In good company* [Motion picture]. United States: Universal Pictures.

Yakin, B. (Director). (2000). *Remember the Titans* [Motion picture]. United States: Jerry Bruckheimer Films, Run It Up Productions, Technical Black, & Walt Disney Pictures.

CONTRIBUTORS

Véronique Ambrosini is a Professor of Management at Monash University. She was previously a Professor of Strategic Management at Birmingham and Cardiff Universities. Her research is conducted essentially within the resource-based and dynamic capability view of the firm. She has articles published in internationally recognized academic journals such as *Journal of Management Studies, British Journal of Management* and *Human Relations* and practitioner-oriented journals such as *European Management Journal* and *Management Decision.* She is the author of *Tacit and Ambiguous Resources as Sources of Competitive Advantage* (2003, Palgrave Macmillan), the editor of *Exploring Techniques of Analysis and Evaluation in Strategic Management* (1998, Financial Times/Prentice Hall), and a co-editor of *Advanced Strategic Management: A Multiple Perspectives Approach* (2007, Palgrave Macmillan). Véronique is an associate editor of the *Journal of Management and Organization.* She is also on the editorial board of the *Journal of Management Studies* and the *Organization Management Journal.*

Emma Bell is Professor of Management and Organisation Studies at Keele Management School, Keele University. She is interested in the critical study

Moving Images: Effective Teaching with Film and Television in Higher Education,
pages 239–244
Copyright © 2012 by Information Age Publishing
All rights of reproduction in any form reserved.

of management and organizational behavior in a range of contexts, including her own. Her research focuses on organizational culture, ethics, learning and change and the role of spiritual and religious beliefs in management. She also teaches and writes about methods and methodologies of management research, including how management knowledge is created. She is co-author of *Business Research Methods* (2011, Oxford University Press) and author of *Reading Management and Organisation in Film* (2008, Palgrave Macmillan).

Jon Billsberry is Professor of Management at Deakin University having previously worked at Coventry University, The Open University and eight years in commercial organizations. He is Chair of the Management Education and Development division of the Academy of Management and served for five years as the Chair of the Organisational Psychology track at the British Academy of Management. Jon's research interests are in the areas of organizational fit and misfit, recruitment and selection, the cinematic portrayal of work and working life, and the development of innovative teaching techniques. His research has been published in *Personnel Psychology, Journal of Business Ethics, Journal of Business and Psychology, New Technology, Work and Employment, Higher Education,* and *Journal of Management Education,* where he is the Editor-in-Chief. He has authored three books and edited four more.

Joseph E. Champoux is a Regents' Professor of Management Emeritus at the Robert O. Anderson School of Management of the University of New Mexico. He received his Ph.D. in Administration from the University of California, Irvine in 1974. Professor Champoux has taught in Austria, France, the Netherlands, Mexico, and Brazil. He teaches graduate and undergraduate courses in Organizational Theory and Organizational Behavior and has received several awards for excellence in teaching since 1982. His research activities focus on film as a teaching resource, work and non-work, job design and motivation, the effects of technology on organizations and management, modern manufacturing systems, and Total Quality Management. He has published articles in several scholarly journals including *Organizational Behavior and Human Performance, Administrative Science Quarterly, Academy of Management Journal, Decision Sciences, Journal of Organizational Behavior, Human Relations,* and *Personnel Psychology.*

Julie Charlesworth is a freelance consultant, author and lecturer. She has a broad interest in public and voluntary sector organisations and management including inter-organizational working, leadership, and community participation and volunteering. Julie takes an interdisciplinary approach to her teaching and research in management and organisations and draws on the various academic disciplines in which she has worked including geography, economics, social policy and sociology. She also has a Masters degree in history, specialising in film history, which is a great influence on her research using visual evidence in understanding organisations and teams, leadership, and communities. She lives in the UK and previously worked at The Open University Business School as well as the Universities of Essex, Leeds and Hertfordshire. She is co-editor of the Policy Section in the new journal *Voluntary Sector Review*. Julie is also a volunteer in a historic garden and researches garden history and conservation.

Nardine Collier is a Research Officer in the Strategic Management Group at Cranfield School of Management. Her research covers areas such as the resource based view of the firm, dynamic capabilities, knowledge, and strategic processes, and she has been published in a variety of journals including *British Journal of Management, International Journal of Management Reviews, International Journal of Management Education* and *Strategic Organization*. Nardine also specialises in teaching quantitative research methods.

Mark Easterby-Smith is Professor and Head of the Department of Management Learning at Lancaster University Management School. His research covers organizational learning, dynamic capabilities and research methodology. He has collaborated with Richard Thorpe over many years on research methodology especially in adapting ideas derived from the broader social sciences into the context of management research. Their well-known book on *Management Research* was first published by Sage in 1991, and has recently appeared in a fourth edition. They have also tried to develop innovative ways of teaching about research methodology, and the chapter here describes one of their classic methods for explaining how and why philosophical underpinnings are relevant to management research. Mark has published several academic articles on research methodology, including papers which have appeared in top US journals such as *Organizational Research Methods* and *Academy of Management Journal*.

Andres Fortino is Campus Provost and Dean of Academic Affairs at DeVry College of New York having previously served at the Polytechnic Institute of New York University, Marist College, and George Mason University. He holds degrees in electrical engineering from the City College of New York and received his PhD in electrical engineering from the City University of New York. Andres has lectured extensively on technology worldwide and has led more than 180 high technology seminars for Learning Tree International. He also worked for IBM Corp. in its advanced technology division where he filed several patents and numerous invention disclosures and received IBM's First Invention Level Award for his work in semiconductor research. The author of eight books, Dr. Fortino has practiced the application of information technology to solving business problems for the past 30 years. His scholarship focuses on information systems development, intellectual property management, data networks, and the diffusion of innovation.

Peter Galvin is Professor of Strategic Management at Newcastle Business School, Northumbria University. He has previously held positions in both Australia and the USA. Peter's teaching has most recently focused almost exclusively upon MBA students where he has experimented with a range of different teaching methods including the use of movies, simulations and other experiential activities. His research has covered a variety of industries from motor vehicles, airlines, telecommunications, bicycles and wine. The focus of this research has been around organizational and industry structures and their impact upon how and where firms compete with each other across industries and the ways in which they seek at attain competitive advantage in different competitive environments. Peter is presently an Associate Editor for the *Journal of Management and Organization.*

Troy Hendrickson is a Senior Lecturer at the Curtin University Graduate School of Business in Perth, Western Australia. He had several years of corporate experience in the pharmaceutical industry in the United States before embarking on his PhD and making the shift into an academic leadership role. He is the Deputy Director of the Master of Business Leadership program and is also actively involved in the MBA program at the CGSB teaching in areas related to leadership, culture and diversity, organizational behaviour and marketing. His research interests in adult learning and teaching methodologies have allowed him to bring a variety of experiential learning scenarios into the classroom which includes the use of films as an approach to deeper learning of key business concepts. He is actively involved in a variety of executive education programs across a variety of industry sectors and has worked throughout Australia, Asia, America, Europe and Africa continually refining and experimenting with unique teaching methods.

Pauline Leonard is Reader in Sociology at the University of Southampton. Her research interests are primarily within organizational change, the construction of gender, race and identity within international organizational contexts and skilled migration. She is particularly interested in innovative methods of research and teaching and exploring the intersections of organizational studies and cultural studies. She has published widely in *Organization Studies, Gender, Work and Organization, Journal of Ethnic and Migration Studies, Social Politics* and *Gender Place and Culture.* Her most recent book is *Expatriate Identities in Postcolonial Organizations* (Ashgate 2010) and she is currently working on two research projects, one looking at careers and identities within not for profit organizations and one exploring changing identities amongst the British in South Africa.

Stephen Sloane is a Professor of Political Science and Public Administration at Saint Mary's College of California. He is a graduate of the U.S. Naval Academy (BS), Harvard University (MPA), the University of California, Berkeley (MA, Ph.D.) and the U.S. Naval War College. His current research interests deal with the role of professionals in modern organizations, novels and film as sources of ideas that contribute to the understanding of organizational systems, critical management studies, and ethics. He retired after thirty years of active duty service as a naval officer (pilot) at the rank of Captain. He is a veteran of the Vietnam War and has been awarded various naval decorations including the Meritorious Service Medal, the Air Medal, and the Navy Commendation Medal. His publications include *Organizations in the Movies: The Legend of the Dysfunctional System* (2002, University Press of America), *Gold Stripe on a Jackass: The Quest for Moral Efficiency* (2008, Hamilton), and a novel, *Cohen's Law* (2010, Createspace).

Janet Sutherland is an Associate Fellow at Curtin University's Graduate School of Business and former Director of their Master of Business Leadership program. She teaches Organizational Behavior and Fundamentals of Leadership. Janet is passionate about enriching the student learning experience through innovation in classroom delivery. She explores the use of a range of existing and new media to enrich the learning experience for her post experience adult students, in the classroom and online environments. Janet's research areas of interest include leadership, organizational behavior, knowledge creation and transfer, and andragogy. She is also involved in executive education, primarily in the area of leadership development. This includes the development and implementation of a leadership development program for elite scholarship students from 66 different developing countries who are studying towards master or doctoral degrees in Australia. Prior to academia, Janet worked in education, media and marketing across government, not for profit, and industry sectors.

Richard Thorpe is Professor of Management Development and Pro-Dean for Research at Leeds University Business School. His research interests include: management learning, management development, leadership and research methods. He has sought to develop these interests in all the institutions in which he has worked. His early industrial experiences inform the way his ethos has developed. Common themes are: a strong commitment to process methodologies and a focus on action in all its forms; an interest in and commitment to the development of doctoral students and the development of capacity within the sector; a commitment to collaborative working on projects of mutual interest. With Mark Easterby-Smith, a long-time collaborator, he has published a number of books and papers on research methods, the most significant being *Management Research* (Sage) now in its fourth edition. He is a fellow of the British Academy of Management and chair of the Society for the Advancement of Management Studies.

Craig Webber is Senior Lecturer in Criminology at the University of Southampton. His teaching is in the area of criminological theory, policing and law enforcement, youth crime and cybercrime. He has researched and published in various areas of culture, media and criminological theory, including the article 'Foreground, background, foresight? The third dimension of cultural criminology' that appeared in *Crime, Media, Culture* in 2007. With Jeff Vass, he wrote a chapter titled, 'Crime, film and the cybernetic imagination', for *The Handbook of Internet Crime* (2010, Willan), which was edited by Yvonne Jewkes and Majid Yar. Craig is also the author of *Psychology and Crime* (2010, Sage).

Thomaz Wood Jr. is a full professor at FGV-EAESP, in São Paulo, Brazil, where he teaches strategy and change management. He is a former director and editor for *Revista de Administração de Empresas*, a leading academic journal in Brazil. Currently, he serves tenure as an associate dean for research at FGV-EAESP. Professor Wood has authored or edited over 20 books and published over 50 academic papers in the field of organization studies. His research interests include: the study of the "spectacularization" of organizational life and the creative industries. He is a partner at Matrix/CDE, a management consulting firm. As a consultant, he coordinated several projects of organizational change, strategic planning and executive education in large Brazilian firms. Professor Wood is also an "accidental journalist" and publishes regularly at *CartaCapital*, a Brazilian weekly magazine. He produced and directed several short movies, but that was many, many years ago.